NEVER IN DOUBT

BY PETER S. PRESCOTT

A WORLD OF OUR OWN
Notes on Life and Learning in a Boys' Preparatory School

SOUNDINGS
Encounters with Contemporary Books

A DARKENING GREEN
Notes from the Silent Generation

THE CHILD SAVERS
Juvenile Justice Observed

NEVER IN DOUBT
Critical Essays on American Books, 1972–1985

PETER S. PRESCOTT

NEVER
IN DOUBT

*Critical Essays
on American Books, 1972–1985*

ARBOR HOUSE / *New York*

Manufactured in the United States of America

10 9 8 7 6 5 4 3 2 1

Library of Congress Cataloging in Publication Data

Prescott, Peter S.
Never in doubt.

Includes index.
1. American literature—20th century—History
and criticism—Addresses, essays, lectures. I. Title.
PS225.P74 1986   810'.9'0054   85-28773
ISBN: 0-87795-803-3

DESIGN BY LAURA HOUGH

FOR
BILL AND JANE-HOWARD,
MARK AND VANESSA

good times, good talk

CONTENTS

TWO
FURTHER PERPLEXITIES OF EVERYDAY LIFE

PREFACE; OR, WHAT I LIKE ABOUT THIS BOOK

WHEN I WAS twelve, my father offered me ten dollars to read H. G. Well's *Outline of History*. I never collected. It seemed a lot of money when I began, but by page 43 it seemed nowhere near enough. I think I was right, but years were to pass before anyone offered me money to read a book again.

Now for nearly thirty years I have been reading books in a professional way—as an editor, a reviewer, an author. I'm dismayed to find the job gets no easier with practice. The trade, or craft, or profession, or art of criticism—no one agrees what reverence is due it, if any reverence at all—is unsettling at best because the kind of stuff we quick-draw artists write in a regular way to meet the deadlines of newspapers and magazines has always been thought a little suspect. My copy of Max Beerbohm's *Around Theatres* falls open to an essay called "The Critic as Pariah," written in 1903: "We are not liked, we critics. The creators of art do not like us, nor do the men in the street. . . . We find there the contempt felt by the man who can do something, and does it, for the man who cannot do it, but does talk a lot about it. . . . As for the men in the street, they may be anxious to learn from the critic. But a thirst for learning does not involve a love for the teacher."

Beerbohm's view of the unlovable critic had been anticipated six years earlier by his predecessor at the *Saturday Review*, Bernard Shaw: "I have never been able to see how the duties of a critic, which consist largely in making painful remarks in public about the most sensitive of his fellow creatures, can be reconciled with the manners of a gentleman. But gentleman or no, a critic is most certainly not in the position of a co-respondent in a divorce case: he is in no way bound to perjure himself to shield the reputation of the profession he criticizes. Far from being the instigator of its crimes and the partner of its guilty joys, he is the policeman of dramatic art; and it is his express business to denounce its delinquencies."

A century and a half earlier still, John Upton, a distinguished critic living in London, spoke out against his colleagues in terms identical to those used by the critics of reviewers today. Upton, in 1746, wrote some seventy-five years before what we think of as modern reviewing was invented: "This is indeed a province for which, however mean our education happens to be, yet by the help of a certain kind of reading, and a proper degree of pilfering from the observations of other men, we all think ourselves highly qualified. Criticism is now no longer, as formerly, the finished production of experienced learning, but the untimely fruit of a confident brow, and a splenetic heart. No wonder, therefore, if from the number of bungling artists, the art itself is brought into contempt; and that now at length the fatal period of time should approach, when critics themselves should be involved in that general ridicule, which long ago has been the fate of divines, philosophers and politicians."

Need we go further back? In Syracuse, twenty-five hundred years ago, a critic named Philoxenus refused to praise a play written by the tyrant Dionysius. For his obstinacy, he was sent to do penal service in the local quarry. Two years later he was released and asked whether he wished to revise his opinion. He replied, "Back to the quarry!" That's the oldest anecdote about a critic that I know, but other stories suggest that the critic has always been with us. Hesiod reports that in the reign of Kronos, Night gave birth to numerous dismal children, but among these was Momus, the god of bantering gaiety. By the second century A.D., when Lucian wrote about him in his satires, Momus had become Olympus's resident critic—a god without stature, of course, but tolerated nonetheless, and licensed by Zeus to tell unpleasant truths. When, for instance, Poseidon created the bull, Momus suggested that the job might have been better done had the animal's horns been placed beneath his eyes so the bull could see what he was goring.

I like those stories. One suggests the antiquity of a tradition of critical integrity in the face of awesome retribution; the other, a certain impertinence, a joy in contumacy. The journalistic critic needs both qualities, if only because he spends much of his time offending his friends as he writes about fairly good books that should have been better, or bad books that are hugely successful. Later on in this book, I'll try to explain why it is that most people in this country who read books at all demand bad books and why only a really talented writer can produce an egregiously awful book. For now, it's enough to say that a journalistic critic who loses his taste for the jugular—and most do, in time—is a writer in need of another line of work. Unlike our colleagues the literary critics, who write at length and at leisure to please themselves, we can't indulge ourselves by noticing only what appeals to us; we are not invited to write only from our particular strengths and interests, but must (to use Northrop Frye's felicitous term) perform as "well-tempered critics." That is to say, we must write, as dexterously as we can, and always in its own terms, about whatever presents itself to us in a newsy sort of way: serious fiction; biography and history; books defining current situations and attitudes, however lamentable; books that have no ambition other than to be useful or entertaining; books that are meretricious trash.

By long tradition, journalistic critics feel obliged to denigrate their work; I don't mean to do so. The role of the book critic writing for a daily or weekly journal seems to me to occupy an exciting and useful middle ground between that of the literary critic and that of what is sometimes called the "mere reviewer." The literary critic, usually an academic sort, is accustomed to applying great labors to narrow areas; he examines the past—old and relatively recent books—and retrieves from it that which is of use to the present. The reviewer lives entirely in the present; he is content to describe a new book's contents and (if he remembers) indicate whether he approves of it. Somewhere in between, the fellow I call a book critic plies his trade. He is concerned with the present, but brings to it some sense of the past. He puts the new books he considers into some kind of context: perhaps the condition of biography today, or the novelist's past work, or the genre to which the book belongs (English mysteries, science fiction), or even the condition of our times that produces such a work. Most important, he demonstrates *how* a book works, or why it doesn't;

he must do this, even if it obliges him to usurp space that a "mere reviewer," his mind coasting in neutral, would decorate with quotations and lengthy synopses of plot.

Sometimes the very badness of a book suggests to me an oblique way to approach it—I've always thought that some of the most dreadful books published today are more revealing of our times and our values than are many of their betters. The business of the journalistic critic is to make use of these books, to show his readers what they really mean; in doing so, he is not obliged to be as dull as their authors are. The temptations of the literary critic are pedantry and obscurity; of the journalist, vulgarity. Forced to choose, I'll risk the latter every time—in vulgarity there is at least energy. Although I could barely read it, and implied that my readers should not bother, I enjoyed writing about Nancy Friday's *My Secret Garden* as much as I did Saul Bellow's *Him with His Foot in His Mouth*.

These pieces are, of course, fugitives, written against deadlines and arbitrary limitations of space that fluctuate even as the piece is in the typewriter, and often beyond. In the interests of economy, I've had to limit this collection; it seemed sensible to limit it to some of the pieces I've written about American books in the past dozen years. Well, *mostly* American books. When I put together my section called "The Art of the Thriller" I concluded that it would be senseless to leave out pieces I had written about John le Carré, Len Deighton, Geoffrey Household. But these are exceptions. I've also tried to include nothing that I did not enjoy writing at the time, nothing that I thought, upon rereading, became mired in a synopsis that might have been useful once but seems deadly the second time around. Thus my reviews of many important books—nearly all of what I've had to say about history and biography, for instance—have been jettisoned, sometimes in favor of books that no one could consider important, except that they gave me a chance to say something of my own about the way we live now, the ideas that we are content to entertain. If this book has any informational value, I will be pleased, but it was constructed with entertainment in mind.

It's customary at this point for the critic to say that he hasn't altered any of these pieces to reflect a changed opinion, but the fact is, I was never even tempted. For the same reason—that is, my vain conviction that I was right the first time—I've resisted the urge to congeal these pieces into a more substantial-looking pudding. Light cosmetics, however, have been applied: a word or phrase changed here; an outdated line dropped there; various printers' errors repaired. I have, too, taken the liberty of restoring to some of these pieces material that had to be dropped because of suddenly constricting space.

Most of these pieces first appeared in *Newsweek*, almost all of them under different titles. I'm grateful to the magazine for permission to reprint them, and to *Newsweek*'s editors for the freedom they've always allowed me. It's a pleasure to thank publicly four of my associates at *Newsweek*—Maggie Malone and James N. Baker, Ray Anello and Ray Sawhill—who have with remarkable patience and integrity steered these pieces through the rocks of revised schedules and the shoals of inadvertent error. My debt to my wife, Anne Lake Prescott, surpasses coherent acknowledgment. She has not only been my most perceptive and demanding editor, but my teacher, research assistant, and, at times, collaborator. "A word fitly spoken is like apples of gold in pictures of silver."

P.S.P.

ONE

The Way We Write Now

SINGER THE MAGICIAN

EVERY THREE YEARS or thereabouts, the gray worthies who make up the Swedish Academy show signs of intelligent life. Charged with annually awarding the Nobel Prize in literature, their taste runs generally to Scandinavian novelists beloved by readers from Reykjavik to Helsinki, to poets who cannot be understood in their own or any other tongue, to Americans (Saul Bellow excepted) who haven't written a good book in years. Tolstoy was not good enough for them, neither was Joyce or Henry James. Nabokov, Auden, and André Malraux fell into their graves without attracting the Academy's notice, and the claims of Borges and Graham Greene continue to be met with a serene indifference. No wonder, then, that when word of his anointment arrived by way of telephone calls to his Miami Beach apartment, Isaac Bashevis Singer responded skeptically. "I thought it must be a mistake or a joke," he said. "I told my wife, 'In any case, let's eat breakfast.' "

It was a characteristic remark: fame has never meant much to Singer. If it had, he would not have written almost exclusively about a way of life that was literally demolished by this century's wars and purges. He would not have persisted in writing his fine stories and novels in a language that is known to fewer people with every passing year. He would not have waited until he was forty-six to publish his first book in an English translation—the step that set him on his way to becoming a world-class writer. "I was prepared actually never to be translated," he says, "never to be known, to remain a Yiddish writer." But translations into many languages followed, and now here he is, a Polish-American who has won the top prize without ever becoming (as so many American writers feel obliged to do) a prominent public figure.

Had his parents had their way, young Isaac would have become a religious scholar. The son and grandson of rabbis, he was

born on July 14, 1904, in a town in that part of Poland that was
governed by the Russian czar. In Warsaw, to which his family
moved when he was four, he observed his father presiding over a
Beth Din, which was (as Singer described it in *In My Father's
Court*) "a kind of blend of a court of law, synagogue, house of
study, and . . . psychoanalyst's office." He lived for a time, too, in
a *shtetl*—the kind of small Jewish town that he was to write about
so often in his stories. Under the influence of his older brother, Israel Joseph, who was to become a well-known Yiddish writer,
Singer tried writing himself, first in Hebrew, then in Yiddish. In
1935, he followed his brother to America, settling in New York,
where he wrote articles, reviews, stories, and (during World War
II) essays on military tactics for a Yiddish newspaper, the *Jewish
Daily Forward.*

More than forty years later, Singer still writes for this paper,
which claims a circulation of forty-six thousand. As he always
has, Singer writes in Yiddish, then revises the work after he has
collaborated with someone else on its translation. In 1961, he de-
fended his use of a dying language: "I like to write ghost stories
and nothing fits a ghost better than a dying language. The deader
the language, the more alive the ghost. Ghosts love Yiddish and as
far as I know, they all speak it." He believes, he says, not only in
ghosts, but in a kind of universal ghostly resurrection: "I am sure
that millions of Yiddish-speaking corpses will rise from their
graves one day, and their first question will be: 'Is there any new
book in Yiddish to read?' "

Ghosts figure largely in Singer's fiction; so do dybbuks,
devils, and household demons. Their existence may prove dismaying to scientists and to Jews who have, as Singer says, "an
illusion that Judaism is a rational religion," but they are nonetheless useful figures through which we may apprehend the mystery
and unexpected joy of living that Singer celebrates in his fiction.
Singer himself is a believer: in God, though he has left the traditional forms of religion behind him; in haunted houses and spiritual creatures that surround us, and of which, he expects, we
may someday know more. His stories are rarely long, but in the
aggregate they embrace all the major themes of fiction: good and
evil; belief and doubt; action and contemplation; patience, betrayal, and the importance of emotions; the nature of illusion and

the joys of the flesh; the falling-out of generations; and the mercy and rigor of the law.

Although in recent years he has begun to write about life in his adopted country, most of Singer's stories are about poor Polish Jews, about injured men and women, holy fools, exiles, and people possessed by a passionate, destructive certainty of purpose. One of his characters attempts to memorize the Torah; another sets out to build in the most exacting detail a matchstick replica of the Temple of Jerusalem. A count who dabbles in black magic creates a she-demon, a perfect woman who comes to him at night, leaving the tracks of goose feet in the snow. In one of his strongest tales, "The Slaughterer," a failed rabbi becomes a butcher; driven mad by his immersion in blood, he perceives the whole world to be a slaughterhouse: even the Torah itself is an object made from an animal's skin.

Some of Singer's characters are scholars, like the one in "The Dead Fiddler" who "rose at dawn and went to the study house to pour over the Gemara, the Annotations and the Commentaries, the Midrash and the Zohar. In the evenings, he would read a lesson from the Mishnah." But study and piety cannot protect these people from the world's irrationality: this particular man must endure his daughter's possession by two dybbuks, the ghosts of a dead man and woman who at first (to the amazement of the townspeople) taunt each other and then get married.

In like manner, the aged scholar of "The Spinoza of Market Street," who has spent his life studying the philosopher who abhorred emotion, falls in love with a pathetic spinster. "Divine Spinoza," he murmurs at the end, "forgive me. I have become a fool." Indeed, there is in Singer's world a special grace allotted to fools. "It is written that the Lord preserves the simple," says one man, and the hero of Singer's best story, "Gimpel the Fool," is redeemed by a simplicity that, though it is mocked by all who know him, allows him to be generous and humane, to take pleasure in life in spite of the evidence of his wife's infidelities.

Books, the commentaries of philosophers, and religion have all, at one time or another, disappointed Singer. Books, even the works of the masters, disappointed him in his youth because they all "concurred that a man could love just one woman at a time. . . . I felt they lied. Rather than literature denying men's laws, the laws had seized literature in a trap and kept it there." Philosophy disappointed him because the commentaries "all led to the same conclusion: we neither know nor could know the essence of things." As for religion, when belief failed, so, for the Jew, did the framework of his life—the knowledge of "exactly what was permitted and what was forbidden, what a person should do from the moment he gets up in the morning until he goes to sleep. My life was one long chain of darkest skepticism." Skepticism, perhaps, but not unalloyed pessimism. In an interview two years ago, Singer insisted, "In life I'm an optimist. If you ask me what I think about humanity, I'm very pessimistic. I don't believe, like the socialists, in a better tomorrow, in a very beautiful future. Far from it. But I behave as if I were an optimist.

"The same questions are bothering me today as they did fifty years ago. Why is one born? Why does one suffer? In my case the suffering of animals also makes me very sad. I'm a vegetarian, you know. When I see how little attention people pay to animals, and how easily they make peace with man being allowed to do with animals whatever he wants because he keeps a knife or a gun, it gives me a feeling of misery and sometimes anger with the Almighty. I say, 'Do you need your glory to be connected with so much suffering of creatures without glory, just innocent creatures who would like to pass a few years in peace?' I feel that animals are as bewildered as we are, except that they have no words for it. I would say that all life is asking, 'What am I doing here?' "

One thing a man can do is seize such pleasures as his straitened life affords. Singer's stories, swift, humorous, and complex as they are, are suffused in sensuality. "I feel no shame in it," he said last week. "The Bible and the Talmud are full of sex stories. If these saints are not ashamed of it, why should I be, who am not a saint? If there is a God, I imagine him as a lover. According to the Cabala, all souls in Heaven make love there. The angels and the Almighty himself have a higher kind of sex, which we may not understand, but they seem to love."

Such whimsy does not charm all of Singer's readers. He has been criticized by some of his fellow Jewish writers for his sensuality, for his concern for a Jewish culture that is now dead in all but literature, for his fondness for ignorant and superstitious

Jews, for his interest in the occult. Why can he not be sentimental and radical in the best Yiddish tradition? For that matter, why does he try to perpetuate Yiddish, a language most Jews can't read? And what are we to make of a writer who not only believes in demons, but seems fond of them? "They steal my manuscripts," Singer said once, "and they keep them for a few days. Then, suddenly, they appear again. Instead of searching for a manuscript as I used to do and getting angry, I know already that the demons have taken it and that it will pop up. They steal my books, they steal my glasses, sometimes they will steal my checkbook, but they give everything back. Once I thought they stole my citizenship papers and I was mad at them. Then after a year and a half, I found them."

Singer today is seventy-four. He has written thirty books, including a number of stories for children. He has won two National Book Awards, and now, thanks to the benign intervention of the Swedes, he is richer by $164,775. His characters may bother each other and themselves by regularly asking, "Who created the world?"—a question to which Singer offers no coherent answer—but he understands the remedies to the dilemma that prompts such a question. Innocence helps, so does love, and the narrow channel through desperation by which we come to understanding and to joy.

October 1978

VEXED BY VONNEGUT

BREAKFAST OF CHAMPIONS provides further evidence that as a thinker and literary stylist Kurt Vonnegut is fully the equal of Kahlil Gibran, Rod McKuen, even Richard Bach. These writers, gurus, and soothsayers apparently fill a need for some of us, adolescents of all ages who clutch at any sentimental positivism:

Gibran's perfumed religiosity; McKuen's mawkish romanticism; Bach's can-do optimism dipped in mystical shellac; and Vonnegut's smug pessimism with its coy implication that the reader is one of the author's initiates, one of the happy few. The comfortable banalities advanced by these writers in place of ideas are totally incompatible, but that doesn't bother the groupies. *Anything* will do for them as long as it tells us it's okay not to think and as long as it's presented in a lobotomized English that these writers feel is appropriate for their audience.

Listen (as Vonnegut likes to say). Here is the plot of *Breakfast of Champions* reduced so small you could stuff it in an earthworm's ear. Kilgore Trout, the prolifically unsuccessful science-fiction writer, is beaten and robbed as he sets off for an arts festival in Midland City, where, when he arrives, his knuckle will be bitten off by Dwayne Hoover, who runs a Pontiac agency and is going insane. Dwayne blows his mind when he reads one of Kilgore's novels, which seems to Dwayne to tell him that only he has free will in a world populated by machines. He runs amok, is carted off. Vonnegut himself comes onstage to bleed for a while and fend off suicide, and then (Oh, massa! Let my people go!) he frees his characters. What that means, I'm not sure, but Vonnegut, who has provided childlike drawings to match his Dick-and-Jane prose, concludes with a self-portrait which, like any peasant's madonna, shows a tear leaking from his eye.

Enough of plot; it serves only as an armature for Vonnegut's specialty: gratuitous digressions. Here we find Vonnegut in his customary pose of satirizing attitudes that only Archie Bunker could love. Vonnegut is against racism and pollution and poverty, oh, my. "A Nigger was a human being who was black." Note the capital N: may as well make the best of a bad thing. Note the past tense: Vonnegut knows all is lost. Taking care to please his audience, he snipes at teachers: they tell kids that human beings came to America in 1492, and they flunk kids who "failed to speak like English aristocrats before the First World War." By any standard, this is sucking up to kiddy grievances. It fits well with the eighth-grade obscenities—the anal imagery and the fascination with measuring penises—and the village blasphemy: for whores to surrender to pimps, he says, is like surrendering to Jesus; they can live "unselfishly and trustingly."

Well. There is just something a little *arrested* about all this. The simpleminded summations: Communists "had a theory that what was left of the planet should be shared more or less equally," but Americans were opposed to communism. The cretinous philosophizing: "There was nothing sacred about myself or about any human being," except, of course, our awareness, "an unwavering band of light." Otherwise, human beings are robots, are machines. In a particularly charmless phrase, Vonnegut calls a girl "a machine made of meat." *That* kind of wisdom. People shoot each other because life imitates fiction, he says, and so Vonnegut, who thinks literature should be therapy, chooses to write aimlessly: "I would bring chaos to order."

Manure, of course. Pretentious, hypocritical manure. From time to time, it's nice to have a book you can hate—it clears the pipes—and I hate this book for its preciousness, its condescension to its characters, its self-indulgence, and its facile fatalism: all the lonely people, their fates sealed in epoxy. Mostly, I hate it for its reductiveness, its labored denial of man's complexity and resilience. Life cannot, as Vonnegut insists, be summed up with "And so on" and "ETC."—or at least not without more wit and insight than Vonnegut can muster. Samuel Beckett is not noticeably more optimistic about the human condition than is Vonnegut, but he does not condescend to Vladimir and Estragon. He does not think they are machines. "We are what we pretend to be," Vonnegut wrote in *Mother Night*, and if we pretend that we are only machines we cannot pretend to be interesting enough for a novel.

May 1973

Postscript: Even though six years had passed since the above was written, my editors at *Newsweek* succumbed to an attack of the vapors when they read a proof of the piece below. They refused to print it. It appeared later in the *Village Voice*.

Slaphappy; or, Breakfast
of Gonfaloons

*In which the reviewer, stunned by Kurt Vonnegut's #1
best seller* Jailbird, *finds himself unable to cope.*

To WHOM IT may concern:
Good news!

You may wonder why a book reviewer, from whom all the
world expects to see a lip disdainfully curled, would begin a piece
with a cordial phrase like "Good news!" I have done it because I
think it is a phrase Jesus would have liked. Did not the four gentle
men who wrote biographies of Jesus call their books "The Good
News" according to Matthew, Mark, and on and on?

For the benefit on my seventeen-year-old readers of every
age, to whom everything must be explained, I must explain that
"gospel" means "good news." You will find the four gospels in
the back of a book called "the Bible," which good people read
once upon a time, and some bad people, too. Imagine that. The
front part of the Bible, the longer part, contains mostly bad news
and poetry. Never mind.

I have three reasons for saluting my readers with such manufactured cheer. The first I forget, but if it comes to me, I will
pass it on to you. Prose like this is easy to write, but it is not useful for pursuing a coherent train of thought.

The second reason is that I received this morning a letter
from a young stranger named Mugger Figleaf of Tumid, Oklahoma. Tumid is notorious for having once been the precise epi-
center of the Oklahoma Dust Bowl. Mugger Figleaf, however, is a
damp young man who, in his letter to me, states that he washes

behind his ears every morning and that he has read nearly every review I have ever written. He is now prepared to state that each and every review of mine has, at its core, an unstated celebration of the work of Kurt Vonnegut, Jr. and his successor, Kurt Vonnegut. This seems to me true and complete. Good news!

The third reason for such a warm sentiment at the beginning of my piece is my conviction that although love may be dying on this ruined planet of ours, courtesy may yet prevail. We genuinely sweet people truly believe this and never miss a chance to write it out for the rest of you. When the green men from the planet Aphrodesia come down to poke among our wreckage, we want them to know that with the last of our technology we wrung acid from the rain to etch our epitaph on the sides of skyscrapers: Let's do go gentle into that good night.

But for a while, life goes on and on. Yes, Kurt Vonnegut has written another and so on. Kurt Vonnegut is a character in some reviews I have written. I have imagined him skipping along the sidewalk, his arms full of money, weeping and sniffling his way to the bank. Readers of *Slaughterhouse-Five* and *Breakfast of Champions* will remember Mr. Vonnegut as a famous sniffler. In his latest novel the narrator exclaims, "What a book this is for tears!" Imagine that.

What surprises Mr. Vonnegut's books have held for me! They have persuaded me that although we are both members of a "little human family," we are not, after all, so dissimilar. It seems we both had mothers, once upon a time. When I was a little member of my human family, my mother would say, "Pull your shoulders back and stop that weeping and sniffling." This was the kind of folk wisdom that my ethnic group brought over with them on the boat from Europe. And I am the poorer for it today. So it goes.

There is more, there is always more. I remember now the first reason why I wrote "Good news!" at the beginning of this piece. For eleven hours after I finished reading Mr. Vonnegut's latest on and on, I amazed my human family by sitting at my typewriter, my middle-aged fingers poised immobile above its keys. From time to time, I would emit a birdlike cry: *"Truwit, cudyews."* My human wife, summoning me to one meal after another, would deride what she called my avian imitations. Little could she understand that, so deeply was I affected by what I had read, I could not find the words to begin my newest celebration of Kurt Vonnegut. My newly emptied mind could only form the words of a song I had once heard children sing as, on spindly legs, they danced among the hopscotch squares. It is the cruelest song that I have ever heard:

> *O melancholy Kurt,*
> *True wit thou never wert.*

Blithe spirits! Fleshlessly jiggling their cabbalistic way, they would cry triumphantly the chorus:

> *True wit! Could use!*

A birdlike cry. Live and learn. "Could use," I thought—not quite the right words with which to begin my celebration. But the sadness of them, the hopefulness, the *sound* of them.
    Good news!

August 1979

SCHOOL OF VONNEGUT

1. Brautigan about Again

IMAGINE ZANE GREY trying to spruce up Book I of *The Faerie Queene* to make it accessible to readers west of Wichita and you'll have some idea of this fable's disarming appeal.* All the ingredients of a Good Old Myth are present: (1) a remote Gothic

---

The Hawkline Monster: A Gothic Western, by Richard Brautigan.

house that maintains its own freezing temperature in the summer heat of the Dead Hills of eastern Oregon; (2) a monster
said to thrash about the ice caves beneath the Gothic house;
(3a) an unmarried woman threatened by the monster; (3b)
her sister, an identical twin; (4) their father, an alchemist
consumed by his search for (5) the proper mix of chemicals that
will solve the ultimate problem of mankind; (6) two professional
killers.

Now for the recipe of the plot. Set aside (4) while (1)
freezes in its simmering container. Separate (3b) from (3a), re-
moving (3b) to (6). Bring (3b) and (6) to (1), then blend (3a)
and (3b). Let (5) boil over until (2) is overdone. Apply (6) to
(2). Allow (3a) and (3b) and (6) to scramble; spice with dirty
words. (The sex is inevitable once you have unmarried women
troubled by a monster thrashing about in their cellar.) And there
you have it. The result, I assure you, is as cute as a bucket of oys-
ter stew: you can suck it right down before you remember to put
in your teeth.

Like Kurt Vonnegut, Richard Brautigan is beloved by college kids. Each is admired for his tenderness toward human vulnerability, for his pose of the *faux naïf*, for his air of sweet,
inexpressible sadness. The difference between them is that Brautigan is a singularly careful writer; unlike Vonnegut, he has not
yet succumbed to portentous postures, gravid with sentimentality. Brautigan is a miniaturist who broods about death, who
builds his novels from small self-contained blocks. He cannot entirely avoid coyness or dead-end digressions. Yet he conveys a
sense of spare economy, of humorous or graceful lines eased in
almost imperceptibly: "Finally they came across something
human. It was a grave"; "The accident barely killed her and she
was quite beautiful in death."

The Hawkline Monster is rather more of a pastiche, more of
a parody than any of Brautigan's other fictions. It lacks the complexity, the many evanescent refractions of his best book, *Trout
Fishing in America,* which taps a central metaphor of American
literature and deserves to survive the time in which it was written. Never mind. There are enough oppositions here (heat/cold;
light/shadow; sex/death) to keep freshman instructors fueled for
a decade. And I like the subtitle. Little old ladies waiting in li-

braries for *Cashelmara* to be returned to the shelves may pick it
up unwittingly. And then won't they be surprised.

September 1974

2. *Bearing Up*

WE WHO HANG ABOUT the literary precincts have been hearing
the phrase "eagerly awaited" quite a lot in recent days. The
phrase is being applied to John Irving's new novel, and it may be
apt, though heaven knows, the awaiters haven't suffered long. It
seems only yesterday the delivery boys were sporting T-shirts
proclaiming their belief in Garp. Only last June, surely, the
speakers at high school commencements who had once exhorted
the serried ranks of surly adolescents with the wisdom of Kurt
Vonnegut were exhorting this season's retired students with the
wisdom of T. S. Garp.

Which is all very well, but it made *The World According to
Garp*, a novel that was not so much read as it was absorbed instantly into our folk culture, a hard act to follow. The bad news
about *The Hotel New Hampshire*—news that was not unexpected by the churlish minority who found themselves less than
enchanted by *Garp*—is that the new novel suffers from a terminal case of the cutes. I finished this book feeling pretty much as I
imagine I would feel having finished a six-pack of Diet Pepsi:
bloated, gaseous, starved for nourishment, and with a bad taste in
my mouth. The finished book was not in such good shape either:
because I had thrown it twice against the wall, its exterior looked
as bent and puffy as its contents.

These contents—and there are a lot of them, for the book is
very long—concern the fortunes of the Berry family and the various hotels in Maine, Vienna, and New Hampshire that must endure their presence. Father Berry teaches at a third-rate prep
school. Mother Berry is an amorphous figure; Irving will presently grow bored with her and kill her off, along with her least interesting child, just to get the second half of his book in trim.

Four children survive: Frank, a loner and a homosexual; Franny, who talks dirtier than any child in the entire history of fiction and has a talent for gouging boys in the genitals; John, the narrator, incestuously in love with Franny; and Lilly, an incipient dwarf with literary ambitions. (The child that is killed is named Egg—yes, really—and says "What?" so often that Irving really had to do him in.) Add to this cast a flatulent dog, a geriatric bear, an ugly lesbian who lives in a bear suit, a circus of midgets, and an Austrian Jewish refugee who is blinded by the Nazis. I haven't forgotten (though I will, presently) the whores who live on one floor of the hotel in Vienna and the terrorists who live on another. The Berrys live "between sin and danger," says eleven-year-old Lilly.

Indeed. Such comments lend this story its charm. Irving is determined to charm us; he applies charm to his pages as relentlessly as a mason supplies cement to an arch he suspects may collapse. Never mind that no one, not even Dickens, has made a wise child seem charming in a novel; the Berry family may be stupider than Salinger's Glass family, but they love each other just as much. They say cute things like: "When you fart, Arbeiter, do the seals in the zoo stop swimming?" Then, when things get serious—as they do when Franny, at fifteen, is raped by three boys—they say serene things: "Just go out and get me yesterday," Franny says, trying to recover, "and most of today. I want them back." Epigrams are never far from these adolescent lips: " 'In this world,' Franny once observed, 'just when you're trying to think of yourself as memorable, there is always someone who forgets that they've met you.' "

A deadly complacency suffuses this novel, a hard-core smugness that might be tolerable in a short story, but that, in a story as long as this, acts as a blotter to Irving's imagination. I don't mean to suggest that he's a pallid writer; far from it. Irving, as if jumping on some giant bladder, can blow up a storm of a scene, only to let it wheeze exhaustedly to death. Like many writers before him—Rabelais, for instance, as well as Vonnegut, whom Irving admires to the point of imitation—he adheres to the idea that truth and beauty are best revealed through the grotesque. John, to take only one example, is taught how to kiss by an older woman who lost all her teeth when *she* was raped, and if you wonder how that kind of education feels, Irving will tell you in detail. Throughout his story, toilets erupt, discharging their cargo upward, heads burst, the dog farts, and the kids seem perpetually to slide in blood, mud, and excrement.

Such an agitated agenda keeps the story churning, even as its significance leaks away between the cracks. Novels don't need messages, but *The Hotel New Hampshire* is so incessantly didactic, so portentous, that I found myself quite ready to grapple with ideas and furious that Irving offered me only marshmallow whip. "LIFE IS SERIOUS BUT ART IS FUN!" he writes at the end, and I guess that's what he intends his story to mean, but here he offers little to demonstrate either side of his argument.

September 1981

LOVE IN RUINS

THE SUREST WAY to start a rush for the exits is to announce the appearance of a young woman writer whose principal theme is love. Nevertheless, a new talent claims our attention most effectively when it treats old themes with fresh energy. I believe Jayne Anne Phillips is indeed a remarkable new talent and if in her first book, *Black Tickets*, she writes about love, or the absence of love, she does so in a way that suggests nothing much can be expected from it. For the women and occasional men in these stories and vignettes, love is not romantic: it is something they may have had once and then lost; it is an obligation, a vestigial link between child and parent; it is something they hadn't known before they got involved with sex; it is above all the unfulfilled promise of redemption.

Phillips's characters are invalids: a few are blind, or mad, or addicted to drugs; others are terminally ill or waiting out their empty lives unloved; others still—the young women whom the author most intimately understands—have reached a dead time in their lives and are uncertain how to proceed. When she is writing at her best, which in this book is about half the time, Phillips regards these people with a tenderness unblemished by so much as a trace of sentimentality. This is an attitude not easy to achieve.

Typically, her protagonist is a woman in her middle twenties, temporarily parted from a lover, who returns home for a few days' disheartening encounter with a widowed or divorced parent. The parent, aging and lonely, is perhaps conscious of having become one of life's supernumeraries and is mildly disapproving of the daughter's muddled life. Conversation is strained; so are the lines of affection, the bonds that were once strong but have now become frayed and entangling. In "Home," the mother, upset by the loss of her own femininity, is embarrassed by the evidence of her daughter's sexuality. In "The Heavenly Animal," a kind of mirror image of "Home," the daughter confronts her father's deteriorating existence, his continuing affection for her, and the loss of a simpler past. In "Souvenir," perhaps the most affecting of these stories about families, the daughter returns to find her mother dying of a malignancy, yet able to provide her daughter with the comfort that should rightly be the mother's.

If Phillips is most consistently successful when dealing with domestic themes, many of the stories in this collection deal with darker matters. Of these, the most striking—indeed, it is the most striking story in the book—is "Lechery," a horrendous, oddly compassionate narrative in which a fourteen-year-old girl tells how, since she was twelve, she has used sex to exert her power over timid and innocent boys. "I do things they've never seen, I could let them touch but no. I arrange their hands and feet, keep them here forever. Sometimes they tell me stories, they keep talking of baseball games and vicious battles with their friends. Lips pouty and soft, eyes a hard glass glitter. They lose the words and mumble like babies; I hold them just so, just tight, I sing the oldest songs." Abandoned by her parents and corrupted by adults, this child remains somehow untouched: "I'm pure, driven snow," she says at the end. Her invulnerability is both touching and alarming.

Of the twenty-seven stories in *Black Tickets*, eleven are of conventional length and sixteen are extremely brief: complete stories compressed into a couple of paragraphs or pages. The

shorter tales are, I think, on the whole less impressive than the
longer; too often they seem no more than showcases for their author's surprising imagination and for her experiments in overwrought prose. No matter. One of Phillips's purposes in this
book is to endow the inarticulate with a convincing eloquence and
in this she often succeeds, as with a topless dancer who says of
her lobsterman father: "He died when I was so young all he is to
me is a furred chest and smell of oiled rope. He died of lobster is
what Mom said, she killed hundreds of them." Like many writers,
Phillips performs best when her prose is plainest. Most of the
time she writes plainly and compellingly; hers is an authentic and
original voice and her debut in this collection just cause for celebration.

October 1979

OATES: OFF AND ON

FEW NOVELISTS worth serious attention are also greatly popular,
and of those who are, few are willing to risk great failure by innovation. Mailer, Styron, and Roth are exceptions, and now Joyce
Carol Oates. This is a polite way of saying that she has finally
written a very bad, nearly incoherent novel. Yet if *The Assassins*
fails to accomplish what its author intended, it is nonetheless a
deliberate enterprise. Oates warned us three years ago what we
might expect from her: an attempted synthesis of dark energies
with a mystical vision, a novel about "our contemporary neuro-
sis—a failure to see how we are all participating in a communal
consciousness."

The murder of Andrew Petrie, a reactionary ideologue and
former U.S. senator, launches his widow and two brothers on
long spirals of solipsistic musing. Like so many of the principals
in Oates's fiction, each is partly mad; each is determined in his
perverse and individual way to reduce or deny his own humanity.

Hugh Petrie, for instance, becomes obsessed by his brother's widow, Yvonne; what he takes to be an all-consuming love for her is in fact only a symptom of his progressively psychotic behavior. In his madness, Hugh translates the external world into unreal interior fantasies, yet for all his preoccupation with himself he cannot see how what is looming inside him will finally do him in. Finally, by an act of violence, Hugh becomes physically what he has always been mentally: a hopeless cripple unable to perceive the world around him; he is locked forever in his imagination.

Yvonne, in her part of the story, is in almost worse shape. A latter-day *belle dame sans merci,* she has ruthlessly cut herself off not only from other people but from her own body. This woman was perfectly matched to her husband, whose detestable social theories gave formal shape to Yvonne's instinctive fears; retribution, when it comes to her, is delivered in a hideously appropriate form.

Stephen, the other brother, neither devours himself as Hugh does nor rejects himself as Yvonne does; he loses himself instead. Stephen has out-of-the-body experiences; he believes that from time to time he is God. His final vision, however, is of demons triumphant; at the end, Stephen has nothing at all.

My interpretation of these interior melodramas may not be the author's, but then *The Assassins* is an obscure novel, long, prolix, and ill-disciplined. At times, Oates seems to be defying the reader to make his way through her pages. Her first chapter, for instance, cannot be understood until the book is two-thirds done, and Hugh's narration is so studded with fragmented phrases, dashes, and exclamation points as to become quickly infuriating. The characters are never made interesting or even credible; each is instead an anthology of psychotic responses, assembled to advance some comprehensive, obscurely articulated ideal of man's essential harmony.

Oates's reputation is now such that no editor would dare touch what she writes, yet this story desperately needs such attention. It is repetitious and sloppily written: "The terrible weakness of men, men of a certain age—what they simply cannot resist and will succumb to every time. . . . They can't help it—can't help it . . . a phenomenon they simply can't help" (Oates's ellipses). With prose of this sort, which is no less intolerable because it reveals Hugh's disordered mind, and her own unintelligible vision of human interconnectedness, Oates has managed to make lunacy more boring than sanity. Which it probably is in reality, but rarely is in fiction.

October 1975

In that divided country over which Joyce Carol Oates presides, the border line of sanity runs right through the middle. Problems of free will do not concern her characters; the condition, in a world where even a head of lettuce is "the size of a baby's skull," simply does not obtain. "How much reality can you credit to all this?" one woman asks, "referring to the street, the busy intersection which she was approaching, a child pedaling energetically on a bicycle, the filmy sky, the day, the world itself." A few pages later she discovers that "her own body was suffused with a sudden vitality, an uncanny strength that had lain in a trance for many years. The body's life is a matter of power, she saw, and one of the manifestations of this power is—simply—to recognize it and pay homage to it." Oates people are possessed by they know not what, but whatever it is, it is isolating and makes knowledge of love impossible. "His essence lies elsewhere," one of her men concludes, "in another dimension, in unspeakable secrecy."

It is, I think, this sense of the irrational, with its potential for destruction, intruding into the banality of modern middle-class life, that makes Oates's fictions—both short and long—so distinctive, so seductive. From reading inelegant newspapers we know, or should know, that the world often presents itself much as Oates defines it. In *A Sentimental Education,* a collection of five stories and a novella, she once again runs through her by now familiar set of changes. Behind a locked bathroom door a naked young woman slashes at her wrist. A teacher fond of quoting Pascal finds himself ineluctably drawn into savage brawls with strangers. A man finds himself unable to cope with the memory of a murder he has witnessed, although he knows that "sooner or later one would probably witness a murder, living here. Living anywhere, in fact."

Garish as her themes may be, Oates's treatments are impeccably assured. She knows as well as any of her contemporaries how to shape a narrative to the effect she means to achieve; she writes as easily about men as about women, as well about teenage eroticism as about middle-aged lust. I enjoyed all of the stories in this collection, but one strikes me as particularly elegant. In "Queen of the Night," an attractive woman in her fifties divorces her husband and succumbs to the infatuation of a much younger, thoroughly useless young man. Within her she feels a power develop that she had not recognized before, and by the story's end—though nothing has been explained—the young man introduces her to his coven of night friends as Queen of the Night: Hecate, goddess of witches and the underworld, a female principle incarnate. This is, I suspect, a story that Jung would have enjoyed, rich in psychic vibrations and evidence that Oates does not draw her inspiration wholly from the police blotter.

January 1981

It says something about serious fiction's uneasy state today that two recent ambitious novels have (with the greatest self-consciousness) returned to discredited modes of storytelling. I mean Mario Vargas Llosa's *Aunt Julia and the Scriptwriter*, which relies on jumped-up soap operas for its several narratives, and now *A Bloodsmoor Romance*, Joyce Carol Oates's pastiche of the nineteenth-century romantic novel. Maybe they're telling us that the old ingredients were the best, or are at least still serviceable—even if no one can write them with a straight face now. Oates begins with an abduction and ends with another; in between, in this story, which is noticeably longer than *Middlemarch*, she gives us a time machine, infant deaths, a ghost, a seance, an orphan found, a great inheritance with a dramatic reading of a will, betrayals, a wedding night, lost lovers returned, various catalogues of nineteenth-century clothing, legends, and assorted oddities, and some curious (but not uninteresting) sex. I think it unlikely that her American models did as well—not Catherine Sedgwick or George Lippard, whose romances nobody reads today; certainly not Louisa May Alcott, read now by none but children.

There were, on an afternoon in 1879, five marriageable sisters attending to their sewing in a gazebo on a great estate in Pennsylvania. Deirdre, the youngest, walks down the lawn and, as her sisters watch, is kidnapped by "an outlaw balloon of sinister black-silken hue, manned by an unidentified pilot." So much for the first page of this enormous novel; on the second, the narrator suggests that Deirdre may have deserved her fate. An adopted girl, she was an uncouth, even froward child, insufficiently grateful to her father, the famous but economically straitened inventor, whose pursuit of a perpetual motion machine will lead him nearly to a nuclear chain reaction by the time of his death. Deirdre will in time surface as a genuine medium, one who is really in touch with the spirit world, but before she does, fates equally odd—and equally disgraceful—will claim each of her sisters. One, for instance, will become a Broadway actress and the mistress of Mark Twain (who is, like Madame Blavatsky, Deirdre's onetime patron, convincingly represented here); another will kill her husband under the most peculiar circumstances; still another will flee her wedding bed to become a man. In these early days, it seems, all the transsexual process required was determined imitation: cussing and drinking whiskey and chewing tobacco and wearing pants would eventually cause the critical interior organ to take up residence outside. This daughter becomes a U.S. deputy marshal in Tombstone.

Good stuff, this; a writer with plot on her mind could hardly ask for better. Oates has always had a flair for what I can only call *Petit Guignol* and here she invests it with wit. Repeatedly—and her story is dauntingly repetitious—she redeems the preposterousness of what happens with the fertility of her imagination, with her humor and scholarship, and with her determination to encase her narrative's improbabilities within an elaborate retrograde design. Oates knows very well that a kind of suspense can be generated (albeit in a hokey sort of way) by muttering darkly about dire events to come and by freezing an unexplained event on the page as she indulges in a long flashback.

Our pleasure in her expansive and funny story, however, can't be unalloyed; the novel does present problems. One is its prolixity. Another is its narrator, an unidentified maiden of middle or late years, who is somehow privy to the characters' most intimate thoughts. How a narrator who is not the author can be omniscient cannot, of course, be explained, which is why (I suspect) Oates never tells us who she is, and that's a pity because we really need to know—I can't think of another long work of fiction in which the relationship of the narrator to the characters is not sorted out at once. Here we keep waiting for a revelation that never comes. Still, this narrator does fulfill a traditional role: she doesn't understand the significance of what's going on. The woman is starchy; she would like us to think her prim, though she clearly relishes the improper parts she claims she blushes to report. She insists that females must keep their place, when the point of the novel is that these repressed young women are busting out all over. Though her verbosity can be exasperating, she's a fine comic creation—and yet even Oates can't always control her: occasionally when the story shifts gear, Oates (as if by instinct) gives it the narrative tone it deserves, never mind what her little old lady would say. Finally, there's a problem that a spoof of romantic fiction can never overcome: the reader can't care for the characters; he can only wait for something bizarre to happen to them. The lack of caring, in so long a novel, becomes a burden. But as for the bizarre events—Oates never fails us there.

September 1982

TROPIC OF CANKER

UNLIKE GREAT COMPOSERS, writers of genius are not expected to perform with any degree of consistency. Bach and Mozart wrote some dull music, on occasion plagiarized themselves, but neither ever wrote anything so appallingly awful that you would doubt its paternity. Not so with writers. Two books written at full throttle, the hand held hard on the horn, will excuse a dozen tepid or egregious exercises. Norman Mailer, who has reason to know this, here celebrates Henry Miller, calls him a great writer.*

---

*Genius and Lust: A Journey Through the Major Writings of Henry Miller, by Norman Mailer.

"When Miller is bad, he may be the worst great writer ever to be bad."

That's a pretty terrible sentence, but then critics of genius (and Mailer is one) spend a lot of time being wrong, too. Mailer is wrong when he says Miller's prose equals Faulkner's, wrong to suggest *Tropic of Cancer* is as good as *The Sun Also Rises* and better than *The Great Gatsby*. No matter: we don't ask genius to be right; we ask it to be provocative. What Mailer means—what anyone who talks of Henry Miller's greatness must confront—is that most of Miller's writing is slight and self-indulgent. Eventually his reputation will rest on two books, *Tropic of Cancer* and *Tropic of Capricorn*, with perhaps a nod at *Black Spring* and *The Colossus of Maroussi*. To say so should not diminish his importance. Mailer is right to say that Miller committed "a revolution in style and consciousness."

Revolution! For a quarter of a century Americans were forbidden by their fellow Americans to read this American's books. Thousands of us, solemnly sworn to study French literature, went to Paris, checked our bags at a pension, and took the first bus to Brentano's, Avenue de l'Opéra, where we bought *Lady Chatterly's Lover* and the two *Tropics*. Later we carried these books home stuffed in our jockey shorts, or we mailed them gift-wrapped with a card ("This won the Prix Goncourt, hope you like it, love, Aunt Tania"), a challenge to U.S. Customs.

And we did this because really there *was* a revolution and we wanted to see what the fuss was about. Henry Miller, a very good writer, wrote about sex as no other serious writer ever had. He could not write about sex with love (which was the only kind of sex that literature was supposed to celebrate), but he was pushing at the limits of what you could do with sex in literature and it was an act worth watching. All the bad words are on display, but in his obscene books it is not the obscenity that matters. "I have no money, no resources, no hopes. I am the happiest man alive." *That* is the essential Miller, the narrator who can admire his love's "beautiful wild hair" just before the lice pour out of it, or "the pleasant sound of water running in the urinals." "I vomit all over the place, in the beds, in the washbowl, over the suits and gowns and the galoshes and canes and notebooks I never touched and the manuscripts cold and dead." Nobody, in a novel-cum-autobiography, had written quite like that before. The smells of armpits and sewers bubbling up pervade Miller's fiction: "There was a touch of spring in the air, a poisonous, malefic spring that seemed to burst from the manholes."

Only fifteen years ago our policemen and judges, the grocers who serve on rural school boards, the suburban bankers who moonlight as library trustees were fighting to protect America from Henry Miller's books—but it seems an age has passed. The *Tropics*, legitimatized, don't carry quite the punch they did when they were banned—when we had no access to the truly degenerate books that followed in their wake—and Miller's "clean" books are now nearly impossible to reread. Mailer is right to say "the experience which makes his literature is precisely his sexual vigor, and he is next to no author without it." But of course, being Mailer, he pushes his point too far: Miller, for him, is "the Grand Speleologist of the Vagina . . . the man with iron in his phallus, acid in his mind and some kind of incomparable relentless freedom in his heart." Recovering, Mailer says of Miller that obscenity was not a pose, "but the natural blood of his mind and the steel in his tools of analysis."

Miller could be funny about sex, or cold-blooded. He wrote better than anyone else about sexual exhaustion, could get across something of the mystery of woman, of sex as an abstract compulsion. That he would seem pleased with such abstractions is a curious fault in a writer who dealt in such realistic detail with what he saw in the streets of Brooklyn and Paris, and keeps him from true greatness. "Kikes" and "niggers" stroll across his pages, and those parts of a woman that lie north of the navel and south of the knees are never closely examined.

For Miller, women are subject to "uterine hysteria"(what other kind did he think there was?); they slaver and drip and shout, "Do it, do it, or I'll go mad." "She wasn't any longer a woman in heat," Miller observes, "she wasn't even a woman; she was just a mass of undefinable contours wriggling and squirming like a piece of fresh bait seen upside down through a convex mirror in a rough sea." One doesn't have to be far advanced into women's lib to wince at that, or at Miller's consistent dehumanization of women. The problem of pornography in his work is for us very real, though he is probably the most forceful pornogra-

pher in history. When he is writing well about sex, as he does in
the *Tropics*, he is lyrical, but when Miller writes badly, as he
does in the interminable *Sexus*, he is only mechanical: "I began to
work on her like a plunger."

Norman Mailer has written a stylish, acute essay about
Miller and has assembled with less than acute discrimination a
large amount of Miller's writing. Curiously, he has ignored some
of Miller's finest, most revealing passages: the account in *Capricorn* of his first seduction (he was fifteen and she was his piano
teacher); the description in *Cancer* of spring arriving in Paris and
the discourse on Matisse and the modern world. "The monstrous
thing is not that men have created roses out of this dung heap,"
Miller wrote, "but that, for some reason or other, they should
want roses." Mailer missed that part, too. Miller is no philosopher
(though he tried hard), but to avoid his philosophical flights is to
misrepresent him. On the whole, readers who don't know Miller
would be better advised to buy the two *Tropics* and the number
24 of *American Review*, which contains the major part of
Mailer's essay.

November 1976

THE NEWS FROM
ANCIENT EGYPT

LISTEN! In every alley in the literary precincts: the sound of
knives being sharpened against steel. Eleven years in gestation,
Norman Mailer's magnum opus, his million-dollar baby about
ancient Egypt, has finally been delivered. Surely a cord needs
cutting here—if not the baby itself, ugly and odiferous as it often
is. But no, the knives are not in order, even if *Ancient Evenings* is
a novel a lot of people are going to love to hate. Stupefying the
book many be, but it's also damned impressive, a book to remind

us that even in his most obsessive wallowing Mailer remains the most talented writer we have just now. *Ancient Evenings* is not just dauntingly ambitious; it's daring, too, because in it Mailer works against his established strength as our most journalistic novelist, the inductive, intuitive reporter whose nose ferrets out the American essence. His nose is still active—to catalogue the smells in this story, most of them fecal, would set any reader against it—but the reporter has stepped out of the room. Here Mailer does what artists do: he invents a world, reconstructing (as he said in an earlier work) "the dinosaur from the fossil bone."

That world is the Egypt of three thousand years ago. Though Mailer remains as true to history as any novelist need do (he has clearly done a great deal of research), this world is stranger than we might imagine; it's a younger world animated by energies that will soon be dimmed by technology. In it, the gods are very much a presence; magic works; ghosts walk; reincarnation is unremarkable; and the people (at least the nobility of which Mailer writes) are sexually omnivorous and often able to communicate by thought alone. Mailer sets the bulk of his story within two frames. In the outer frame, the ghost of a young man awakes in a tomb to encounter the ghost of the great-grandfather for whom he was named, Menenhetet. Menenhetet embarks upon the story of Isis and Osiris, one of the most haunting legends in all mythology and one that Mailer develops eloquently and at length.

What the younger Menenhetet then remembers serves as the story's second frame. He remembers an evening when his family dined with Ramses IX, at the pharaoh's palace in Memphis. It was a night for ambition: the boy's great-grandfather hopes to become the pharaoh's vizier; his mother hopes to seduce Ramses and to persuade him that he is the real father of her son. Because the elder Menenhetet remembers in detail each of his four lives, Ramses asks him to tell the story of a great battle fought 150 years earlier, in which the Hittites nearly annihilated the forces of Ramses II. Encouraged by his host, Menenhetet talks the night (and the book) away, enlarging his assignment to include his entire autobiography: how he rose from the peasantry to become Ramses's best charioteer, general of all the armies, keeper of

Ramses's harem, and finally confidant to, and conspirator with, two of Ramses's wives.

It's Mailer's conceit to filter this violent, elaborately detailed story of splendor and decadence through the eyes of a six-year-old boy. Now there are two complexities of everyday life that six-year-old children cannot be relied upon to grasp: the ambiguities of lust and power. Yet power is what *Ancient Evenings* is about: the power of the gods, of warfare, of magic, of sex used as a tool for aggression, of kings, and of family connections. Its message (if it has one) seems to be that the concentration of power at the top of the pyramid unhinges all stability: to rule all is to fear everyone. That's lofty enough; now for the matter of sex, which is here used as an instrument of humiliation. Mailer, we know from past novels, has thought long and hard about anal rape, but here he outdoes himself. The news he brings us from ancient Egypt is not just of sex that is unfailingly exploitative, but of pandemic buggery. (The Nile itself is likened to the cleft between two buttocks; a chariot wheel to "a strange anus." No wonder the Hebrews, who took a dim view of sodomy, left Egypt at just this time. In Mailer's story, the Egyptians are hardly aware of the Exodus: Moses appears offstage for only a page—the Yasir Arafat of his day.)

The effect of this anal obsession is at first mesmerizing, then anesthetizing, but finally, like so much else in the book, it assumes an incantatory quality. Mailer is a great list maker—of weapons, perfumes, clothing, the ingredients of the most sacred incense. He makes up Egyptian folk tales, songs, ceremonies of magic and initiation. Unlike most historical novelists, he has shorn his story of any reference to ideas or cultural attitudes that came later. His people are not twentieth-century figures in fancy dress; the metaphors they use develop from the life they know. When the river rises, "the sluggish green of the Nile, which had been like a soup thickening on the fire, began to ripple, and we used to say that a crocodile as long as the river was stirring beneath."

That's grand stuff, and so is Menenhetet's account of the great battle of Kadesh, which involves a warrior lion that Rider Haggard would have envied, and the retreat of the Egyptian wounded: "Some lived. Some died. They all stank. The Divisions of Amon, Ra, Ptah, and Set traveled behind each other in so long a line that it took a day to move from the van to the rear. Now we were truly like a worm cut in four pieces. Yet the smell connected us. We moved slowly, a thick river, full of rot, and the screams of the wounded were terrible when their wagons shuddered over the rocks of the gorges."

You'll have to push your way through this book, part of the way in four-wheel drive, but you'll never mistake it for so many of those that crowd publishers' lists today: the thin volumes about thin marriages into which even thinner adultery intrudes, and all of them sounding the same, as if they had been patted into shape in some national creative writing class. *Ancient Evenings* is worthy of our irritation, our respect, and perhaps our awe.

April 1983

THE HEMINGWAY LETTERS

IMAGINE, if you will, this scene, preferably as a sequence of panels in a comic strip. We are in the bar dining room of the "21" Club, or the editorial rooms at the *New Republic*—anywhere that literary hangers-on hang out. Suddenly, a fat, bearded man appears, wielding a submachine gun. He is—no doubt about it— Ernest Hemingway. *Brrup-bup-bup-bup-bup-bup!* The floor is strewn with editors, book reviewers, academic critics. One of *Mad* magazine's deranged fantasies, you will say; possibly the *National Lampoon.* Wrong: the fantasy is Hemingway's own, conveyed in a letter to John Dos Passos.

It is this kind of *jeu d'esprit* that makes his letters worth reading, yet for a time an embargo was imposed upon them.*

Ernest Hemingway: Selected Letters, 1917–1961, edited by Carlos Baker.

Hemingway did not want them published—they were, after all, personal, libelous, rambling exercises composed by way of relief from the day's work of controlling the language—and his biographer, Carlos Baker, was prohibited from quoting them directly. Hemingway constantly apologized for his letters: they were too long, too dull, too badly spelled. They do not read, as Shaw's letters do, like argumentative essays; few are as affecting as Scott Fitzgerald's letters to his daughter. Hemingway liked gossip, scraps of news, body counts of birds and fish he slaughtered— none of this very interesting now. Often he couldn't take the time to be acute: of Gerald and Sara Murphy he wrote, "They're grand people. Nice people are so damned nice," and of Thomas Mann's *Buddenbrooks*, "a pretty damned good book. If he were a great writer it would be swell." Some of his early correspondence is so cute as to affect a disinterested reader's glottal sphincter: "Dearest Wicky," he addresses his first wife, Hadley, "Poor dear little Wicky Poo."

Nevertheless, despite these fallings-off, and despite Hemingway's fondness for such words as "kike" and "nigger," the letters are fascinating—precisely because they are so unguarded, so intense, so expressive of the author's mood of the moment. Hemingway emerges from these pages as close to life as we shall ever see him: blustering, aggrieved, courteous, malicious, determined, funny, profane, and increasingly obscene. These letters emphasize what is perhaps most important about the man: that however careless he seemed to be about his life, he was obsessively careful about what he wrote for publication, a tireless craftsman conscious of the revolution he was working in American prose.

Of his first major book, *In Our Time*, he wrote to his publisher: "The stories are written so tight and so hard that the alteration of a word can throw an entire story out of key." And to his father: "You see I'm trying in all my stories to get the feeling of the actual life across—not just to depict life—or criticize it—but to actually make it alive." If this meant using words that were then unpublishable, he would use them and argue with his editors for them, though always maintaining that he never used obscenities for effect and would accept a substitute where possible. "Invention" he wrote to Fitzgerald, "is the finest thing but you cannot invent anything that would not actually happen. That is what we are supposed to do when we are at our best—make it all up—but make it up so truly that later it will happen that way." Finally, there is no excuse for a bad book: "I happen to be in a very tough business where there are no alibis. It is good or it is bad and the thousand reasons that interfere with a book being as good as possible are no excuses if it is not. . . . Taking refuge in domestic successes, being good to your broke friends etc. is merely a form of quitting."

Sound words, surely, and this book should be read by apprentice writers for them, but it is more likely to be read for its author's famous posturings and prejudices. Hemingway on what fun it was to beat up Wallace Stevens. Hemingway on how cool he was as he murdered an unarmed German prisoner. Hemingway on raising babies: "Main thing with baby is have good nurse." Hemingway on women who write memoirs: "The only way, I suppose, is to find out what women are going to write memoirs and try to get them with child." Hemingway on how he saved his wife Mary's life after the doctor had given up. Hemingway on boxing dead writers: Turgenev went down easily, but "it took four of the best stories" to beat de Maupassant. "I wouldn't fight Dr. Tolstoi in a 20 round bout because I know he would knock my ears off. The Dr. had some terrific wind and could go forever and then some. But I would take him on for six. . . ."

When he isn't strutting admiringly before the mirror, he offers condescending appraisals of his fellow writers. Mary McCarthy "writes like the most intelligent trained flea that ever lay between Fortune's Favors." T. S. Eliot is "a damned good poet and a fair critic; but he can kiss my ass as a man and he never hit a ball out of the infield in his life and he would not have existed except for dear old Ezra, the lovely poet and stupid traitor." Faulkner "has the most talent of anybody and he just needs a sort of conscience that isn't there. Certainly if no nation can exist half free and half slave no man can write half whore and half straight." To his publisher, who had sent him James Jones's *From Here to Eternity*, he replied, "I do not have to eat an entire bowl of scabs to know they are scabs; nor suck a boil to know it is a boil; nor swim through a river of snot to know it is snot. I hope he kills himself as soon as it does not damage his or your sales."

Reading other people's mail is a primary human instinct, yet

I doubt whether anyone would pay (with tax) thirty dollars for a
look at nearly six hundred of these letters if they didn't support
and extend the legend that Hemingway assiduously cultivated
and at times resisted. Fortunately for his reputation and our sensibilities, however, there is much of a more serious and humane
substance here as well. An early letter from young Ernest to his
mother protesting that his stories were not written to pander to
the lowest human responses is quite moving—the kind of letter, I
suspect, that many of this century's authors have written to their
parents. Hemingway's efforts to see that Ezra Pound was not
crucified for his treasonous wartime broadcasts are entirely laudable. Most affecting of all are the letters he sent to Scott Fitzgerald in the thirties, urging his friend to finish *Tender Is the
Night*, reminding him what good writing is and what good writers must do.

Hemingway knew Fitzgerald better than anyone and was
appalled by the spectacle of tragic waste. "I often wonder if he
would not have been the best writer we've ever had," he wrote to
their mutual editor, Max Perkins, "or likely to have if he hadn't
been married to someone that would make him waste *Everything.*" Later, he wrote, "Work would help him; noncommercial,
honest work—a paragraph at a time. But he judged a paragraph
by how much money it made him and ditched his juice into that
channel because he got an instant satisfaction. . . . It was a terrible
thing for him to love youth so much that he jumped straight from
youth to senility without going through manhood." And to Fitzgerald he wrote, "Forget your personal tragedy. We are all
bitched from the start and you especially have to hurt like hell
before you can write seriously. But when you get the damned
hurt use it—don't cheat with it. Be as faithful to it as a scientist. . . ."

Such concern, such perceptions, excuse any amount of vanity and clowning. The collection that Carlos Baker has assembled
provides as much of both as anyone could ask for. It deepens our
understanding of one of America's most important writers without offering much news—Baker had, after all, access to the letters,
and paraphrased many of them, when he wrote his biography.
Indeed, one will need the biography at hand when reading the
letters, for the notes that Baker appends to them are often inade-

quate, leaving many persons and events unidentified. I would have preferred him to replace perhaps twenty of these letters with a skeletal life of their author, or an appendix identifying each correspondent. A small complaint; this book, while barely moveable, is indeed a feast.

March 1981

DONALD BARTHELME'S WONDERFUL MACHINES

Notes for the Barthelme review:*

He has said somewhere he trusts only fragments. Yet clearly he trusts irony, too, so he will appreciate my impression that not only are some of these stories better than others, but some parts of his stories are better than other parts, and sometimes parts of his sentences are better than others. I have not found this true with other writers.

His joke:

At a recent dinner party an elderly, much decorated writer smiled benignly on the bearded man to whom he had just been introduced. "And what do *you* do, Mr. Barthelme?" The instantaneous reply: "I repair typewriters." A mad jest, perhaps rehearsed, yet not inaccurate.

His wonderful machine:

Like the Wright brothers, who repaired bicycles, the typewriter repairman has a marvelous invention, the Distant Early Warning Cliché Detector with exclusive Recycling Attachment, which he wheels out into the late afternoon of America. Bring me

---

*Here I have made the form of my review of Donald Barthelme's *Sadness* accommodate some passages from a later review of *Guilty Pleasures* as well.

your tired words, your poor phrases, your huddled sentences yearning to breathe free.

In the late afternoon the light falls sideways on drowsy people and language, heightening colors to fever flush, deepening shadows, pockmarks, fissures; it is an uneasy time of day. "We are adrift in a tense and joyless world that is falling apart at an accelerated rate," says one of Barthelme's narrators. He's right; what to do? The typewriter repairman's machine sends up puffs of colored smoke, warnings against the unreliable blue of the sky. And sometimes a pink party balloon, rising through the smog.

"Ennui is the absence of games," says someone else, ". . . the modern world at its most vulnerable."

Things to be taken into consideration:

He is a mannerist. In each of his stories he attempts to dance on the crest of the waves. For this purpose, he has another wonderful machine, a wave-making device, which other writers, like Robert Coover, borrow from time to time. It produces creditable waves, but occasionally Barthelme sinks to his knees.

His stories are elusive. Some are more accessible than others. They are also very short.

Sources of Barthelme's work:

Borges is the name that springs from the critics' lips, but French films and surrealistic painting seem more apropos. Alain Resnais juxtaposes banal dialogue with nuclear holocaust, flashes fragments of narrative at the viewer. Magritte piles up ugly houses and calls the arrangement *The Bosom;* he plucks away the silhouette of a *petit bourgeois* in a bowler hat to reveal a sky full of clouds beyond. This is Barthelme's line of work.

His techniques: his themes:

Irony is his principal tool. He relies also on fragmentation, the apotheosis of banality. He is playful, yet fearful of life's viscosity. What he has previously called "the trash phenomenon" is overtaking us all. And Barthelme is its chronicler. The metamorphosis of everything into trash: our acquisitions, our speech, our lives. The awesome moon rocks, for instance, are just so much more trash: "the moon rocks gave off a slight hum, which cleaned your teeth, and a brilliant glow, which absolved you from sin."

It is not always clear in his stories precisely who is speaking. His occasional college humor ("I visit my assistant mistress") and more than occasional gloomy aphorisms ("What an artist does, is fail"). His targets are often broad—Ed Sullivan, the Cosmopolitan Girl, the verbs favored by newsmagazines—and tattered, but Barthelme comes on like Robin Hood: his shafts split whatever arrows he finds standing in the bull's-eye.

The speed and economy with which he begins: "While I read the *Journal of Sensory Deprivation*, Wanda, my former wife, read *Elle.*"

The recurring theme in many of these stories is man's temptation toward conventional life.

Examples:

In a story about Saint Anthony at large in the city today, the former ascetic and recluse concedes that "ordinary life" is indeed a temptation. "You must fight against the cocoon of habituation," says a voice in another story, "which covers everything, if you let it. There are always openings, if you can find them. There is always something to do."

Against entropy:

A certain optimism, then; it has always been lurking about Barthelme's fiction, but never much remarked. Snow White, in Barthelme's only novel, tells the dwarfs she doesn't like their world and is trying to learn to imagine a better one. In one of his stories, "A City of Churches," a girl threatens to disrupt the city's hermetic placidity: "I'll dream the life you are most afraid of," she says. In another, he seems to demonstrate that we cannot, through words, approach the idea of Nothing. The interfering plenitude of life continually nudges us away from an excuse for stopping. The typewriter repairman keeps us in working order still.

November 1972 and November 1974

In literature, as in psychoanalysis, it's always open season on fathers.* The legal limit, the one who wears your name, never suffices—we are drawn to stories of bigger game, of heroic sons who did their monstrous fathers in. Kronos, Oedipus, and Samuel Butler. There are exceptions. Aeneas bears his father, Anchises, on his shoulders from the flames of Troy. Medieval literati sighed in admiration: a pious son. Yet Anchises hung around to

---

*The Dead Father, by Donald Barthelme.

share his son's further adventures and begins to look (to our modern eyes) like a pain in the neck. How to get rid of the father? Freud considered the problem and chewed on his cigar. You can't kill the father in your head. The father, like the poor, we have always with us. In modern fiction, fathers tend to prevail, viz., Kafka's story "The Judgment," in which the father tells his son to drown himself and the son does, loving his father as he vaults from the bridge.

The dead father in Donald Barthelme's second novel is being dragged from here to there by a small band of faithful, occasionally mutinous, subjects. The dead father is thirty-two hundred cubits long, has one mechanical leg, and from time to time walks around with a sword laying waste clusters of musicians and animals. "He is dead only in a sense," one of his followers explains. The dead father performs the traditional paternal roles of controller, confessor, and constrainer of children; he puts out ukases and punishes transgressors; he makes male children wear cap-and-bell hats and deflowers the girls. His followers mock and rebuke him; yet, as one remarks, he still has "Authority. Fragile, yet present. He is like a bubble you do not wish to burst." Another replies, "But remember there was a time when he was slicing people's ears off with a wood chisel. Two-inch blade."

Into his novel Barthelme has bound a pamphlet, "A Manual for Sons," which offers useful information ("The best way to approach a father is from behind") and examples of paternal discourse ("Son, you got to get your natural impulses curbed"). Certain other truths emerge as the dead father is hauled along his course. "A son can never, in the fullest sense, become a father. . . . At what point do you become yourself? Never, wholly, you are always partly him." The true task of the son is to become a paler, weaker version of the father, "thus moving toward a golden age of decency, quiet, and calmed fevers."

In a similar way, Freud tells us, was religion born. A small band of men killing the father, hauling him away and eating him (instead of burying him, as these men do), feeling guilt. Barthelme may or may not have had the history of religion in mind, but when you write a fable about one kind of archetype, it's hard to avoid colliding with others. What's more, Barthelme's fables tend to be oblique, as does his dialogue, long runs of it in this book. The scraps of speech are tangentially related but continually turning away from whatever course the conversation may have had; phrases are repeated as leitmotifs, but there is no center at all. The result, a theme-and-variations approach to what fathers mean to us, is always witty and occasionally beautiful. Barthelme's business is to draw beauty from banality, to assemble fragments into mythic structures, to help us to tolerate, as one of his characters says, "the anxiety. To do otherwise is to jump ship, ethics-wise."

November 1975

Perhaps half of the pieces in Donald Barthelme's new collection, *Great Days*, show him at his most adventurous; none, I think, shows him wholly at his best. More than most writers, Barthelme is willing to make difficulties for himself, discarding the fiction writer's traditional resources to invent new forms with which to mirror our complacency, our discontent.* Occasionally—in his shortest pieces especially—he seems complacent himself, content just to hum a jig or two, to be no more than charming. And why not? Must we constantly flog our best writers, demanding from them only the most strenuous exertions? Besides, Barthelme really *is* charming:

—Love, which is a kind of permission to come closer than ordinary norms of good behavior might usually sanction.

—Back rubs.

—Which enables us to see each other without clothes on, for example, in lust and shame.

—Examining perfections, imperfections.

—Which allows us to say wounding things to each other which would not be kosher under the ordinary rules of civilized discourse.

---

*"If you are trying to make art," Barthelme told me in 1973, "you have to go where difficulty is. Any writer in the country can write a beautiful sentence, but it is more interesting to write an ugly sentence which is also beautiful." Difficult writing, however, presents its own problems: "You limit your audience drastically. You exclude people, cut them out. As good socialists, good democrats, we don't want to do that."

Antiphonal voices such as these remind me that of all our present crop of prose writers, Barthelme is the most concerned with sound. Our most musical writer, he has never been particularly concerned with plots, or with descriptions and analyses of character, but advances his fiction by working variations on a theme and by the sound of voices playing against each other.

In *Great Days* Barthelme pushes this kind of writing to the limit of comprehensibility by constructing seven of his pieces entirely as dialogues between unidentified pairs of men or women. No scene is set; no names are given; no movement occurs; the disembodied speakers are not allowed so much as an ash can to cover themselves. Nor do the voices necessarily speak to each other—sometimes they talk at tangents. In "The Crisis," for instance, a man speculates on the progress of an unsuccessful rebellion while another offers a barrage of self-centered clichés. From this, many changes are rung on certain attitudes that cannot be unfamiliar to those who have lived through our recent history, and, because Barthelme rarely leaves his clichés alone, but alters them subtly to make them fresh and pleasing to the ear, from such banality comes something rich and strange. It is all done with the ear, and I am tempted to say that Barthelme writes as a blind man might—except that blind writers are usually the first to tell us the news of how things appear to the eye.

Perhaps because they are so ambitious, these dialogues are not all successful. One in particular, "The New Music," contains so many kinds of references that it seems to need further decoding; its very privacy, and the repetition of certain phrases that have not been made quite resonant, suggest a kind of self-indulgence. Barthelme, running through his riffs and licks, seems sometimes more enchanted by his music than I can be. As if in contrast, *Great Days* includes a number of Barthelme's least ambitious works: short sketches, playful *jeux d'esprit* that offer a cute phrase ("Mine is the art of the possible, plus two") or an easy joke ("He has this mysterious power over people and events which is called ten million dollars a year, gross").

By my count, seven of these sixteen pieces show Barthelme performing either daringly and well or efficiently and well—and that may be all we can ask. It is in the nature of the way he writes that his pieces (and I keep using that word because *story*, in this

collection, really will not do) can be no better than the invention,
the controlling metaphor, that he chooses for each. If his inventions are sometimes slight, it doesn't matter much, for the least of
Barthelme's stories must make us smile, and over the years he has
assembled an impressive body of work.

February 1979

SCHOOL OF BARTHELME

LIKE A CHILD who pats a pile of wet sand into turrets and crene-
lated ramparts, Robert Coover prods at our most banal distractions and vulgar obsessions, nudging them into surreal and
alarming forms. His fictions—novels, stories, and, in *A Theological Position*, plays—sound at times like incantations, which, as
they progress, mount to frenzy. What began slowly, seemingly
grounded in homely realistic details, lurches, reels a bit, becomes
possessed by manic excitation; the characters' faces dissolve to
reveal archetypal forms beneath; time and direction come un-
glued; the choices a writer makes to send his story one way or another are ignored so that simultaneously all possible alternatives
occur and, at the end, as often as not, we find our laughter con-
tracting in our throats because some of Coover's stories can be
fearsome indeed.

From fantasies that crowd our minds in idle moments
Coover's best tales come. At first simple distractions, the fantasies
assume control. A miserable accountant improves his loneliness
by playing baseball games in his mind; in time the players become more real than the man imagining them. A baby-sitter arrives and, for a moment, her employer is distracted by lust.
Images gnaw the corner of this man's consciousness; certain
scenes recur, theme and variations, as the pace accelerates. Which
are "real," which imagined? Where, in fact, is the point of departure, the tonic note?

This is Coover's most intriguing skill: while casting his stories loose from time and realism, he maintains the form and pace that narrative requires, shaping from shopworn details stories and symbols that have the timelessness, the compelling but oblique reality, of myth. He plays, too, with literary stories that have the qualities of myth, revising them to remind us of the eternal attraction of the gingerbread house even if, behind the cherry door, there is a "sound of black rags flapping."

The only direct statement of Coover's intention that I have seen comes toward the middle of his last book, *Pricksongs and Descants*, in the form of a dedicatory note to Cervantes. "For your stories," he wrote, "also exemplified the dual nature of all good narrative art: they struggled against the unconscious mythic residue in human life and sought to synthesize the unsynthesizable, sallied forth against adolescent thought-modes and exhausted art forms, and returned home with new complexities." All this is evident in these four plays.

In the longest, *The Kid*, the conventions of the western story, often satirized before, are given a scathing beating. Every line spoken, every stage direction, is a cliché ("I'm *skeered*, Sheriff! . . . Glass shatters, bullets whine"); the Kid is a psychopath programmed to respond only to certain stimuli, particularly injuns, and the local hero has to be ceremoniously sacrificed. In another play, the "theological position" is that virgin birth is no longer possible and therefore the priest had better have sex with the pregnant maiden; toward the end, only the players' genitals are talking—which should have been funnier than it is, or more profound, or something. Never mind; Coover takes extraordinary risks and deserves forgiveness for his failures.

The two remaining plays are better. Both are monologues. In one, a director, perhaps God, urges two actors to show some feeling in their love scene, but they respond only with impassive motions. A scene with intriguing reverberations: perhaps Coover is suggesting that the first attempt to create love failed, or that love cannot respond to the clichés this director uses ("It's the sweetest story ever told! It's chasing rainbows through heavens of blue"). Coover's effect here, as elsewhere, derives in part from the deliberate artificiality of the actors. His most recent story, in *New American Review*, number 14, begins with a long scene that turns out to be a pornographic movie observed by the story's characters, and in *The Kid* the actors' voices are twice replaced by microphone voices, as if from some dreadful radio serial.

The other monologue, *Rip Awake*, may be Coover's *Emperor Jones*. Rip van Winkle toils up his mountain again, half dreading, half looking forward to his next encounter with the little men: "I mean, listen, I don't entirely regret them twenty years." Rip is in bad shape. He can't remember things well, can't sleep now, wonders whether the dwarfish bowlers get their importance from him or he from them. He worries about the Revolution: did it really happen, and if so and he slept through it, does he need his own? Are the "little buggers" in fact real? Anyway, Rip is, as he says, "proceeding back up the mountain to rassle with the spooks in his life." Internal or external, *those* are real, and that is what Coover writes about so well.

May 1972

ADVANCED MANDARIN

1. Thomas Pynchon

IF *Slow Learner* were Thomas Pynchon's new book, we'd have to reckon it a major disaster, the kind of book that sends critics reeling back to their warrens to reassess its author's earlier work. Fortunately, it's not new; call it a minor disaster. This aptly titled collection brings together five of Pynchon's earliest short stories, four of them written while he was in college. In an introduction, which is quite the best part of the book, and as artful in what it omits as in what it says, Pynchon suggests cogent reasons for disliking his juvenilia. Other reasons will necessarily occur to the reader, for once the introduction is done, there lie the stories, dead on the page.

Each fails in its own way, but over all an arty aura looms. Either Pynchon is, as he admits, forcing his characters and events

to conform to "a theme, symbol or other abstract unifying agent,"
or he's whipping his prose into a viscous pudding. Sometimes he
does both at once. The story "Low-lands," for instance, is a good
example of the forcing process. The protagonist is a *schlemiel* of
the kind Pynchon later developed more fancifully. Kicked out of
his house by his wife, the *schlemiel* and some drinking buddies
seek refuge in a shack owned by the "king" of a vast rubbish
dump. During the night, a nymph, forty-two inches high, calls to
the *schlemiel;* he follows her through tunnels under the rubbish
to a chamber she shares with a rat named Hyacinth. Now anyone
who went to college in the fifties, as Pynchon did, knows exactly
what he's reading: he's reading a prose variation of *The Waste
Land.* Eliot's imagery, somewhat translated, mounts as—well, as
rubbish does in a dump; it finally smothers the story.

Of the earliest story in this lot, the less said the better. It's
about disaster, death, sex, and the military—just the kind of thing
you expect to find in a college magazine. Lest any reader be so
dull as to miss its labored point, Pynchon spells it out clearly at
the end. The latest story, written after *V* appeared, shows Pynchon jettisoning what he had learned about writing fiction to produce a plastic artifact for the *Saturday Evening Post.* The plot
involves some prankish schoolboys who treat a "colored" boy just
as if he were one of them—which their parents won't do. A coy
performance, it's sentimental, much too long, and has a trick ending reminiscent of Ray Bradbury on one of his windy days. Another story, "Under the Rose," is of marginal interest because,
in greatly ventilated form, it became the third chapter of *V.*
This early version is remarkable only for its extreme turgidity
and its alarming prose: "Hearing the languishment in that
voice, Porpentine wondered idly if she were bud or bloom;
or perhaps a petal blown off and having nothing to belong to any-
more."

It's no sin for a writer to begin with stories like these, but
why, after his novels have made him justly admired, would he
want to resurrect them? Pynchon's groupies, and the graduate
students who even now are hacking out dissertations on Pynchon's use of nineteenth-century physics, will doubtless want to
paw over each of the master's shards, looking for signs of better
things to come. The story called "Entropy" will give them what
they want: two models of the world grinding to a halt, one cere-

bral, the other instinctual; allusions to Henry Adams; some college humor; some chatter about communication theory ("I don't know anything about communication theory") and entropy ("He . . . envisioned a heat-death for his culture in which ideas, like heat-energy, would no longer be transferred"). Pynchon is right on target when he writes of the "bleakness of heart" he experiences when he rereads "Entropy"—it's as crisp and tasty as a salad left overnight in the refrigerator.

April 1984

2. Don DeLillo

ONCE IT WAS thought fashionable, particularly among writers of the Bloomsbury persuasion, to condescend to American literature. How vigorous it is, yet inelegant. How magnificent its country energy, yet its language lacks breeding. Virginia Woolf could play this game until they came after her with a tea tray: Whitman she thought an admirable writer, and Lardner, Sherwood Anderson, Sinclair Lewis—but they didn't write English. Not with words like *boob, hobo, graft,* and *hiking.* Now all has changed: among serious writers of American fiction Mandarin is the most admired style. The reader is confronted with cleverness, skittering symbols, pockets of amiable pedantry, a language so musical that he can almost sing the paragraphs. Plots have been jettisoned for a theme-and-variations effect—a story that extends but does not progress. Characters have been dumped with the result that all the voices in the story echo but one voice—the author's.

The trouble with Mandarin writing is not that it hasn't produced good fiction—it has produced some of our best—but that it is by definition an elite line of work, as difficult to perform well as it is tempting to imitate. Our very best mandarins are stalked by talented disciples: Donald Barthelme by Robert Coover, Thomas Pynchon by Don DeLillo. I have no doubt at all that if we hadn't had *V* and *Gravity's Rainbow* we would not now have *Ratner's Star.*

The time is 1979, the place a remote think tank where two thousand scientists are preparing for interstellar contact by learning to "think as a single planetary mind." Among them is Billy Terwilliger, fourteen, a Nobel Laureate in mathematics who does pure work in zorgs: "A lot of it is so abstract it can't be put on paper or even talked about." Billy must decipher a message the center thinks has come from a planet circling a distant star. The message is in mathematical language: 101 pulses and gaps composing the lowest three-digit prime.

Billy stewing over a math problem would have killed the novel, so his author trots him around the center, makes him listen to the grotesque theories of his colleagues. Many of these are studying "alternate physics" and the theory of invisible mass, which developed from the rumor that most of the universe is missing. Moholean relativity presumes that "the mass holding the galaxies together is trapped in moholes. This is why we can't find it." It also presumes "that in a mohole the laws of physics vary from one observer to another." There's quite a lot of this kind of thinking in the novel, some of it charming and witty, some not; in fact the characters in the story have nothing to do but lecture Billy in their perverse obsessions—as insistently as, but with less style than, the Red Queen and the Caterpillar once lectured Alice. In time, Billy and his friends retreat to a gigantic cavern beneath the center, there to continue nattering, to solve the cipher, and to work at composing an intergalactic language.

To be really disappointing a novel cannot be really bad. What's needed is a developing tension between the author's talent and the reader's hopes on the one hand, and the author's performance and the reader's frustration on the other. *Ratner's Star* provides such exquisite tension in large measure. DeLillo knows how to write brilliantly, even movingly, but he doesn't know when he's writing dully, doesn't know when his book has started to die in his typewriter. *Ratner's Star* is twice too long; as its terminal signs (failing inspiration, metastasis of exhausted ideas and dialogue) progress in the second half it becomes virtually unbearable. There are too many cartoon characters, too many familiar situations, and too much talk without insight, without any real *vision* at all.

Part of this failing may come from running too closely in

Pynchon's tracks (the story even has a mysterious recurring symbol, a boomerang, embarrassingly like Pynchon's V's and rockets), and part from the difficulties of writing satire in an ambiguous age. What's gone wrong with much of our recent satire is that it hasn't changed at all in the past fifteen years, and our society has—or at least the way we think about society has changed. We need to rethink what's actually grotesque about the way we live now, and to that end I propose a moratorium on such stock figures as life-denying scientists, mad generals, obsessive Jews with New York accents, evil psychoanalysts, sane lunatics, and lecherous ministers. We can revive them in a few decades with their energy restored from lying fallow.

June 1976

ANOTHER NOVEL TO RETIRE

I'VE LIKED THIS novel less each time I've read it over the past twenty years.* At its recent best, it was called *The Ginger Man;* earlier, *Tom Jones*. At its worst—well, no one knows, for the worst still molder in manuscript form; every publisher has one or more floating unread in his slush pile. Invariably, it is a story about a sensitive rogue, a bright young man who once knew a good life but is now reduced to squalor in a big city; he has problems with women, money, and the law, yet his heart is pure, and the grotesque derelicts he cultivates are pure as well.

A respecter of tradition, Craig Nova gives us Stargell, a sensitive rogue who once invented things to help cripples, but who now lives shabbily in "the dark furrows of New York" with his

---

Incandescence, by Craig Nova.

wife, an emotional basket case who drinks beer and watches television when she is not "trying to kill herself with sleep." For
some reason, Stargell loves his wife, but she won't let him touch
her. He loves his father, who is dying of cancer. He even likes his
wife's father, a retired Greek colonel who packs a .45 and dreams
of instant wealth. Stargell, bless his heart, becomes involved with
a loan shark and some ingenious grand larceny. He takes care of
those who need him, God's people all: the pornographer, the
drunken cripple, the blind waiter. "Being alive is like praying,"
Stargell observes, a bit of philosophy worthy of Kurt Vonnegut
in high gear.

Well, this is sentimental stuff to be sure, all mush at the core
despite the surface wordplay, the scabrous details and scatalogical
imagery. I don't mind sentiment, but I do insist that this particular sentimental novel, so stereotyped in the effects for which it
reaches, be given a rest, put out to pasture for a decade or so.
Haven't the men (they are always men) who write it yet realized
that the more bizarre their characters are, the more predictable
they are? Apparently not. Nova is often a skillful and energetic
writer, though at times the similes and metaphors on which he so
heavily relies seem fatigued: a voice on one page is "like a cat in a
garbage compactor"; on another, two voices are "like a parrot in a
garbage disposal." He can do better, I'm sure, and so can his publisher, who has inexplicably fitted this novel with a jacket that
suggests it is a pornographic work. It is nothing of the kind.

March 1979

PAUL THEROUX AS
JOSEPH CONRAD

I'VE SUSPECTED for some time that there's a clear affinity between Joseph Conrad and Paul Theroux. I don't mean to compare their achievements (Conrad, at Theroux's age, had written nothing), but merely to note certain parallels: two expatriate writers living in London and drawing upon their extensive travels to provide exotic backgrounds for their stories about vulnerable human beings faced with moral collapse. Theroux must have noticed; toward the end of his new novel he tips his hat to the author of *The Secret Agent*. And so he should, for *The Family Arsenal* is clearly inspired by Conrad's story: the subject, themes, and imagery of the earlier novel are here displayed in contemporary dress.

The Secret Agent was developed from a scrap of old news: an anarchist's attempt to blow up England's Royal Observatory. *The Family Arsenal* deals with four apprentice terrorists loosely connected with the IRA who wait for an offensive to begin in London. The authors of both books lay heavy lashings of irony onto their stories and look on their characters as pathetic shams, not revolutionaries at all. "The criminal futility of the whole thing, doctrine, action, mentality," Conrad exclaimed in a preface to his novel, ". . . exploiting the poignant miseries and passionate credulities of a mankind always so tragically eager for self-destruction." Theroux doesn't write prefaces, but he plainly agrees. Like Conrad, he writes about spiritual despair, a London from which moral and spiritual sanity have fled, a world waiting, possibly deserving, to blow up.

London itself—that crowded, sweating, stinking, disintegrating city—is as much a presence in this story as are any of the characters. One of them looks forward to "a cleansing holocaust. . . . The overheated world had split its shell like a cooking egg. Deranged, deranged. The news was written in blood. . . ." The book swells with such images: sewers rise, bricks bleed poisons, buildings sink into rubble. Here it is that the American Valentine Hood has come to hide.

A consul in Vietnam, Hood was sacked when he hit a government official. He lives now with Mayo, "a barbarian with taste," who works for the IRA—she has just stolen for ransom a Flemish painting that nobody wants to recover—and with two scruffy teenagers, a boy who makes bombs and a girl who delivers them to railroad luggage lockers. Their menage is a parody of marriage, of a family. The kids prance about the city imagining buildings exploding. Hood, a truly violent man (and therefore distrusted by the IRA), murders a drunken bully and finds himself suddenly heir to the bully's widow and a cache of weapons for which the IRA has lusted. When the violence comes, it is not even remotely in aid of a social idea.

"Perverse unreason," Conrad wrote in that same preface, "has its own logical processes." Theroux's novel may be read as a gloss upon that text. The revolutionaries in his story haven't the least idea of what they're about. "These rich people—they're messing the other ones about," say the bomb-making boy. "And like the other ones don't have anything. I don't know." He himself would like a cabin cruiser, or maybe a stereo. The IRA lacks the enterprise to launch its fabled offensive. Only an accountant, a bourgeois defender of financial proprieties, actually wants the city to blow up, but when the bomb explodes he's looking the other way.

Comic, ironic, and brooding, abounding in as many coincidences as a Restoration comedy, *The Family Arsenal* is an excellent novel, the work of a mature and self-assured artist. Need I add that the homage Theroux pays to Conrad does not diminish, but increases his accomplishment? It is a fact not often noticed that young novelists are always challenging their elders and betters, jostling them, running along to wring their hands, and by such contact developing and strengthening their own identities.

July 1976

If, as Paul Fussell tells us, there's no art or adventure left in travel, and therefore no reason to write about it, why would anyone take on Great Britain?* Travel in the land that Paul Theroux calls "the best-known, most fastidiously mapped and most widely trampled piece of geography on earth" is a cinch and its natives are numb from analysis. Perhaps the challenge is reason enough. An American writer, Theroux had lived eleven years in London without seeing much of the rest of the country. Why not go to the country to write about "its discomforts and natives and entertainments and unintelligible dialects"? For centuries the British had done it to other places—they had "virtually invented the concept of funny foreigners"—so why should not a foreigner do the same to them?

---

*A Kingdom by the Sea: A Journey Around Great Britain, by Paul Theroux.

We can see the travel writer preparing his kit. Knapsack, leather jacket, oily shoes. A distempered ear for dialogue, an illiberal eye for detail. He will travel by foot and branchline train. Beginning in May of 1982—season of the unpleasantness in the Falklands and the papal visit—he will move clockwise around the perimeter of Britain, Ulster included, because "in many respects, Britain *was* its coast." Above all, he will avoid Britain's past: "no sightseeing; no cathedrals, no castles, no churches, no museums. I wanted to examine the particularities of the present." The landscape excepted, Theroux means to avoid everything that a traveler would want to see.

Clearly there's a scheme here with just enough self-flagellation in the prospectus to suggest a sound result. It's not surprising that his dyspepsia sets in early and stays late. On the train from London to the coast, roughnecks shout obscenities; his first night out, he's cheated at his hotel. He eavesdrops on traveling salesmen bullying waitresses and middle-aged men commenting on their impotence. "I saw British people lying stiffly on the beaches like dead insects." He also saw naked men watch copulating couples. Other vacationers, shirtless under a dark sky, emitted "hog whimpers" as they slept. A holiday camp reminds him of Jonestown; a fat naked woman wakes him at night by rummaging through his luggage. Wales offers a pornography shop; the train stations, graffiti: "Wogs ought to be hit about the head with the utmost severity."

As for the landscape, the sole aesthetic indulgence he allowed himself, he speaks of "long coastal stretches of unexpected decrepitude": "All the bungalows were ugly in the same way; all the gardens were ugly in different ways." Did the seaside communities offer relief? "Brighton was full of disappointed and bad tempered visitors." "As soon as I saw it, I wanted to leave Cardiff." "I walked on to Cogan, an awful-looking place." "Dery was frightful." "Cleethorpes looked a terrible place." "I came to hate Aberdeen more than any other place I saw."

So monotonous a litany suggests that his oily shoes put blisters on his feet. Not at all: Theroux insists he is "the cheeriest visitor. . . . All travelers are optimists. . . . Travel itself was a sort of optimism in action." It's hard to understand what the man's talking about. One of the problems with his book lies in the discrepancy between his protestations of high spirits and his testimony of squalor, decline, and degeneracy. Very likely, working-class Britain today can appear as tacky as he makes it out to be, but there's nothing entertaining about that, nothing specifically British about that—and one of the things a travel book must do is to be entertaining, or at least interesting, about the news of another place.

What Theroux has done—what he set out to do—is to apply past attitudes of travel writers to a book about the present. With two exceptions—his chapters on Ulster, which is a genuinely terrible place, and on northern Scotland, where he finds self-reliant people he admires—his method fails. Travel writers like Sam Johnson and Evelyn Waugh epitomized the bigotry of their age; the wit that sprang from their intolerance remains funny today. Theroux's mistake is to think that he can apply a similar disdain to a generation of levelers, alert to every slight. In fiction, he could get away with it; in reporting, not. It's embarrassing to see him lay funny names on the people he meets: Crapstone, Mould, and Witherslack, Swineham, Smallbone, and Wockerfuss. Even the generalizations traditional to travel writing seem in Theroux's hands both sour and untrue. Britons on the beach, he observes, face the sea: "Perhaps another of their coastal pleasures was being able to turn their backs on Britain." Nonsense. People on any beach face the sea; another crusty American, Robert Frost, wrote a poem about it.

October 1983

A LION AMONG THE FOXES

A FAVORITE TOPIC among Europeans is the chaos that has overtaken American civilization. They profess shock and dismay. How could Disneyland and Times Square have happened to the

land of de Tocqueville and Lord Bryce? The better sort of
American novelist, however, takes for granted our native lunacy,
our creeping entropy, and makes a virtue of the wit with which
he pleads the guilt of his compatriots. *JR*, William Gaddis's second novel (his first, *The Recognitions*, was published twenty
years ago) is specifically about chaos and disintegration, about
the detritus that we have packed into our lives and discourse to
the point that both have become unintelligible. "What America's
all about, waste disposal and all," says one of Gaddis's many detestable characters. Gaddis winces, grins, does not entirely disagree. It should not be so, of course, but probably is. "Order,"
says Jack Gibbs, who seems to speak for the author, "is simply a
thin, perilous condition we try to impose on the basic reality of
chaos."

In *JR* everyone tries to impose order on chaos by talking.
The book is made up almost entirely of talk—talk to explain what
is happening or to fend off knowledge of what is happening—but
no one listens to anyone else. If two people talk, they carry on
two conversations at cross-purposes. Everyone talks in a kind of
manic frenzy, interrupting and interpreting each other, stunning
one another with irrelevancies, persiflage, euphemisms, evasions,
jargon, clichés, and stubborn refusals to understand. None of the
speakers is ever identified; we must sort them out from internal
evidence, and that is not always easy. Nor is it always easy to determine *what* is said, for the characters are sometimes drunk,
usually desperate, and always uncaring of syntax. Gaddis's novel
is four times as long as most and runs without so much as a break
between scenes. He means us to work at understanding it: "Most
God damned writing's written for readers perfectly happy who
they are rather be at the movies," Gibbs says.

Difficulties aside, *JR* is an extremely funny novel. Through
the many sequences of incoherent conversations a complex, coherent plot develops. JR, a scruffy eleven-year-old kid, manages
to accumulate a business empire by answering ads in magazines.
He works from a phone booth, coerces adults to front for him,
becomes an early master of lease-backs, write-offs, and deficit
spending. JR deals mostly in trashy products and exhausted properties; his operations, just barely legal and never plausible, are a
paradigm of the larger world of school administrators, stockbro-
kers, tycoons, lawyers, all of them fossilized in their own jargon,

their obsession with public relations, and the diversion of their energies into talk—which is what entropy is: the amount of energy unavailable for work. "It's all so, just so absurd so, lifeless," one of the characters observes, "there aren't any emotions it's all just reinvested dividends and tax avoidance that's what all of it is, avoidance. . . ."

The artist, however, may prevail. He must endure the sludge that is flung at him, overcome self-doubts, and, when the roof falls in on art, as it literally does at the end of this story, he must set about pulling the plaster out of the canvas—a pleasingly conventional moral for a novel that is eccentric only in form, not in substance. I wish I could be sure that scores of thousands of readers will invest the effort that *JR* requires, for it seems to me one of the most brilliant and complex of recent comic novels, one that can fairly be compared to *Catch-22*, *The Sot-Weed Factor*, and *Gravity's Rainbow*. Gaddis has managed to write about chaos without slipping into the condition himself and he is constantly funny about matters that are not, of course, finally amusing. His is a major achievement; I think it will endure.

November 1975

Postscript: JR went on to win the National Book Award, though I have yet to meet anyone who has read it, or intends to read it. The newly formed National Book Critics Circle, which I had helped to found, refused even to nominate it for its first fiction award; when several members of the NBCC's executive board told me that they hadn't bothered to read it ("It's too long, too difficult, you know how busy we are"), I resigned.

Aesop reports that a fox once sneered at a lioness: "You give birth to only one cub at a time." "Only one," replied the lioness, "but it's a lion." So it is with William Gaddis, who has given birth to only three novels in thirty years. The foxes have sneered—his books are too long, too difficult, and certainly none has yet proved commercially successful—but to those who have eyes to read, *The Recognitions* and *JR* look like lions among American novels. So, too, does his new one. It's possible that *Carpenter's Gothic* will for the first time get Gaddis the audience he deserves, if only because it's short, confined, and more accessible than its predecessors.

The plot develops within the space of a few days on a single set: a Victorian house on the Hudson River rented by Paul and Elizabeth Booth. Liz is an heiress who has to scratch for a dollar; she can't get at the fortune amassed by her father, who died just before he might have gone to jail. The estate's executors are battling lawsuits and dissipating the capital as expeditiously as possible. Liz's brother, Billy, is only slightly more useless than her husband, Paul, a wounded Vietnam vet who's trying to promote himself as a consultant. Paul's only client, whom we never see, is a black television evangelist, Reverend Ude, who dreams of missions in Africa as he battles the IRS and charges of bribing a reactionary senator. Add to these the owner of the house, McCandless, a geologist who may have found precious minerals in Africa. McCandless drops in from time to time to rummage among his papers in a locked room and eventually to take Liz to bed. Finally, there's a CIA agent who wants McCandless's secrets. Unprepossessing though this crew may be, they have no difficulty nudging the world toward Armageddon, which, like the human race, begins in Africa's Great Rift Valley.

That, in carpenter's terms, is the shell of the story, but the shell can't convey how funny this book is, or how angry, or even what it's about. Like Gaddis's other novels, *Carpenter's Gothic* develops on several fronts simultaneously. With its emphasis on an old house, a secret in a locked room, a mysterious and masterful proprietor who woos the patient heroine, it's a spoof of gothic romances—specifically *Jane Eyre*. Here, as before, Gaddis plays with his usual themes, the four quadrants of his personal literary mandala: fakery in American life, our obsessions with money and with publicity, the importance of religion. But if in the past Gaddis resolved his tumultuous narratives with endings that suggest optimism, some hope that man's muddles may yield to "a vision of order . . . some connexion between the earth on which he walks and himself," he doesn't do so here. Far from being the way out of our dilemma, religion now becomes its cause. "Despairing" is too strong a word for this story (true despair precludes anger), but *Carpenter's Gothic* is surely Gaddis's most pessimistic, his most savage, novel.

His main concern is with stupidity. "Stupidity's the deliberate cultivation of ignorance," McCandless says. He means specifically the stupidity of "revealed truth," the determinedly preserved ignorance of fundamentalist preachers like Reverend Ude and the antievolutionists who censor textbooks. These are the people who have all of the answers, none of the questions. "Revelation's the last refuge ignorance finds from reason," McCandless says. "Stupidity like that, you put a hammer in its hand and everything looks like a nail." The carpenter image emerges again: tack this stupidity to the specter of communism and you get people who are quite willing to go to war—they know the bombs are meant to fall, releasing the faithful to reassemble at the Great Picnic in the sky.

Thus with only five visible characters (two more have walk-on parts) and without leaving his single set, Gaddis brings us to the end of the world. To the old "carpenter's Gothic" house on the Hudson, news from the outside world arrives by telephone (in this book, the phone is always ringing), newspaper, and radio. The difficulties of Gaddis's novels have been much exaggerated; the reader need only adjust to one of the most distinctive voices in American fiction. He need only be alert to Gaddis's manner of playing with an action or a phrase: everything Gaddis puts into one of his stories—a door left open, a room being cleaned—returns, amplified, an altered significance. Appropriately, for a novel that denounces fundamentalist religion, this one begins with the Holy Ghost literally taking a beating in the opening paragraph. *Carpenter's Gothic*, like *JR*, proceeds almost entirely through dialogue—torrents of fragmented, distracted, self-seeking talk, which may or may not be heard. Liz is the only reticent character; she actually listens to the bullying diatribes to which Billy, McCandless, and particularly Paul subject her. What these men say is appalling, but the way they say it—their self-deceptions and monstrous obsession with their blighted concerns—makes for high comedy in the grand manner.

June 1985

THE VOICE OF THE AMPLIFIED CUCKOO

NO MONUMENT OF ancient Rome has weathered as well as Juvenal's observation that considering the world's present state, it is difficult not to write satire. Very well, but what happens when everyone writes satire? When shrieks and cackles have become the tone of the day? In our age of electronic amplification, must the satirist who means to be heard above the general cacophony raise his decibel level to an intolerable degree? From the evidence of his new novel, *Good as Gold*, Joseph Heller seems to think so. But that way danger lurks. Satire is a delicate craft; it will founder if one line is not tied precisely about the neck of its victim and another is not fixed firmly to some standard of decency or restraint. Swift and Pope, who wrote the most effective satires in English, never cut loose these lines; now Heller has. Forsaking the buoyant inventiveness of *Catch-22* and the morose chilliness of *Something Happened*, he turns strident in despair. *Good as Gold* resembles nothing as much as a self-indulgent ventilation of private spleen.

To his traditional targets—imperturbable bureaucracies and insufferable families, the rise of incompetents and the decline of logic—Heller adds another: the experience of being Jewish in America. His protagonist, though Jewish, claims to know nothing about it, but he is writing an article and a book on the subject anyway. At forty-eight, Bruce Gold professes English at a New York City college; his undistinguished writings have been noticed in the White House. Gold understands himself well enough: he is a liar and a melancholy hypocrite who has cultivated his image as a radical moderate, a pragmatic progressive, and a liberal reactionary. He understands our society, too: nothing can be done to retard its slouch toward entropy; it would be futile even to try. "In the long run, failure was the only thing that worked predictably."

Unlike Heller's earlier hero, Yossarian, Gold pants to embrace the insanity of our time. His need for money and the chance to escape his suffocating family prick his ambition. So does a presidential aide who urges Gold to join the White House staff to "do whatever you want as long as you do whatever we want. We have no ideas, and they're pretty firm." A good joke, this; recognizing it, Heller repeats it perhaps seventy-seven times. Gold, says the aide, may pick his assignment—attorney general, director of the CIA, even secretary of state—and to get such a job he need only divorce his dowdy wife and marry his gentile mistress, who won't marry him until the job is already his. A veritable catch-22, but the girl's influential father offers encouragement: "I pray you will not let being a little sheeny inhibit you, you kike. I hear they're giving mentions now to coons, Greeks, dagos, spics and women."

If Gold does not recoil from this assault—he wants a job and will endure countless humiliations before admitting he would prefer not to be a Jew—the reader must. Were Heller's ear in working order, his aristocratic bigot would not yell "kike" and "sheeny"; he would instead purr over "gentlemen of the Hebrew persuasion" and "keeping Louisville clean." Satire exaggerates, of course, and Heller legitimately means to show us Jews and gentiles whose undifferentiated anger results from a lifetime's frustrated egocentricity, yet in this novel Heller operates as if he were a jewel thief wearing boxing gloves. The author of *Catch-22* might have KO'd Washington's bureaucracy had he troubled to close with it. He might have thoroughly pummeled the Jewish family (an overly pummeled target, to be sure) had he not settled for writing one funny scene and repeating it half a dozen times. Even his elaborately documented attack on Henry Kissinger, the "socialite warmonger," is overdone: having made his incontrovertible point for six pages, Heller rests and then resumes for another sixteen.

Excessive wear on some of this material and a refusal to engage the rest account for only part of Heller's failure here. The book could have used an editor—someone to warn Heller that he will lose much of his audience when he writes "the *vontz* was *nisht aheyn, nisht aher*. . . . The *chuchem hut gezugt,*" and so on, and to insist that he cannot, as late as page 308, introduce himself in the first person to tell us of his problems writing his novel. Always a pessimist, Heller presents for the first time a protagonist who acts irrationally because all moral, ethical, and intellectual restraints have vanished from our society. The tension between what should be and what is has disappeared. True as this conclusion may be, it does not lead to art; art requires tension. When, early in the story, Gold observes that he has always spoken in a humanitarian sort of way, "yet he no longer liked people," and his author offers no further perspective, we must recognize that something, perhaps all, has been lost.

To be truly fierce, satire must offer an alternative vision. Swift writes to Pope in 1725: "But principally I hate and detest that animal called Man, although I heartily love John, Peter, Thomas, and so forth." The saving remnant. Heller clutched it once and, talented writer that he is, will doubtless clutch it again.

March 1979

A DECADENT NOVEL

LEGEND HAS IT that Hemingway, broken in mind and about to die, spoke well of Vance Bourjaily's talent. Once a writer would have framed such praise—the consummation of ambition—and hung it on his wall just below his stuffed tarpon, but Bourjaily may have felt a cold sweat flush away his pride. Would Edgar be pleased if Lear had told him he had a talent for government? And is not *talent* a chilling word to apply to an author of four novels? At what point does talent yield to achievement? Fifteen years and three novels later, Bourjaily still hovers in that penumbra where able writers try and fail to write a book of real importance. His new novel, *Now Playing at Canterbury*, has been twelve years in

the writing, but it is not that book, not the book Bourjaily meant
it to be: the Big American Novel that would let him bask finally
in the glare of a major literary reputation.

It's a big book, all right, and the talent that Hemingway observed glitters fitfully among its many pages, but as a novel it's a
mess—pretentious, shallow, complacent, and mannered often to
the point of self-indulgence. Indeed, if we agree with Lionel
Trilling that a novel is an "agent of the moral imagination," this
must be perceived as a decadent book—a travesty, really, of the
novel it might have been. I'll come back to this matter of decadence in a moment, after struggling briefly with the plot.

An opera is about to be performed at a midwestern university. The score and libretto are by local talents, but some prominent performers have been imported. There are a great many
characters and, as rehearsals progress, virtually all have stories to
tell: dreams, fantasies, snatches of autobiography, tales of violence, sex, and romance. A *Canterbury Tales* of contemporary
America, you see, and "the hooly blisful martir" these pilgrims
seek must be the opera's première. To stress the Chaucer connec-
tion, Bourjaily includes an animal story and another in lame iam-
bic couplets. But Chaucer had the wit to keep the frame of his
tales either unobtrusive or witty and dynamic; Bourjaily has not.
His characters, drawn so thin as to be translucent, scratch at one
another and constantly change beds; most speak only in the author's tone of voice, so, when everyone changes beds once more at
the end, it seems that Bourjaily is straining for confusion, for self-
parody.

The idea for the novel that Bourjaily has not written is
sound. One could, from such a framework, write stories that illustrate some truths about America. But the novel that Bourjaily
has written is not about American truths, or human truths, but
about fantasies: the orgy fantasy, the pot-bust fantasy, the
student-power fantasy, the Vietnam War–resistance fantasy. I do
not mean that what Bourjaily writes about is untrue, but that his
treatment of what is true, or is a good myth, is false, that he gives
us America at the same remove from reality that television gives
it to us. His stories offer no narrative or moral perspective that is
new or freshly observed, no information about students or blacks
or bombings or drugs that could not have been researched from
TV news or TV situation dramas. His characters, strong and

weak guys all, at their best resemble characters from old movies that we see on late-night television.

A perspective limited by television is not enough to make a novel decadent, but to rejoice in the confinement is. Bourjaily has traded in the author's omniscience, as Tolstoy and Hardy understood it, for a smug knowingness. "Billy Hoffman, in he shuffles," is not just a bad sentence, it's corrupt because the author is clearly pleased with its badness, has worked hard to make it just as awful as it is. This sort of writing, combined with a plot that is not developed, but simply extended by the yard, results in a book that few caring readers will want to finish.

September 1976

Postscript: Not surprisingly, Vance Bourjaily was miffed by this review. He told his friends he was miffed (in the small world of books, such news always gets back to the source) and, years after the event, he wrote a short piece for *Esquire* to say that he was still miffed. The question arises: is a reviewer ever justified in attempting to blow a bad book out of the water? I think the answer is yes, but the reviewer must choose his targets with the greatest of care. It's not enough for a book to be bad; other elements must be present: smugness; pretentiousness; an overinflated reputation; clear evidence that a book's badness is not the result of incompetence, but of deliberate design. Such books represent an assault on the republic of letters and should not be ignored. A reviewer confronting a routinely bad book simply criticizes it and leaves his reader to disagree if he will. But a reviewer confronting a genuinely meretricious piece of work assumes a greater obligation. The book is an offense and must be labeled such: to shrug or say, "I didn't like it," is insufficient; the essence of its awfulness must be laid bare—and that requires more art, more critical effort than a reviewer usually expends. Above all, the reviewer must make sure that nothing he says will induce his reader to try the book for himself. Contempt and wit are his best weapons here. If he does his job right, he'll leave no room for argument; if he backs away from the task, he might as well admit that books really don't matter.

Readers of this book might conclude that demolition work is my usual line of business; in fact, I'm rarely tempted. Kurt Vonnegut, Jim Harrison, Vance Bourjaily, Nancy Friday—these

proved irresistible, and so did Edna O'Brien, so greatly praised
by others. My review of her novel *I Hardly Knew You* doesn't
properly belong in a collection devoted to American work, but it
illustrates what I've been talking about in this note.

Trying to Read Edna O'Brien

GARBAGE PUT OUT in winter will not smell as soon as garbage
put out in summer, which is doubtless why Doubleday has put
out Edna O'Brien's new novel now.* Twelve years ago, O'Brien
wrote a novel since dropped from her list of credits: *August Is a
Wicked Month* it was called, and it seemed to me meretricious
trash, but lately she has been widely praised for novels and stories
I have not read. "Writes beautiful prose," says one reviewer.
"Loves language with an almost sensual delight," says another.
Anthony West says she "writes with extraordinary effectiveness
and power," and Erica Jong does the old soft shoe: if James Joyce
had been a woman, if Dylan Thomas had been Irish, that kind of
thing.

Time to look again, I thought, and this is what I found: "It
was a night of indescribable beauty and happiness"; "Being
kissed by him had all the freshness and innocence of a spring
day." I screwed my spectacles into my eyes and persevered: "Just
as well, I thought, not to be entering the mad bazaar of love
again"; "I had a sudden mad message to peel off my clothes."
Joyce would surely applaud, and Thomas nod over his beer. I
pressed further: "Oh ornamental gates that guard a beautiful
house, oh stone house with arches, turrets, and long low loggias,
will I ever forget you." Well, I won't. O'Brien is fond of the
Gothic: "Any more monkey business out of you and I will have
you committed," says the husband, to which the narrator replies,
"There is no monkey business," and he says, "You will do as you
are told. From now on I am master."

By now you will be panting for news of the plot. Nora, the

I Hardly Knew You.

narrator, has murdered her boy lover: in jail, she awaits trial and reflects, in a distracted manner, on her life and loves. She hints she is mad, but madness in fiction requires its own fixed logic, and Nora is not up to that; she offers weather reports instead and country rambles, and the hope that we will wait to learn *why* she killed her man. When it comes, the explanation beggars belief, but I don't complain. While waiting I was treated to a lesbian scene in which Nora told me that the part of her lover which attracted her attention "was as warm as jam that had just been lifted off a stove." My cookbook tells me that the warmth of jam lifted off a stove is 221 degrees Fahrenheit. What a surprise for Nora. Ah, Joyce; ah, prose.

January 1978

THE LAST OF JAMES JONES

JAMES JONES died last year at the age of fifty-five, leaving undecided the question whether he was the worst novelist ever to write good novels or the best ever to write such bad ones. *Whistle*, which he did not quite complete, won't settle the issue, for if Jones's bad novels are appalling, even stupefying performances, his good novels are pretty bad, too. An honest reader must admit his ambivalence: Jones could write a complex scene involving only the crudest of characters, a chapter that is at the same time both good and bad, a book that is simultaneously both true and false. Few writers give us such unease. And so, somewhat guardedly, I can report that *Whistle* is Jones's best novel in sixteen years, that it recovers much of the passionate intensity that animates his better work, and that it returns to thwack again at the only theme he ever handled with authority: the effect on men of war and the military life.

In a note written more than four years ago but published

only now, Jones discloses that he had always intended his large
war novels to form a trilogy. *From Here to Eternity* is his har-
rowing report on the lives and attitudes of professional peacetime
soldiers. *The Thin Red Line*, set on a Pacific island, is perhaps
the best novel about combat to come out of World War II. *Whistle* shows how soldiers are destroyed, not by the war but by their
removal from the war and the fraternity of army life, by that re-
laxation of responsibility that prompts them to destroy themselves. Unfortunately, the idea for the story is the best thing
about it.

In 1943 four soldiers from an infantry company in the Pacific are sent by boat and train to an army hospital in Tennessee.
These soldiers are familiar, having appeared under slightly different names in the preceding novels. Jones has injured each of them
with care: a damaged hand for Mess Sergeant Strange; a smashed
ankle for Landers, the company clerk; shattered thighs for Prell,
the company hero; fever and hypertension for First Sergeant
Winch. These men, who have known no security except what the
company provided, are quickly unhinged by faithless wives and
intolerable families, by their rage and despair at the human condition—"for," as Landers puts it, "all the sad members of this
florid, misbegotten, miscreated race of valuable creatures." Death
and discipline held the outfit together once, but replacements and
reassignments are ungluing it now; the hospital half-life they find
worse than the horrors of Guadalcanal, and the Tennessee
women, all foaming in heat, threaten to "split the common male
interest."

To stave off disintegration, these out-of-work warriors resort
to traditional defenses: drink and brawls, politics and sex. Of
these, only the latter are of much use to the novelist. Politics, at
least of the kind practiced within the army, has always been
Jones's strength. He understands better than anyone the mind of
the professional enlisted man and the elliptical processes by
which favors are bartered and officers outflanked, the tricks by
which the army's bureaucracy can be exploited. Jones's top sergeants are masterful executives; by far the best scenes in *Whistle*
are those in which Winch, who unobtrusively mothers his small
crew, negotiates with his fellow sergeants—to prevent Prell's
leg from being amputated when the officer-surgeons have said it

must come off, or to finagle for Prell, who loathes him and whom he pretends to despise, a Congressional Medal of Honor.

Sex, as usual, is another matter. Jones, the dedicated realist, the expert in the way things work, wrote nothing even remotely convincing about women, but he wrote a great deal about them, nonetheless. It is as if, distrusting them, he wanted to harry them into formation, where they must all do his bidding by the numbers. The women in *Whistle* are all amateur whores, assembled only for men's sexual ease: slap them, leave them, train them to your preferences—they remain constantly, instantly available. They perform here in scenes that are executed with all the artistry of an X-rated movie—a strobe light glares on the exposed flesh and the camera crowds in as close as it can without blurring the focus.

For all I know, Jones may have drawn his women as coarsely as he did for some misconceived artistic purpose—to set them apart, say, from his men, who alone are capable of a tragic sense of life. Jones's women can think no further than their next orgasm; they will survive. But Winch and Strange, Landers and Prell, sense that they are doomed; apathetic and bitter, hating the army but unable to let it go, each is aware that his experience of war has been a sorry one, that his only investment is in his buddies—and even that is collapsing. Clear-eyed (in spite of all the booze), they step firmly toward the particularly senseless fates that their author has conceived for them. It's all rather oddly romantic, even baldly sentimental in a quaint, old-fashioned way.

Jones died with little more than three short chapters of *Whistle* yet to write, though it seems to me that he left his story as nearly complete as it need be. An often clumsy writer who could not resist making a point three times where once was perhaps too much ("Where did your responsibility end? Nowhere, apparently. Never. It never ended"), he preferred not to surrender an episode or scene until he had flogged it to death. The outline for the conclusion of the book, which has been pieced together from Jones's note and conversations by his friend Willie Morris, suggests that the unwritten scenes would most likely have proved the least convincing. Jones may have died young, but there seems little doubt that he had said what he had to say.

February 1978

THE JOURNALIST AS FIRST NOVELIST

FOUR YEARS AGO, Tom Wolfe announced that the novel had
ceased to be literature's main event. Able writers, he assured us,
were no longer haunted by the specter of a first novel as yet un-
committed to paper—they were too busy converting journalism
into a fine art. More recent evidence, however, indicates that the
immaterial first novel hovers like ectoplasm about the edges of a
reporter's ambition. Eventually he will feel compelled to give it
some kind of tangible form. A young writer, ignorant of any life
except his own, will stuff his autobiography into it. Curiously,
older writers—hardy journalists like Francine du Plessix Gray
and Renata Adler, who have written quite a lot about other people—do the same.

Why? Because the first novel is a good place to put things
that would be awkward to use elsewhere. No one requires much
fiction from a first novel, or even a coherent form. It can be intimately confessional, like Gray's *Lovers and Tyrants*, which was
apparently reconstructed from memory and diaries, and laid out
like a line of sizable, freestanding stones, or it can be coolly ironic,
like Adler's *Speedboat*, which resembles snapshots that have been
hoarded over the years before being glued in order in an album.
No one minds much if a first novel runs on too long, as these do,
because a writer who builds a book by sections is hard put to
know when to stop. And no one objects to narrators who see
themselves as victims; that's part of the convention, too. Gray's
describes herself as "a case of spiritual nymphomania and emotional frigidity"; Adler's suggests "it is possible that we are really
a group of invalids, hypochondriacs, and misfits."

Love as tyranny is Francine Gray's theme. The selfish tyranny of a governess's love that leaves the child she cared for with a legacy of guilt; love for a father whose death has yet to be accepted; bondage to a lover so narcissistic that he defines himself as "style incarnate"; a marriage so placid that it threatens to extinguish feeling. "What do you want in life?" asks Stephanie, the author's narrator and alter ego, of herself. She replies, "Ecstasy and tenderness. And to be heard, eventually." Torn between opposing desires, Stephanie yearns for love and self-sufficiency, for freedom and security; she will settle for oppression when it comes in the guise of shelter. "The most tyrannical despots," she observes, "can be the ones who love us the most."

In an elegant prose, developing scenes and characters generously and with a sensuous attention to detail, Gray fashions Stephanie's story into eight self-contained episodes. Stephanie: a French aristocrat's child, moving in a world of old estates and eccentric relatives until the Germans come and her father is killed. Stephanie: a natural survivor brought by her mother to New York, where she contends with a chic school, adolescent attachments and rivalries. Stephanie: the mistress of a French prince. Stephanie: married into "calm and silence," to which she is entirely unsuited. Stephanie: always discontented. Fearing "that morbid descent from bliss which any permanence entails," she wants to live disreputably but finds there's no tradition for such a female role in a society arranged by men. Our lovers are our oppressors, she concludes, and she must chafe against them until she has exorcised herself and can begin her life anew.

For three-quarters of its route, *Lovers and Tyrants* is a remarkably convincing, even exhilarating performance. Toward the end, in a long section written in the third person, I sensed the author striking poses, lecturing us a bit to emphasize points already amply developed, introducing two characters—a radical Jesuit and a homosexual youth—who are not as engaging as I suspect the author means them to be. But the rest is impressive. Francine Gray is as self-assured when she describes the social and aesthetic problems that beset children assembling packs of trading cards as she is when she prepares the intensely moving scene in which Stephanie reconciles herself emotionally to her father's death. Through her narrator, Gray offers an absorbing study of the complexity of a woman's erotic psychology: the desire to desire, the sense of boredom and absurdity, the suspicion that the act of sex is less important than "that delectation of privacy so directly lacking in modern life."

If Gray's novel is passionate and engaged, Renata Adler's is witty and detached, a wry report on selected foibles of our time. *Speedboat* offers no story at all and little more by way of characters. Arranged as a collage of snappy anecdotes and aphorisms, incidents and observations, it proceeds (if that's the word I want) by means of theme and variations. A subject, a phrase, even a sound dropped in one brief section will be echoed in the next. Adler, I suspect, has been writing this book for years on little file cards—jokes she has heard, night thoughts, surplus grotesqueries that didn't fit into her regular reporting—and now the cards are laid out like a game of patience. You could probably start reading anywhere, leave off anywhere. It's a brilliant, funny enterprise, lapidary to a fault and, I'm afraid, evanescent—I'm forgetting it even as I write this piece.

Jen Fein, the narrator, is a journalist and sometime teacher, trained to precise observation and condensed writing, a traveler ("I stole a washcloth once from a motel in Angkor Wat"), and perhaps too fond of scotch and Valium. Her tone, appropriate to our post-Vietnam and Watergate days, is cool, inquiring, resigned to despair: "When I wonder what it is we are doing—in this brownstone, on this block, with this paper—the truth is probably that we are fighting for our lives." Jen goes to flight school and Biafra, she studies at the Sorbonne and teaches college English. She is adept at satirizing students, faculty politics, telephone operators. She is particularly good at observing the deterioration of language (" 'Phenomena' is another singular, taking the plurals 'phenomenas' and 'phenomenums' ") and of conversation ("Well, I am a personality that prefers not to be annoyed." "We should all prepare ourselves for this eventuality").

Speedboat is the quintessential "New York book." It's hard to imagine anyone west of the Hudson or south of Langley, Virginia, reading it with anything but indifference, or perhaps hostility. In fact, it's hard to imagine anyone at all being able to understand it twenty years hence—and yet if it were stashed in a time capsule and dug up a century from now it would be worth deciphering, a latter-day Linear B that would show how some of us lived and what passed for thought in the seventies. If there *is* any truth, that is, or anyone left to read it. "The truth," says Jen, "I would like to say here, is as follows. But I can't. In some places, it may already have begun, the war of everybody against everybody."

A little later she says, "I don't think much of writers in whom nothing is at risk." Agreed. Both Gray and Adler have written very nervy books, risked much, pushed what they were attempting further than it could reasonably go. Never mind; literary excess is no mortal sin. These are classy performances, both.

October 1976

THE APOCALYPSE ACCORDING TO JOAN DIDION

JOAN DIDION is our foremost practitioner of the literature of permanent nervous collapse. The geography in her books may vary slightly, but the spiritual landscape alters little, if at all. The West has completed its decline. Desolation squats like smog upon the streets. Bleak comedy flickers like brush fire on the darkened hills. Dutifully, the natives continue to suffer and inflict damage upon one another, though their reasons for doing so have become obscure. Memories weaken, cancers prosper, babies are born deformed. A sudden shift of the polar caps just now would be no bad thing, if only to stop the pain. For Didion's people are all emotional invalids, all terminal victims of their own violence, corruption, or helplessness. And only the helpless may be redeemed, may attain a frail nobility by hanging on, by prayer— which for Didion is any ritual that is repeated for the preservation of sanity or in aid of a naïve hope.

A Book of Common Prayer, then. The deserts of which
Didion has written before yield here to a sterile Central American
republic called Boca Grande, a country without culture or contrasts, without tourists or a history anyone remembers. Grace
Strasser-Mendana narrates. An American, a scientist, the widow
of Boca Grande's richest entrepreneur, Grace observes with contempt the meaningless machinations of her brothers-in-law as
they joust for political control. Grace, who has reduced fear of the
dark to "an arrangement of fifteen amino acids," cares only for
Boca Grande's "opaque equatorial light. The bush and the sea do
not reflect the light but absorb it, suck it in, then glow morbidly."
Grace is sixty, "a prudent traveler" and "a student of delusion."
She is dying of cancer. This is not, she says, her story.

It is instead the story of another American, Charlotte
Douglas, which Grace has reconstructed. Charlotte walked out on
one husband, then on another, then on her first again. She arrived
in Boca Grande for no clear purpose one year and was murdered
there the next. Grace discovers that Charlotte, who made a fool of
herself at parties and hung around the airport, had simply determined to stop walking away. She was there to wait for her daughter who, at eighteen, had helped to bomb a building, steal and
burn an airplane. Her daughter, a fugitive, would surely soon
show up. Charlotte's purity of purpose prevents her from understanding that she has been caught up in one of Boca Grande's
tawdry coups d'état, so, still waiting, she is killed. Or perhaps she
understood that her daughter was forever lost and elected to lose
her life.

For such a distinction we cannot rely on Grace. Grace (the
irony of her name cannot be unintended) is a rational pragmatist:
"I learned early to keep death in my line of sight, keep it under
surveillance, keep it on cleared ground and away from any brush
where it might coil unnoticed." But Charlotte eludes her; Grace
cannot quite grasp the metamorphosis of Charlotte from a figure
of fun into a figure of passionate resolve, though she is finally
aware that her condescending gaze is inadequate to assess Charlotte's history. There is something of Conrad in this morally ob-
tuse narration, and in the story's rotting ambience, something of
Graham Greene: "Her clothes mildewed. The untouched butter
in the little crocks went rancid by noon and by dinner was dusted

with a fine volcanic ash still falling from an eruption two years before."

The precedents don't matter. Nor do Didion's occasional, inadvertent parodies of herself: "I will sit in the dark reciting Matthew Arnold as usual," says Grace, and Charlotte, during periods of depression, "endured the usual intimations of erratic cell multiplication, dust and dry wind, sexual dysaesthesia, sloth, flatulence, root canal." What does matter is the intensity of her personal vision and the brilliance of her technique. She is the most economical of writers, able to condense into a single paragraph what others would take three pages to expound. Unerringly, she seizes the exact phrase that not only describes but comments on a scene: ". . . the pool was filled with prematurely thickened young girls celebrating a forthcoming marriage." Her laconic prose, compressed into short chapters and staccato paragraphs, allows for occasional repetitions that lend a liturgical echo to her tale. Her exposition of situations and details adroitly conceals their significance—until much later their meaning flares before our eyes.

March 1977

LETTERS OF LIBERATION

BECAUSE I HAVE an uneasy feeling that any attempt I make to describe what happens in this story is likely to start the summer rush for the beaches, I want to say at once that *The Color Purple* is an American novel of permanent importance, that rare sort of book which (in Norman Mailer's felicitous phrase) amounts to "a diversion in the fields of dread." Alice Walker excels at making difficulties for herself and then transcending them. To cite an example: her story begins at about the point that a respectable

Greek tragedy reserves for its climax, then becomes by immea-
surably small steps a comedy that works its way toward acceptance, serenity, and joy. To cite another: her narrative advances
entirely by means of letters that are either never delivered or are
delivered too late for a response, and most of these are written in a
black English that Walker appears to have modified artfully for
general consumption.

The letters begin with Celie addressing herself to God because she's ashamed to speak to anyone else. Celie is black, ugly,
not good at schoolwork; she lives in rural Georgia in this century's second decade and is fourteen when the man she takes to
be her father begins to rape her. She bears this man two children,
who are taken away; at his insistence, she marries a man who
would rather have had her younger sister, Nettie. Others call
Celie's husband Albert, but she cannot; unable to muster his
name in her letters, she refers to him as "Mr. ————." "You
black, you pore, you ugly," Albert tells his wife, "you a woman,
you nothing at all." Albert invites to their home his old mistress,
Shug Avery, who arrives ill, with "the nasty woman disease."
This event, which should break up any household, proves oddly
restorative; a bond between Celie and Shug develops, almost to
the exclusion of the useless Albert.

In time—the course of this novel covers more than thirty
years—Celie discovers that the despicable Albert has been withholding letters written to her by Nettie, who has gone to West
Africa as an apprentice missionary with the couple who adopted
Celie's children. There among the Olinka tribe, Nettie finds herself an object of pity and contempt. In Africa as in Georgia, men
expect women to serve them, yet there Nettie discovers what
Celie does at home: "It is in work that women get to know and
care about each other." Celie now writes to Nettie letters that her
sister never receives. There is, in this parallel correspondence in
which no letter ever hopes for an answer, something deeply moving: these sisters need each other desperately, but each must mature and survive without response from the other.

Love redeems, meanness kills—that is *The Color Purple*'s
principal theme, the theme of most of the world's great fiction.
Nevertheless—and this is why this black woman's novel will survive a white man's embrace—the redemptive love that is cele-

brated here is selective, even prickly. White folk figure rarely in its pages and never to their advantage, and black men are recovered only to the extent that they buckle down to housework and let women attend to business. For Walker, redemptive love requires female bonding. The bond liberates women from men, who are predators at worst, idle at best. As Celie says of Albert, "One good thing bout the way he never do any work round the place, us never miss him when he gone."

In the traditional manner, Walker ends her comedy with a dance, or more precisely with a barbecue. "White people busy celebrating they independence from England July 4th," says Celie's stepson, "so most black folk don't have to work. Us can spend the day celebrating each other." In this novel, the celebration has been painfully earned.

June 1982

WOMAN'S DESPERATE LOT

Two BRASS-BRIGHT first novels with a common theme: woman's desperate lot.* Men still write about women in the old way, disliking them mostly: think of Mrs. Portnoy or John Updike's women, who have all become harridans, shrews, and amateur whores. But women writers, the good ones today, seem curiously of one mind. They write about women as victims of their own neuroses, victims of waiting and wasting, victims of other, grotesque women and of brutal men. In these novels, as in *The Bell Jar* and *Play It as It Lays*, we see women at the edge, close to violence and mental collapse. The clamor of women's liberation is never heard in these stories about women who are grounded in

---

Maiden, by Cynthia Buchanan, and *Thinking Girl*, by Norma Meacock.

their sex, who would reply to Freud's famous question "What does a woman want?" with no more than a request for decency, kindness, and love, for recognition as a person. Their astonishing availability to men is matched only by their astonishing tolerance of men's shortcomings, which has not been my experience of the sex, but let it go: we are talking about women writing about women.

Maiden is a bright, if not finally successful story—a curate's egg sort of book, by which I mean that parts of it are very good indeed. Its heroine, Fortune Dundy, is thirty and a virgin: "her virginity had burrowed in," Cynthia Buchanan writes in the most dazzling opening three pages that I have seen in some time. "So she was a little crazed, a little abstract. . . . She was waiting for the summons, the tap on the shoulder, the visitation, the different drums." Fortune is nervous, romantic; when she talks she uses too many words, as if to hold at bay the perils of communication; she tries not to think about sex, is uncomfortably aware of the imminent tedium of the flesh: "Clothes had been invented for a purpose. Out of kindness, consideration to the human eyes of your neighbor." Still, Fortune thinks she has "a certain subterranean something." Because she is not vulgar, because she cares for integrity and love, she is no match for Dionysius West, the California swinging-singles club she goes to live in, looking for a man, a place "packed with wild-eyed—here we are!—good people over 25 but under 40," a place where "all the women shall wear grass skirts! Boooooo! But all the men—ah—*hah!*—shall drive LAWN-MOWERS!!!"

Buchanan, whose photograph suggests that she has what Yeats warned against—"Beauty to make a stranger's eye distraught"—tells her story with a dancing intensity, writing wittily and playing on words. She plays, too, with at least five perspectives on her narrative, four of them Fortune's (she is always observing and explaining herself and her fantasies) and the fifth the author's own. Her novel is funny, delightful, not very well welded together. The end is bloody and abrupt; not tragic, because it violates what we expect from the characters, but simply a mistake, a rush to be done, to be sad because (maybe) stories like this are meant to end sadly.

Norma Meacock's novel about an English girl who reads

Wittgenstein and Sartre and rolls over for any man who puts a
hand on her, is even better. Lindy, the "thinking girl," has been
kicked out by her first lover, a girl who wants to take up with a
man. Lindy is crushed, but her sexuality is not basically lesbian;
men are just fine by her, but she would like to *talk* to men, about
politics and philosophy, about art or her medical problems—and
the result is always the same: "I just seem to end up in a position
where only one thing is required. I'm seduced all the time."
Lindy marries, finally, a self-centered slob, an appalling lout who
collects graffiti and dithers over a monograph on sex. She works at
loving him and keeps a notebook on her "thoughts." "I'll live to
think," she says. "Somebody's got to do the thinking." Her husband screams abuse; Lindy, who once rejected him, now attempts
to endure him. "I needed responses," she says. "Any responses. I
lived in relation."

Woman's contingency, her need to be endorsed by man, is
not endorsed by either of these writers, but it is the matter of
their novels. The idea of *la belle dame sans merci* is not, apparently, one that women writers feel comfortable with today.
Wretched wights they give us in plenty, but it is the women in
their fiction, now, who are alone and palely loitering. Like
Maiden, Thinking Girl is weak in its links and its transitions—
one can almost see the holes where hunks must have been torn
from a previous draft. In fact, an English edition of this novel appeared four years ago without some of the explicit sex scenes that
Meacock handles so expertly. All writers today are self-conscious
about representing sex in fiction, but Meacock writes her sex
scenes with wit and élan; they work, and we must be grateful for
that. More important, she writes tightly and with precision; each
scene emerges sharply in focus. Hers is a tense story, erudite and
witty as well; the sadness she achieves at the end is honestly arrived at.

February 1972

Like most feminist novels, Diane Johnson's *Lying Low* represents a triumph of sensibility over plot. Why a strong, credible
narrative line that leads to a satisfactory resolution of conflicts
should visit these stories so infrequently, I do not know. Because
the ability to tell a good story is unrelated to gender, I sometimes

suspect that the authors of these novels are simply indifferent to
the rigors of narrative. Violence they give us in plenty, but the
violence seems somehow laid on—an external, almost gratuitous
manifestation of a deeper internal disorder. These novels are always most convincing when least dramatic. Condition, not action,
is their true concern: the problems of women confronting, or trying to ignore, their desperate lot.

The scene in this one is the Sacramento valley. A useless
man and three neurasthenic women inhabit a large old house,
amid premonitions of suffering and disaster. The man, Anton, is a
photographer of trees and mountains; deserted by a succession of
wives, he does little now but irritate his sister, Theo, who owns
the place. Theo, once an undistinguished dancer, teaches ballet in
town—and plans to teach it as a kind of therapy to convicts in the
local prison. The other women are boarders. Ouida, a Brazilian
with a precarious command of English, has lost her passport to an
unscrupulous employer; "too innocent for America," she embraces every kind of occult foolishness while waiting to be de-
ported. None of these three knows anything about the beautiful
Marybeth, who is hiding there under a false name. Marybeth,
formerly a radical student, is wanted for the murder of a man who
was working on a new kind of napalm when Marybeth and her
cronies threw a bomb into his laboratory.

Until the outside world intrudes, bringing death and disar-
ray, each woman lives entirely inside her own mind: waiting,
fearing, regretting. Except for her opening pages, Johnson nudges
her story along entirely through her women's perceptions, jumping nimbly, restlessly among their thoughts, never lighting for
long. She treats them lovingly, satirically, wittily, all at once; it is
a virtuoso performance, really, a kind of balancing act that seems
from the beginning impossible to sustain. But she does sustain it,
using a prose tempo that is entirely her own and some amiable
misanthropy: the men in this book are all useless, inadequate, or
deluded. "What do men think of?" Theo asks. "It's hard to imagine the mind of a man, she thought, minds lacking the rich full-
ness of a woman's mind, all kinds of ideas cut off from them, no
ideas about sewing or the colors of things."

It's hard to dislike so clever and deftly observant a novel, and
I don't really dislike it. I'm disappointed by it because I don't

think Johnson knows where she is taking her people, or to what purpose. In the end, she is unjust to them, killing one, humiliating another, leaving the fate of a third unresolved. Unable to conclude her story, she simply lets it go.

October 1978

From the evidence of much of the fiction written by our abler women novelists today, men are useless articles, fit to swell a scene or two but not to be closely regarded. In *Hearts*, a man is introduced drinking a martini; three pages later, "he poured more whiskey into his glass." And why not, I ask. This fellow is not as badly off as are Hilma Wolitzer's other males. One enters only to die at once; another lies disabled by a stroke; others attempt indecent advances; still another pours coffee while, a room or two away, the women talk about the business of life. When, finally, one man does prove capable of offering the support and comfort that the heroine briefly, intermittently requires, he is kissed off, left to run futilely after the car that carries the women away. We may not have come as far from *Shane* as once we thought.

Hearts draws upon another distinctively American myth: the story of two people, one dependent on the other, packing a few belongings and hitting the road or the river to start a new life, to find through a sequence of adventures and eccentric encounters a better understanding of their own humanity. Widowed at twenty-six after six weeks of marriage, Linda Reismann finds herself pregnant and saddled with her husband's thirteen-year-old daughter, whom she hardly knows. Robin, a perpetually sullen and hostile child who already looks like a woman, is her stepmother's natural antagonist: "Linda the Wimp," she calls her when she doesn't call her something worse. Poor Linda: decent, responsible, a worrier, she does seem (for one who grew up middle class in Pennsylvania) impossibly innocent.

Taking only what she can stow in the trunk of her car, Linda drives Robin west from New Jersey. She has three items on her agenda: an abortion, the surrender of Robin to her grandfather in Iowa, and her own new life in California where she hopes to see movie stars pushing carts through the all-night supermarkets. None of this will come about, of course. Robin has her own agenda: to find and take revenge on her mother, who ran out on

her when she was five. Besides, the point of a story like this is that
this woman and this girl, so incompatible at their journey's beginning, must come to know and care for each other. In Linda's
words, they must learn "that you can become a family by the
grace of accident and will, that we have a duty to console one another as best we can."

Hearts is a nice, sentimental novel, for the most part expertly
wrought. I think it should please a great many readers—most of
them women, I suppose, though the mildly feminist cast to the
story ought not to frighten away the men. Through a sequence of
flashbacks (the journey forward is also the journey back) we
learn what we need to about Linda's joyless youth: her cruel and
(need I add?) witless father; her mother, who was too often
away. There is just a touch of comfortable sex, and a moving end.
I don't really object to the men being as pallid as they are because
the two women are fully realized. I do object to some of the plot's
absurd contrivances, but then fiction of this sort rarely offers
credible narratives. The author's attention is elsewhere: on the
condition of women and on the development of sensibilities.

December 1980

THE CHRISTIAN NOVEL NOW

WALKER PERCY is a Christian novelist, which is not to say that
he's a Christian who writes novels—there's no shortage of
those—but that he's a novelist who writes about Christian concerns, and our supply of these is at present diminished. Once, in
an essay, he likened the Christian novelist to "a man who has
found a treasure hidden in the attic of an old house, but he is
writing for people who have moved to the suburbs and who are
bloody sick of the old house and everything in it." An overstate-

ment, perhaps. One need not profess the faith to recognize the mythic structure that Christian themes can lend a narrative, or the fine opportunities for moral perplexity that they afford. In any event, Percy's fourth novel, *Lancelot*, is his most specifically and rigorously Christian. An urgency has replaced his customary gentle amiability; in this story about moral ferocity, the author's wit and comic playfulness have been carefully tamped down.

The story is told as a monologue. Lancelot Lamar, like the protagonists of all of Percy's novels, is a "somewhat lapsed" man, a victim of *accidie*, that splenetic sense of uselessness and alienation, who has come to the end of his rope. From a cell in what is either a prison or an asylum, Lance explains his recent history to his former college roommate, now a priest-psychiatrist. Lance's antebellum mansion in Louisiana, restored with the fortune of his second wife, has burned down. His wife and two movie people died in the holocaust. Lance often digresses as he relates his decline from college football hero to adult idler and dilettante in law and history, a man whose life slipped away until, by accident, he discovered that his daughter's blood type could not possibly derive from his. With the evidence of his wife's infidelity before him, Lance sets out after further proof—a quest, of sorts, for "the sweet secret of evil," the sexual transgression that may reveal to him for the first time what sin is.

"The Knight of the Unholy Grail," Lance calls himself and, indeed, he is a mirror image of his Arthurian namesake, ironically aware that "it was not so much the case of my screwing the queen as the queen getting screwed by somebody else." This Lancelot can glimpse his grail, can become violent, can withdraw through madness from our degenerate society. "I will not tolerate this age," he tells his visitor, "and I will act."

Lance, the atheist, proposes a revolution in morality, a stern code imposed by a few righteous men who are prepared to act violently if need be. "Don't talk to me of love," he says, "until we shovel out the shit." But *love* is the magic Christian word; without it, Lance's program for reform is exposed as the ludicrous thing it is. At the very end, Lance admits his quest has failed: he has found sin but felt nothing. "Christ," he says to the priest, "you of all people should understand." Is this Christ just another oath, or has Lancelot always known to whom he has been talking?

So ambitious is *Lancelot*, and so complex, that you might think the clangor of symbols and allegory would drown the story. Not at all. Percy is a seductive writer, attentive to sensuous detail, and such a skillful architect of fiction that the very discursiveness of his story informs it with energy and tension. From the start we know that there are violent deaths and the destruction of a great house to be explained, but the distracted Lancelot cannot quite focus on his story; his digressions increase the suspense and we must wait a long while for the horrific climactic scene in which a number of lethal forces converge and this corrupted southern Camelot is literally blown off the face of the earth. This is a fine novel, not so much a departure from what Percy has done before as an extension of it, and, as he has said elsewhere, a portrait of "a new breed of person in whom the potential for catastrophe—and hope—has suddenly escalated."

February 1977

The phrase is not generally offered as a compliment, but when I say that Frederick Buechner's new novel seems longer than it is, I mean to praise it. It seems so because Buechner, working as a novelist ought, constructs in small space a universe entirely his own, which he reveals through a language invented for the occasion. Of course, neither is altogether unfamiliar. *Godric*'s world resembles what we think we know of England in the eleventh and twelfth centuries, a world set forth in accents that retain an Anglo-Saxon flavor: "In Saxon soil that Harold hallowed by his falling there." This is also an England that only a saint and poet might perceive, an anthropomorphic land in which "rock and river clap like hands in summer sun," of loyal, loving snakes and wraithlike figures appearing to beckon a sinner on toward Christ.

Buechner's narrator (who is based on a historical figure) is a crusty hermit of more than one hundred years. For half that time Godric has devoted himself to prayer and mortification of the flesh: he wears a punishing iron vest and crouches, every day of the year, in the icy waters of a river that flows near Durham. Blessed with second sight and the power to heal ("it's as if my hands are gloves, and in them other hands than mine"), he is tormented by memories of his rough-handed past—memories reawakened by a young monk who has come to write the story of his life. Distrusting hagiography, Godric tells us what he knows the monk will not: of his early years as a lecher and seagoing trader, of his skill at bilking pilgrims, of cruel months spent in the service of a villainous lord, and most particularly of the ill-starred love that he and his sister bore each other. Aware that he has become an object of reverence—"How holy must he be to rest in one place, rooted like a tree, so he may raise his shaggy arms to God alone while holy thoughts nest in his leaves like birds"— Godric offers a dissenting opinion: "Is the past a sea old men can founder in before their time and drown?"

From the book's opening sentence—"Five friends I had, and two of them snakes"—any sensible reader will be caught in Godric's grip. Obsessive and unyielding, saints are almost without exception intolerable human beings; certainly the God-racked Godric is no exception, though he has decent instincts and his anguish is affecting. Like all good writers of historical fiction, Buechner strives less for verisimilitude than for a vision of the past, a tone of voice that is not so much intended to be accurate as useful to his purpose. In telling his long story in such a short space, and from both of its ends at once, Buechner glides deftly from the fanciful to scenes that are nearly realistic: his description of Godric's pilgrimage to Rome, for instance, and of the corruption of that city at that time, seems to me a remarkable tour de force. I think Buechner has risked much in attempting to define the ambivalences in the life of a saintly man, and risked even more by adopting a language that could easily have become overwrought. In a year in which most American novels have seemed either tedious or flaccid enterprises, *Godric* glimmers brightly.

November 1980

PHILOGOREY

A rod is the very best thing to apply
When children are crying and cannot say why.

THAT'S ONE OF my favorite couplets—I quote it to my children constantly—but it's not by Edward Gorey. You might think it was. Gorey's curious little books combine macabre, unmistakable drawings with macabre, elusively familiar lines of verse. Like Hilaire Belloc, whose ironic *Cautionary Verses* relate the baroque deaths of naughty children, Gorey writes edifying stories that are part put-on, part parody, reminding us of the earnest morality tales of the early Victorian era.* Unlike Belloc and the Victorians, Gorey never suggests that the fate of his characters is in any way deserved. Gorey is an extreme economist: not a word is wasted in his children's books, limericks, grisly tales, and rhymes about children who, in alphabetical order, succumb to dismal ends. Now Gorey's first fifteen books have been collected under a title that plays on a Greek word for "a nonsense verse or composition."

Take one of his milder efforts:

> *An innocent maiden named Herridge*
> *Was cruelly tricked into marriage;*
> *When she later found out*
> *What her spouse was about,*
> *She threw herself under a carriage.*

Here, as elsewhere, suggestion is all. The deadpan narration hints at more alarming limericks that we all have heard, once upon a time. We don't know what the girl encountered in her marriage and are just as glad we don't. From the accompanying drawing,

---

*Amphigorey and *The Awdrey-Gore Legacy,* by Edward Gorey.

we know the lady is a Victorian, though some of Gorey's characters evolve into the Edwardian and flapper eras. In Gorey's tales and verses, people disappear without explanation, are slaughtered in the most abominable ways, are obliged to entertain supernatural creatures in their homes (one wears a college scarf and basketball shoes; another, which we never see, sinks slowly from one floor through the next). Nobody seems to mind much; the intervention of such visitors, if odd, is not particularly sinister: the world contains such things. Madness, depravity, deterioration: all are commonplace in Gorey's universe. Weird reptiles prowl inconspicuously through some of the more caustically sentimental stories, but everywhere we look there is solid furniture, patterned wallpaper.

Gorey is a master of leaving our expectations unfulfilled. His stories are fragmented in a surrealistic way: the elements are banal and the connections that might link them are missing. Sometimes he plays conventionally on names: Harold Tyne-Forque, Weedhaven Laughing Academy, Collapsed Pudding in Mortshire. His meticulous drawings, in which space, angles, and the presence of walls are all more carefully considered than a triviality like gravity, are quite likely to show such wonders as a wan child drinking gin; beside her is a doll: a skeleton in a nightgown. One of Gorey's best books, *The West Wing*, has no words at all: only ominous doors standing open, a mirror reflecting a part of a door with part of a something coming through it, four tentacles (which upon prolonged examination prove to be the legs of a chair) edging around a corner. The prose in the other stories poses and abandons dramatic situations without explanation.

The Awdrey-Gore Legacy is a lovely spoof of Agatha Christie's detective novels. Here, Gorey gives us all the ingredients of the classic English mystery: the characters, rooms, maps, time tables, and jargon, each with its special nimbus, but there is no plot at all. Astonished, we look again: the absolutely familiar world of the detective mystery is here, but it doesn't mean anything. There are details and clues abounding, but none that you can seize. Everything is precisely accounted for, but the specifics, the details, only symbolize the specifics and details that, in a real detective story, are significant. As always, the pictures are exquisite: murder weapons are arranged according to bluntness and limpness so that Gorey can amuse himself with visual correspondences. And there are portentous quotations from something called *The Ispsiad,* which, of course, means an epic about itself. That's what Gorey's delightful tales have always been about.

October 1972

THE ART OF THE THRILLER

1. The Ear of Elmore Leonard

IN NEW ORLEANS, where you drive west across the bridge to reach the east side of the city, Police Lieutenant John Schluter, Jr. describes a scam that hooks the tourists.

"Man says, 'Bet you a dollar I can tell you where you got your shoes, what city, what state.' No way he can know, right? You take the bet. Man says, 'You got your shoes on your feet, in the city of New Orleans, state of Louisiana.' You lose."

The scam has a naïve charm: it works by exploiting the semantics of the spoken language. Schluter's audience, a spare, bearded man in a Kangol cap and tennis shoes, is in a similar line of work. Elmore Leonard, the author of twenty-three novels and fifteen screenplays, is the best American writer of crime fiction alive, possibly the best we've ever had. He has come from his home in Birmingham, Michigan, to renew his acquaintance with this city in which he was born fifty-nine years ago. He's come to listen to what people say here, the *sound,* the rhythm of what they say. "Listening," he says, "is hard work." He won't use most of what he hears in his new novel, which will be set in New Orleans, but you can't tell that from his face, which registers only polite attention.

Elmore Leonard, called "Dutch" by everyone who talks with him for more than five minutes, is the author of *Glitz*, a novel now floating near the top of the best-seller lists. Above *Glitz*, like an algae mat on a eutrophying pond, lie books by Sidney Sheldon and Danielle Steele—an impenetrable barrier, but Leonard's nonetheless pleased: with 185,000 copies in the stores, *Glitz* has already far outsold his previous novels. Film, reprint rights, and a fee for writing a screenplay earned him nearly $1 million last year.

Leonard's belated recognition is in part the result of a calculated full-court press by his hardcover publisher, Arbor House. Reviews of Leonard's recent books have been uniformly enthusiastic, but readers didn't respond: *LaBrava*, his previous novel, sold about twenty thousand copies. Arbor thought they could do better. They spent six months studying the pattern of how his previous books were ordered, then kicked in $100,000—a huge amount by publishing standards—for advertising deliberately designed not to look like advertising for a book. To sell a lot of books, a publisher is wise to make his product look like something else.

The strategy paid off, with no visible effect on Leonard, who, except for his sudden access to big money, in no way resembles the characters of whom he writes. "They tell me I can drive a Mercedes," he says. "I don't want to drive a Mercedes." Leonard was raised as a Catholic; in 1934, when he was nine, his parents moved him to Detroit. He is today a recovered alcoholic, a heavy smoker, and a modest, reticent man. Only rarely in his conversation can one detect a glint of his steely professionalism.

Uninterested in writing literary novels, Leonard chose a genre: he began by writing westerns and turned to crime fiction when the market for westerns collapsed. He sold his first story to Argosy in 1951, but ten years would pass before he earned enough from his fiction to write it full-time. So Leonard wrote advertising copy for Chevrolet trucks. Then, too, he would go out to do research, use his ear. He would ask, "What's the best thing about this truck?" One driver replied, "You don't wear that sonofabitch out, you just get tired of looking at it and buy a new one." Leonard proposed the line for an ad campaign; Chevrolet was not prepared for such authenticity.

This same care for authenticity characterizes all of his books;

it prompts him to write without benefit of similes and metaphors. Like its predecessors, which include *Stick, Cat Chaser, Unknown Man #89,* and *Split Images, Glitz* is a crime novel so artfully wrought that its interest extends beyond the usual audience for thrillers. Leonard writes about urban human predators; some are incompetent hustlers, others are clearly insane. Part of his stories' appeal is their tacit implication that if the reader wasn't careful, if he let his guard down just a little, people like these might move into his life.

In *City Primeval,* for instance, a man lends his apartment to his girl friend while he's out of town; she moves in her main man, a murderer who's soon trying on the other fellow's suits. In *52 Pickup,* a rich man conducting a banal affair runs into blackmailers who murder his mistress while making a movie of the event. These and Leonard's other stories are violent in the extreme, his finely tuned dialogue as coarse as his characters themselves. Yet all this sociopathic stuff is made tolerable by a fluctuating degree of satire, a mordant humor that sharply distinguishes his books from those of the writers to whom he is frequently, and inaccurately, compared: Hammett, Chandler, Ross Macdonald.

Take *Glitz.* If it's not his best story, it's his most carefully textured novel; besides, the margin of difference between Leonard's better and lesser works would admit, with difficulty, a butterfly's wing. The plot isn't as strong as some that Leonard has conceived, but it's representative of the confrontational story that Leonard has often written. Vincent Mora, a Miami police detective, goes to San Juan to recover from bullets adminstered by a drug addict. Vincent likes women, including a hooker who's been offered a job by the owner of a casino in Atlantic City. In San Juan, Vincent runs up against a man he once sent to prison: Teddy Magyk, a psychopath who wants revenge.

Because Teddy's ambition dovetails with his hobby—killing women—he follows the hooker to New Jersey and pitches her from a terrace eighteen stories high. He wants to attract Vincent's attention, and he does. Vincent works unofficially with the local police—he's the guy who doesn't have to obey the rules. While Teddy stalks him, he tries to nab the hooker's killer and stay alive in the process. The climax, like those of many of Leonard's novels, involves a bloody confrontation between the good guy and the bad guy.

A brief sketch of its plot can't begin to suggest what an Elmore Leonard story offers. Not in his plots, but in the way that he defines a chapter, a character, a point of view, and a few lines of dialogue do we see a serious artist at work. Leonard doesn't begin with the plot in his mind; he doesn't know how his stories will come out. "After writing thirty years, I know there'll be a plot, a beginning, an end. I'll pull something out of here and put it there." Instead, he thinks of a situation and a handful of characters. First, he needs to get their names right, then he begins to develop them in a large notebook. "I start out hearing a person. Not so much what his background is, I know a little about that. But what does he sound like? I'm not sure yet. I want to learn his attitude." In his notebook, his characters speak of their lives directly to him. Here's one from the book he's working on: "My dad supported himself through school playing poker. He went to Oklahoma, took geology, but didn't finish. He sold oil leases at first. . . . I heard my dad tell my mother, 'Well, we've got $300,-000 in this new lease block,' and my mother say, 'If no one buys the deal, what do we eat?' My dad says, 'We eat *it*, honey; that's the business.' "

"If it sounds like writing, I rewrite it," Leonard says. The result of such care is that the secondary characters in his novels, even those who appear for no more than a page or two, are entirely credible. Vincent, clearly, is an archetypal Leonard hero, honest and caring, yet violent when he needs to be, a rogue male who must work his own justice—just as they do in westerns. In contrast, Leonard gives us three vulnerable women, each sharply characterized. The women in his stories tend to be especially exposed to mayhem; considering what happens to them, it's a wonder women like his books, but many do. "My women are getting better and better," Leonard says. "God knows, I'm working hard enough on them."

He says, too, "I'm not a good narrative writer. I put all my energies into my characters and let my characters carry it." Because he doesn't know where his novels are going, he builds them from a series of expertly crafted scenes that hang in the memory long after the narratives dissolve. The scene in *52 Pickup* in

which the hero is forced to watch a snuff film made of his mistress's murder may be the most alarming in any American crime
novel. It's tolerable only because the woman was never a character in the story; Leonard had the good sense not to let us care for
her. By contrast, there's a chapter in *Glitz*, in which a former
beauty queen tells Vincent about the hooker's humiliation in a
way that keeps coming back to herself; it may be the most sensitive scene he's written. "I look at each scene separately," Leonard
says, "not as part of the whole."

His books depart from the hard-boiled tradition in another
way: from Hammett to Mickey Spillane, from Macdonald to
Robert B. Parker, writers have generally told these stories in the
first person. By jettisoning the security of first-person narration—a unified point of view, a single sardonic tone of voice, a
sense of the hero in control—Leonard can let his characters
breathe more easily, show us how matters seem to them. In this
way, the reader knows more about what's going on than the hero
does (it takes Vincent a long time to figure out that Teddy killed
the hooker). Leonard asks himself: what's the *purpose* of this
scene? He writes it and then decides that it works better if presented from another character's point of view. In one scene, for
example, a shark lady who's married to the casino's owner lays
down the law to her alcoholic, impotent husband and his fatuous
manager. In the original version, the wife had the last word—but
somehow the scene didn't work. Leonard recast it from the manager's incompetent perspective; *now* it works.

When asked how he knows so much about underworld entrepreneurs, Dutch Leonard says, "I make it up. I listen to cops. I
spent most of three months sitting around squad rooms in Detroit
listening to cops. Sitting around police headquarters in New Orleans, he listens to Lieutenant Schluter and Detective Sergeant
Delsa talk about the sixth sense cops develop to tell whether a
man in a car is carrying guns or drugs. "You can tell if a guy's
dirty by looking at him," Delsa says, "how he carries himself."
Leonard likes the sound of that and makes a note; he makes another when Schluter tells him that Dixie beer, the local brew, is
best drunk from long-neck bottles, not from cans. Delsa tells a
story of the man who stole a Mercedes from a dealer, then

brought the car back to the same dealer for service. "Where else would you take a Mercedes?" The dealer didn't recognize his car. Leonard likes that, too: it has a real-life implausibility that will make a good paragraph. He likes the sequel even better. The man was a hotel thief. When he was finally caught, the only evidence that stood up was a monogrammed briefcase the cops found in his room, its contents untouched. The thief had never opened it; he just wanted it. "It's like human nature," Delsa says. Leonard nods: human nature is what does you in.

Because one of the characters in his new novel will be a hotel thief, Leonard wants to learn how to rob hotel rooms. He gets Lieutenant Schluter to introduce him to the chief of security at one of the city's largest hotels. The security man is polite, consents to an appointment, then makes himself unavailable, doesn't return Leonard's calls. Who *is* this man who looks like he might be found floating down a hotel corridor at 4:00 A.M.? Even if he is what he says he is, who needs precise instructions in burglarizing hotels broadcast in a best-seller?

Leonard shrugs: "I'll make it up." And he can be pretty sure he'll get it right. Leonard's books contain the odd technical error—one reader wrote, "Please quit putting safeties on revolvers; they don't have any!"—but he has a novelist's talent for making up things that turn out to be just so. In *Swag*, his crooks hold up Hudson's, a department store in Detroit. Hudson's wouldn't tell Leonard how it moves its cash about, so Leonard "made it up" and got the complicated procedure right. In *The Hunted* he made up the details of a quarrel between two real ball players. The widow of one called him: "How did you know all that?" "It was in the papers?" Leonard suggests. No, it wasn't.

Leonard has written two television pilots and thirteen feature films, of which five have been produced to date. Among these is the script for Burt Reynolds's production of *Stick*, but Leonard doesn't like what's happened to it, doesn't see how it can succeed. "When I'm writing I see real people," Leonard says. "When I see the movie I see actors acting." In *Stick*, "they've taken out the plot and put in machine guns and scorpions."

Leonard saw the first cut last June—the movie was supposed to have opened last fall—and wrote a four-and-a-half-page letter to Reynolds. "I didn't get into the technical aspects—he could get that from anybody. I did say specifically there were too many re-actions between the characters. My characters don't react to each other. They don't laugh at each others' lines. They're saying seri-ous things. It's all right for the audience to laugh, or the reader, but not the people who are involved. This is all pretty much low-key, deadpan stuff." Which makes a good novel, of course, but not a movie. Reynolds reshot some of the film and showed the new, improved version to Leonard three months ago. Leonard was not encouraged, but there's nothing he can do and, besides, he's got the new book to work on.

He has the gimmick: an ex-convict, just released from twenty years in the Louisiana State Penitentiary at Angola, meets a former nun who tells him of a cache of money about to be sent to the rebels in Nicaragua—it will, she says, be used to "finance murder." (Large caches of money, usually being moved about in suitcases, are a Leonard trademark; another is photography: stills, movies, videotapes, play important roles in his stories, saying something, perhaps, about the voyeur that lurks in most Ameri-can men.) The ex-con sees a chance for one last big haul, one that he can morally justify. He enlists the aid of three men he knew in Angola.

Leonard will tie these three to a heist he heard of from Lieu-tenant Schluter and Sergeant Delsa. It's a marvelously compli-cated story involving a rogue cop, his senior mistress, his junior mistress, and his sister, who worked for Wells Fargo in Memphis. Together they stuffed $6.5 million into a van; they would have taken more, but that was all they could squeeze into the van. It was the second biggest robbery in American history, the largest involving a cop. Over a year passed before the crime unraveled. When the police found the cop's share hidden in his wall, they noticed he had torn off the bands containing the cash and thrown them in a corner of the room—where anyone could see them. "Like human nature," as Delsa would say. Another writer would make a whole book out of this story, but for Leonard it will be only a few pages of background: "I don't like to know how my story will come out."

At this point, he doesn't even know "who the good guys and bad guys are," so he drives up to Angola, on the Mississippi bor-der, to learn something of how they lived as convicts. Nobody escapes from Angola's eighteen thousand acres; it's where all of Louisiana's hard cases go. Accompanied by two wardens, Leonard inspects the penitentiary's more hospitable areas, then spends two hours with a lifer in for murder and another man in for armed robbery. Wilbert Rideau, the murderer, is, as convicts go, a famous man. A slim, personable man of forty-three, he's won numerous major journalism awards for editing the prison journal, *The Angolite*, to which Leonard subscribes. In the words of Louisiana's governor, presently to be indicted for corruption, Rideau is "the most successfully rehabilitated prisoner in the state." Nothing about him suggests that twenty-four years ago he cut the throat of a woman in the course of holding up a bank, then spent eleven years on death row.

Leonard suggests situations; Rideau doubts they could occur: "You're going to have to use your creativity on that." Leonard presses him on prison vocabulary. Rideau feeds him "free man" for guard, "fresh fish" for new convict, "turn you out" for the ritual in which the fresh fish's manhood is tested: he's beaten, raped, forced to fight with knives. "If you're raped," Rideau explains, "you're no longer a man: you're a 'galboy,' a 'bitch,' a 'whore,' and you become the property of whoever turned you out. He traded you, prostituted you, gambled you at cards. Slavery was pretty widespread." Rideau remembers knife fights between inmates with books strapped to their chests. The winner would volunteer to rush the loser to the hospital—but only to make sure he never got there. Rideau's art director, the armed robber, recalls a convict who gave up proving his manhood with his knife. "I fought thirty, forty times," he reports the convict saying. "It didn't do no good. So I went the other way. It don't hurt as much."

Novelists seldom get so much good stuff all at once. Leonard may use some of it, but he's attracted now by the power plays inmates use to determine what TV show a group will watch. Muscle decides the matter. A scene rises in his mind. One of his characters will be watching the news. Half a dozen tough guys— "hogs" in prison parlance—walk in, switch the channel to Bugs Bunny. What will his man do then? "I don't know," Leonard says. "I'll think of something."

April 1985

2. The Best of Ross Macdonald

ASTONISHINGLY, Ross Macdonald has written his novel again, even more skillfully than before. I don't mean that he has probed further into moral exhaustion, into the vulnerability of the innocent or the corruption of a family than he did in *The Chill* and *The Underground Man*—in writing detective stories, which depend on surprises and reversals, one can only press so far in such directions—but that the architecture of *Sleeping Beauty* is particularly complex and satisfactory. Reading a Macdonald novel is like watching dots appear on a three-dimensional graph of a mathematical equation—we try to guess where the other dots will fall and the shape of the line that will connect them—and on this graph Macdonald makes us account for more than the usual number of factors, of dots deceitfully arranged.

A beautiful and unstable young woman, heir to a California oil fortune, disappears with a lethal dose of sleeping pills on the day that her family's offshore oil explorations result in a disastrous spill. The woman's husband asks Lew Archer to find her, and so, as the lake of oil moves in toward the beaches, Archer races around interviewing the woman's family, sorting the skeletons as they fall from three generations of well-appointed closets. The woman, it appears, is being held for ransom; it appears, too, that the present oil disaster is linked to a ship's fire in World War II, and the present crop of corpses to a murder more than a quarter century old.

As always in the Lew Archer novels, a great many people are linked together by avarice, adultery, and anger; all are suspect because in the closed world of a family's affairs those who do not breed corruption are eroded by it. In this novel, too, we see all of Macdonald's other motifs elegantly developed—the search for the lost child; the idea that family determines fate; the need to restore order to the past as well as to the present; the balance between natural and moral disaster; scattered images suggesting the imminent end of man and his endeavors; and a harmony of structure: the bird that is washed up from the oil-slicked ocean at the book's beginning is paired a little later with a man who is similarly oiled and destroyed.

Most interesting of all is the pairing that Macdonald has made uniquely his own: that of the victim, who is immobilized by her consciousness of the world's violence and cruelty, with Lew Archer—"thief catcher, corpse finder, ear to anyone," as he says of himself—the competent man. "It seemed to me," Archer says of a character in this story, "that he allowed himself to feel too much, and that it interfered with his power to act." Archer does not let that happen to him; more aware than anyone of the world's wickedness, he allows himself only minimal involvement with other people, and can therefore remain free to act, to restore order. It is a marvelous formula that Macdonald has found; the wonder is that he keeps improving it.

May 1973

3. In the Theatre of the Real

A STORYTELLER who attempts to break new ground is well advised to go easy with the pick and shovel. The trick is to leave intact at least some of the soil that has yielded profitable crops for him before and may do so yet again. That's what John le Carré has done in his tenth novel: while working a new terrain and pressing to extend the limits of what a spy novel can accomplish, he's kept the romantic attitudes, and much of the black and polished pessimism of his earlier books. A tag from *The Looking Glass War*—"Love is whatever you can still betray"—might easily serve as an epigraph for his new book. The argument advanced by the man called Control in *The Spy Who Came in from the Cold*—"We do disagreeable things so that ordinary people here and elsewhere can sleep safely in their beds at night"—is precisely the argument advanced by the hero of Israeli intelligence in *The Little Drum-*

mer Girl. In fact, these two novels, separated by twenty years, share an identical theme: the discrepancy between what a country says it stands for and what its operatives, to preserve these ideals, are willing to do.

As for new ground broken: in the past, le Carré has treated places like Germany and Hong Kong as arenas in which the people who really matter—the British and the Russians—conduct their secret war. Espionage is the pursuit of empire conducted by other means. Now he reverses himself: his principal locations are again England and Germany, but his antagonists are the Israelis and the Palestinian terrorists. Neither nostalgia for a lost empire nor the compulsion to revive old conflicts motivates these warriors; survival and a sense of justice do. For the first time, le Carré suggests that his villains, the Palestinians, have a legitimate case—George Smiley would never have granted that to the Russians. Artfully—because it is dramatically effective and because it will help to allay the anxieties of his Jewish readers—le Carré puts the pro-Palestinian argument in the mouth of one of his Israeli heroes. It's a fine romantic touch: these amazing Israelis! Despite their excesses, they really do understand.

Always attentive to mood and scene, he develops his story slowly and from several angles. A suitcase bomb explodes in a diplomatic community near Bonn. The intended victim: an Israeli with hawkish views on Palestine. This incident is linked to others, all the work of a shadowy man who directs the Palestinian terror in Europe. The problem of catching him falls to an Israeli intelligence team headed by a grizzled survivor of Nazi concentration camps, a veteran of Israel's struggle to be born.

Marty Kurtz is the new novel's George Smiley. A loner, a man of mesmeric intensity and ability, Kurtz finds that he and his methods are viewed with increasing impatience by the new, politically minded men of Israel's intelligence bureaucracy. To put an end to Palestinian terrorism, Kurtz's masters incline toward an invasion of Lebanon. Kurtz's alternative plan is to find "a window that was wide enough to slip someone through and so take the enemy from inside his house." The question becomes: who's to go through the window? Whom will the terrorists accept? Kurtz's answer: "You want to crack the terror target these days, you practically have to build your own terrorist first." With little time allowed him, he sets out to do just that.

The unlikely agent he means to recruit is an engaging young Englishwoman, a gentile. At twenty-six, Charlie (we never learn her last name) is a talented regional actress. Warm, intelligent, brave, often witty, and blessed with the kind of memory her profession requires, Charlie offers other qualities Kurtz needs. She's promiscuous and accustomed to abuse by men. More important, she's a flaky radical whose unfocused idealism pits her against what she perceives to be the deadness of bourgeois England. Kurtz correctly sees Charlie as a loyal girl looking for a place to invest her loyalty—but first he must get her attention.

To this end he dispatches his best operative—Gadi Becker, an indomitable warrior who "fought the battle for the Golan from behind the Syrian lines." Becker meets Charlie on the beach at Mykonos, where she and her little family of traveling actors are relaxing. No sooner is he drawn into their group than he draws Charlie away—kidnaps her, in fact, to a safe-house in Athens where Kurtz and his team of tough young Israelis await.

Le Carré tends to build his novels from sequences of set pieces—some no longer than a page, others very long indeed. The scene that follows Charlie's abduction runs forty pages and, for its complexity and imaginative brilliance, it the most extraordinary that le Carré has yet written. Charlie is subjected to an interrogation—the mirror image of the standard-brand interrogations in countless more conventional spy stories. Intending to bring Charlie close to breakdown, Kurtz conducts it strictly, but his intention is benign. He means to enlist Charlie in his mission, but at the same time he must strip her of her weaknesses. He doesn't want truth from her; he wants lies.

Kurtz knows that he can attract this young actress: "to the uninitiated, the secret world is of itself attractive. Simply by turning on its axis, it can draw the weakly anchored to its centre." Knowing, too, that actors sometimes think of themselves as hollow people, he offers Charlie the chance to play the role of her life in "the theatre of the real." For her drifting, he offers a straight line; for her duplicity, zeal, a true allegiance. At the same time, he implicitly offers her what she requires even more: in himself, a father; in Becker, a lover; in the tough young commandos who stand about the room politely applauding Charlie's performance, a family to replace that from which he took her.

Of course Charlie accepts. She never had a chance. Becker

takes her education in hand: "On the old reality we impose the new fiction." He invents for her a Palestinian lover, playing the role himself so fervently that his own identity wavers. In fact, this Palestinian (if not the lover) exists. The younger, feckless brother of the terrorist chief who is Charlie's target, he is a prisoner of one of Kurtz's special teams in Munich. Once the details of his life have been wrung from him, and the fiction of his love for Charlie documented by forged letters, he will be killed. At that point, it's only a matter of time before his brother's people get in touch with his grieving mistress.

To synopsize even the first half of one of le Carré's remarkable stories is to betray the manner of its telling. In nearly all of his novels the narrative advances on three fronts at different speeds. (1) *The strategic front:* the goal toward which his undercover agents move is always clear. Smiley intends to smoke out the mole in the Circus, or force Karla to defect; Kurtz means to nullify the director of Palestinian terrorism. (2) *The tactical front:* a plan is launched, but the reader can't put the pieces together. What is the relevance of all this elaborate activity? Sometimes le Carré relents and lets the reader run briefly ahead of his characters' understanding of events, but then he pulls him back again. (3) *Individual skirmishes:* each scene develops clearly enough, but sometimes its significance isn't revealed until it's over. At other times le Carré simply tells his reader what happened before circling back for a leisurely description of how it came about.

Similarly, le Carré sustains throughout all his stories a number of constant themes. One, treated at length in *A Small Town in Germany,* involves people's need to expose their vulnerabilities when only disaster can result. Another suggests that in the kind of lethal conflicts that le Carré chronicles, every victory contains its own defeat. Le Carré's agents are individual entrepreneurs—anachronisms, really—working against time lent to them only grudgingly by their bureaucratic masters; the ultimate victory, just off the pages of the book, will belong to the bureaucrats. A third theme suggests very clearly that for a professional, death is the price of yielding to passion. Such was the fate of Jerry Westerby, who fell in love with his quarry in *The Honourable Schoolboy,* and such is the threat that Charlie confronts when, her loyalties confused once more, she goes to bed with the terror-ist leader.

Le Carré's most important theme is a mirror image of this last: the violence done to the competent man's personal life by his dedication to clandestine work. The "cold" from which the spy Alec Leamas wanted to come in was the loneliness of his pro-fession, which had divorced him from the comforts of human un-derstanding—indeed, from all human values. Le Carré, however, had struck his tonic note even earlier, in the opening pages of his first novel, *Call for the Dead:* "It saddened [Smiley] to witness in himself the gradual death of natural pleasure. . . . He guarded himself warily from spontaneous reaction. By the strength of his intellect, he forced himself to observe humanity with clinical ob-jectivity, and because he was neither immortal nor infallible he hated and feared the falseness of his life." Smiley, who could take no pleasure from his wife, who gave so much pleasure to other men, is perhaps no worse off than Becker, who has put such a damper on his emotions that for much of the book he seems inca-pable of human response.

Literature is made from such stuff—and from the social sat-ire and the often elegant prose with which le Carré shapes his stories. With each book, le Carré improves and expands the po-tential of the genre in which he works. Thus *The Little Drum-mer Girl* is not only a spy story; it's a political novel and a love story, too: a love story in which the anticipation of sex is used as a weapon to gain a political end.

Le Carré writes this kind of thing better than anyone has ever done—intelligent and exciting stories attentive to the credi-bility of character and informed with a moral vision. That he writes romances—stories that subordinate every element they contain to the tyrannous demands of plot—in no way lessens his claim to a place in our literature. Stories precede literature and remain fiction's essential element still.

March 1983

4. The Art of Trash

MY MAILBOX is a creature of habit. Fatigued by its daily obligation to disgorge perhaps a dozen new books, it has for some years now offered me each day the same novels it produced for me the day before. One of these invariably has a picture of a pretty young thing in a Regency dress on its jacket. Another sports a swastika. A third displays an ominous-looking child with weird eyes that imply God-only-knows what telekinetic powers. Usually I find my mailbox's assembly-line production eminently resistible, but last week I succumbed to curiosity. These fearful children, for instance: surely there is some archetypal myth at play here? The oldest story in Western literature is that of the usurping child. Though it did him little good, Kronos acted prudently when he chose to swallow his children.

Stephen King has made a lot of money from such children. In his first novel, *Carrie*, a young girl with odd mental powers sets fire to a building full of people who have abused her. In *Firestarter*, Charlie, a young girl with odd mental powers, sets fire to several buildings full of people who have abused her. The essence of a good myth is that it stays essentially the same.

Charlie's lot, however, is more desperate than Carrie's. At eight years old, she is the child of parents who participated in an alarming drug experiment conducted by a ruthless government agency called "the Shop." The experiment left her father with the ability to "push" people—that is, an ability to make others see and do what he wants. Her mother, as befits domesticated women, can only shut a refrigerator door from across the kitchen. Charlie's inheritance is more disturbing: not only can she will fires to start, she can't entirely control the force within her. The mad villains at the Shop fear that as she matures her talent will achieve nuclear, perhaps doomsday, proportions. Hit men are sent in pursuit of the family. Imprisoned at the Shop's headquarters, prefatory to the novel's great climactic conflagration, Charlie

is put through her paces incinerating steel and burning up cin-
der-block walls.

Dare you ask how the story ends? Come, now: what chance
has a government agency that couldn't give Castro an exploding
cigar against this third-grader who can raise thirty thousand degrees of heat? I can say only that Coleridge's dictum about the
willing suspension of disbelief takes a merciless beating in the
course of these many pages. And yet, says Stephen King, "There
is nothing in *Firestarter* that isn't documented or based on actuality." Indeed. The key to successful trashy fiction lies in its author's belief that it is truly the genuine article.

October 1980

At the University of Langley, where I teach a doctoral sem-
inar in spy-novel writing, I must constantly remind my students
of priorities. To their surprise, plot stands at the bottom of my
list. Using W. T. Tyler's *The Man Who Lost the War* as my text,
I demonstrate that the first priority is weather. Cold, light snow, a
drenching freezing rain; it is always winter in spy novels. The
second is light, or the lack of it; because spy novels take place in
the dark, if it isn't evening or night, the sky must be overcast. The
third is geography. Spy novels take place in East Berlin, whose
ravaged landscape must be lovingly detailed—though I let my
advanced students try their hands at describing the KGB in Moscow and MI6 in London. The preferred time for a spy novel is
1961, the year the melancholy wall went up.

Long before I allow them to frame a plot, my students must
construct an atmosphere. The proper atmosphere for a spy novel
is entropy, a general grinding down, "a sense of great things
dwindling to a small, mean end," as George Smiley put it several
years ago. Bitterness, pessimism, a weary romanticism: these
spices must be ladled in with a generous-size spoon. Light love is
permissible, but only if no happy marriage can result; explicit sex
is forbidden because it introduces a kind of energy at odds with
the attenuated mood my students must develop. I encourage long
flashbacks to promote nostalgia; even if, as in Tyler's novel, they
do nothing to explain character or to advance the story, they take
up a lot of space. For a spy novel to make the best-seller list, it
must be long, so the rule in my class is: twice as long is twice as

good. And from my most ambitious students I require a lot of fine
writing, too. Fine writing takes up as much space as flashbacks—
besides, it snows the reviewers.

Once they have attended to the priorities, my students find
the plot takes care of itself. As Tyler's novel shows, there's no
need for variation. A disillusioned, retired American spy encounters a disillusioned, aging Russian spy in East Berlin. Each is
more inclined to work for his own vain purposes than to serve his
masters, so some impressive, possibly real information changes
hands. The Russians are relentless; the British are worried about
a mole in their tunnels. There is a chase, some treachery, a grand
gesture. And no one, I tell my students, will notice how hollow
and fatigued all this is because hollowness and fatigue, cloaked in
fine writing, are the point.

March 1980

> *Fare thee well, for I must leave thee,*
> *Do not let this parting grieve thee,*

And I'm sure it won't. Len Deighton and Eric Ambler number
their readers in the hundreds of thousands and will never notice a
disappointed lover tiptoeing tearfully away. I have been faithful
to both of them in my fashion, but a suspense story, like a love
affair, requires a modicum of energy. If a writer in the genre
shows signs of contentedly repeating his old familiar motions, as
Deighton does, then it's time to throw him over; if, like Ambler,
he seems to take himself seriously, seems to want to regularize the
relationship, then it's time to jilt him, too.

First, Ambler. When his most recent novel, *The Levanter*,
appeared, I grumbled that nothing *happened* until page 80, a poor
showing for a suspense story. It seems I missed Ambler's drift: in
Doctor Frigo nothing happens until page 240. Ambler is going
straight now (his publisher suggests that we start taking him
seriously as a political novelist), and we all know that straight
fiction doesn't require the lashings of fear and muscle that made
Ambler's early stories famous. Talk and politics will do instead,
with lashings of local color.

Dr. Frigo (his nickname is French slang for refrigerator),
son of a martyred politician from a Caribbean coffee republic,

plies his medicine in exile on a French West Indian island. Frigo doesn't know who killed his father and doesn't much care; like his nickname, he is singularly cool—but he is also naïve, which is why he gets into trouble when the local intelligence officer bullies him into spying on his father's political heir, who has arrived on the island to prepare a coup in the coffee republic. The coup is what happens on page 240; in the preceding pages we get a lot of talk in the *préfecture* and doctor's office, a lot of debate in cars, restaurants, and private homes. Ambler is generous with authentic-sounding medical detail and precise observations of Caribbean islands, and it seems to me that if you can stand the boredom you may find much in this story that is skillfully performed.

The boredom will not inhibit *Doctor Frigo*'s reception—most hugely popular novels are hugely boring—but it is fatal to the book's posture as serious political fiction. Political novels are difficult to write because political events, so fascinating in real life, are distracting in fiction except as catalysts of theme or character. (This is why some of the best have the narrowest focus: C. P. Snow's *The Masters*, set in a college, is a better political novel than is his *Corridors of Power*, which concerns the national government.) Political novels, until further notice, are stories about men who are unequal to occasions. Their true subjects are the effect of ambition on integrity and of power on process, of men subjected to stress that will make them squeal, of men confronted rudely by their own weakness and failure of vision. Ambler is not up to a real political novel; having written for nearly forty years suspenseful romances about men who prove less frail than first they seem, he lacks a vision of man's essential frailty.

As for Len Deighton, he has returned from writing straight fiction to his reluctant spy, and the result is middling-okay, not as crisp and stylish as *The Ipcress File* or as fat and grotesque as *The Billion-Dollar Brain*. Deighton's specialty has always been a nearly incoherent plot—you could barely grasp it as you read it and forgot it immediately afterward—told with such smooth assurance that the reader felt quite comfortable.

In *Spy Story* our nameless hero has retired from British intelligence and acquired a new identity; he works for an organization called the "Studies Center," which plots elaborate war games to be used for training NATO's high command. One night he discovers by accident that somebody is impersonating his old spy self . . . and then (of course) he is bulldozed back into hair-raising undercover activities involving a Russian defector and a nuclear submarine in peril under Arctic ice. It is all pleasingly muddled, and there is a lot of knowledgeable technical data scattered about. In fact, Deighton seems to have set for himself three different areas—war games, polar subs, impersonation—which would each sustain a more interesting spy novel than the one he wrote.

I have a great fondness for Deighton's early work. In it there was a kind of tautness: part wit, part comic lunacy, part cynical disenchantment, part parody that was exactly appropriate to the early sixties. That tautness is gone now, and so is the energy and relevance. Ambler should go back to what he was doing before; Deighton should stop writing spy stories.

October 1974

If it's true that we are what we eat, it's lucky that we aren't what we read, for if we were, readers of Michael Crichton's *Congo* would be taken out with the trash in the morning. Having identified the specimen before us, I want to put in a good word for trash. Scientists know that the genus trash comprises four distinct species, three malignant and one benign: boring trash, meretricious trash, fallacious trash, and entertaining trash. Most trashy novels are one or the other, but Michael Crichton's distinction is that his latest romance combines the latter two.

First, the entertainment. Properly educated readers, whom I define as readers brought up on H. Rider Haggard's romances, will sense from the start that they are in safe hands. "It was all going routinely," Crichton writes, "until one day around noon when the porters flatly refused to proceed further." The scene: a remote corner of the country we now call Zaïre. The native cannibals are in revolt. The pygmies aren't friendly. Volcanoes threaten. The characters: some armed thugs from a nefarious Euro-Japanese consortium; a white hunter, no stranger to gunrunning and atrocity, who behaves like a perfect gentleman; a lovely young woman from a computer-based corporation that sells its customers a competitive advantage; a young male ethologist interested in communicating with our primate cousins; Amy, an adolescent gorilla who talks to her keeper by means of American Sign Language. The target: the lost city of Zinj, a.k.a. King Solomon's mines, home of blue diamonds essential to the computers that will wage the next world war. The problem: Zinj has remained a lost city not because explorers haven't found it, but because those who have are destroyed by what appears to be a new species of homicidal gorilla.

Who can resist such an unabashedly silly story? Not I. That Amy the gorilla is the book's only fully developed character matters not at all. That to Haggard's Africa Crichton brings the wonders of modern technology—computers, laser beams, holographic night goggles, and the rest—only adds to the fun. What does matter is that Crichton, in his enthusiasm for his "talking" ape, ignores recent studies that have concluded that apes cannot do what Amy does. Apes do not seem to be able to organize language or generate syntactical sentences of their own. Does it matter? Is not *Congo* pure fantasy? I think it does matter. Crichton's novel, made plausible by its footnotes and bibliography, will be read by thousands who will come away from it thinking that apes can "talk"; in years to come they will remember that they read that somewhere, they forget just where. Crichton has pushed science, myth, and history past the point of fact before, usually seductively. Recently he wrenched the Beowulf story four centuries away from its context to incorporate it into his fictional version of a historical Arab document, thereby diminishing both. But, as mehitabel would say, wotthehell. That's only pseudo-literature and this is pseudo-science, and to us literary folk the sin of disregarding contradictory scientific evidence seems the more offensive crime.

December 1980

5. Love of Honor

AMONG WRITERS of elegant suspense stories perhaps none has been as erratic in the quality of his performances as Geoffrey

Household. A reader might, with some confidence, slap grades on
his books—an A for this, but no more than a C— for that—though
the disparities are difficult to detect in early chapters. In one specialized subspecies of thriller, however, Household remains pre-
eminent: the manhunt novel. No one has written a better chase
story than *Rogue Male*, though many have imitated it, including
Household himself in *Watcher in the Shadows*—certainly the
next best of its kind—and in other stories.

Manhunt novels are exceedingly difficult to write well. In
addition to the usual suspense paraphernalia of plot, pace, and
minimal stabs at characterization, a good chase story provides a
contrast between the terror of what is happening and the cozy fa-
miliarity of the landscape within which it happens. Whether the
setting is urban or rural makes no difference, but it must be precisely realized through lovingly informed detail—and I think that
only a writer who is more than ordinarily fond of, and knowledgeable about, his city or his part of the countryside can bring it
off. Here's an example of the way Household, in his new novel,
Red Anger, uses this effect to heighten suspense. The narrator, a
hunted man, is walking over the English countryside by night:

"Eventually I found the right opening and started downhill.
There was not a sound and I could not hear my own footsteps on
the short turf until I was walking through a mush of last year's
brown stems which had fallen across the path. The swishing disturbed some creature so close that I could just make out the waving tops of the fern as it pushed through the stems. I stood still,
instinctively alarmed, for the hillside was as lonely as any in
England and the forest of waist-high bracken, an intangible surface stretching away like the top of a cloud, could hide anything. . . . The only common animal I could think of, too bulky to
slip between the stems but able to wriggle away at ground level,
was man."

The narrator, a young Englishman who grew up in Roma-
nia, finds on his return to England that he must leap from one jam
into another. Threatened with blackmail by his unscrupulous
employer, Adrian Gurney decides to fake his own suicide and to
reemerge as a Romanian refugee who has just jumped from a Soviet ship into the English Channel. He convinces British intelligence of his authenticity. A mysterious Romanian, however,

persuades Adrian to take a message to a lady living in the country to the effect that one of her relatives, thought to be a British defector to the Soviets, is safe in Moscow. In fact, the "defector," Alwyn Rory, is hiding out in the countryside hoping to prove his innocence of charges of treason. Like Adrian, Alwyn has no official existence—if either was to disappear no one would know—which makes their position the more perilous when they are chased by rival agents from the CIA and the KGB.

The plot grows so complicated that it is difficult to follow—why do these people do such improbable things?—let alone summarize. Household's new device—a double quarry pursued by two teams of villains—works pretty well (give the book a B+), though this kind of story is more effective when it offers a classic simplicity of plot and motive. I wish Household had kept us guessing about the good faith of Alwyn and his family; were he an ironist like Len Deighton he might have twisted his tale at the end to show that Alwyn was indeed a villain, Adrian a dupe, and the foreign agents stout good fellows.

But Household has never been an ironist; he is instead a romantic, a deeply conservative writer for whom it is an article of faith that an honorable man in danger in his own land will prevail. "The fields have their own honor," Adrian observes, and woodland, pastures, harvests are "the result of unremitting work, unremitting love." It is this love of honor, land, and the simple life that Household celebrates in all his violent stories.

September 1975

6. How to Write the #1 Best-Selling Novel

THE TORPID SEASON is about to engulf us all again. Sand, salt, and sunlight conspire to unmoor a person's reason; his wits float adrift on a tide of humidity and gin. Chances are, you will be tempted to resume work on your best-selling novel. Chances are, this summer, as last summer, you will fail to finish the thing, or finishing it, fail to persuade a publisher to unlock his chest of gold. Why? Because you failed to think through your undertaking in an orderly manner. Indeed, so profound is the combination of awe, innocence, and contempt with which the novice novelist surveys the fiction-writing industry that he rarely remembers to think at all.

This is an oversight, if only because the writers who are actually going to produce the best sellers are out there furiously thinking. One is Martin Cruz Smith, whose superior thriller *Gorky Park* has not only sold 140,000 copies in the past few weeks, but drawn praise from readers who scorn best sellers. Smith's own story has a nice reverse twist to it. Many authors spend a decade churning out profitable hack work to support their efforts writing an uncommercial, literary novel. Smith spent the past decade churning out unprofitable hack work to support his efforts writing a novel that would earn him $2 million before publication. A story like that makes you proud to be an American capitalist, particularly when you bear in mind that the hero of Smith's novel is a Russian Communist policeman.

I'll return to Smith's story presently because it illustrates all you need to know about how to write a best seller except how to acquire the talent, which no one can explain but which all aspiring best-sellerists know they already possess. Instinctively, they sense that one need not delve deeply into the art of fiction to construct best-selling dialogue (not to mention best-selling names of characters) of the kind that James Clavell offers in *Noble House:* " 'And fornicate those foreign devils from the Golden Mountain if they don't arrive tonight,' Goodweather Poon said. 'They'll arrive,' Four Finger Wu told him confidently. 'Foreign devils are glued to schedules. Even so, I sent Seventh Son to the airport to make sure.' "

Instinctively, they comprehend that E. M. Forster's musings over plot have little to do with Harold Robbins's near-monosyllabic approach to best-selling narrative in *Goodbye, Janette:* "The cat slashed across her. She bit her lips against the pain. . . . He gripped her by the hair, forcing her to look down at him. 'Look at your master, slave bitch!' "

But instinct is insufficient. With best sellers like these afloat on the lists, the apprentice novelist would do well to ask first not how such stuff is written, but why anyone would want to read it. Why do the novels most widely read tend to be innocent of just those qualities that make a novel worth reading? A novel by James Clavell or James Michener is forbiddingly long and written in what S. J. Perelman has identified as "peristaltic prose"; it makes not the slightest attempt to entertain its readers with any grace or originality of language or construction, any play of ideas or character, any leavening of wit. The traditional best seller is as humorless as its reader, and that (need I say?) is not its weakness, but its strength. Everyone admits that best-selling novels appeal to readers who don't give a damn for modern fiction, but what (for reasons of taste) is never said is that these gigantic dull books make their readers feel *secure*. No one need fear that he will be threatened by a novel's complexity or originality, its ambiguity or wit, when he knows in advance there's none there.

Of these qualities, the most detested by readers and producers of best sellers is originality. Sometimes the Repetition Factor is blatant. The text on the cover of an advance copy of Clive Cussler's *Night Probe!* reads, "The hero of *Raise the Titanic!* Returns"; should anyone miss the point, the picture shows a locomotive sunk beneath the Hudson. Sometimes the RF is more subtle. When Peter Benchley proposed to his editor a novel about an oversize homicidal chondrichthian, he intended a variation on previous disaster novels dealing with floods and earthquakes; when he came to write it, he borrowed elements from *Moby Dick* and *An Enemy of the People*.

The trick that the most successful writers rely upon is the wedding of a profoundly hackneyed formula to what at least appears to be a great load of information about an intriguing subject. We Americans are a nation of autodidacts, reluctant to take our fiction straight without a chaser of education: some credible dirt about Jackie Onassis will do if James Michener hasn't got another saga ready to tell us more than we need to know about Nicaragua from the Jurassic through the Somozan eras. "Americans are in love with different technologies," says Martin Cruz Smith. "If you can combine Zen and the art of motorcycle maintenance, you will do well. If you show how anything is done well—how upholstery is done well, the *inside* of the upholstery industry—

people will read it. Because Americans have a great respect for
professional skills. Europeans have a greater respect for philosophy. If you ever marry the two, you'll have a book that would do
well in the U.S. and Europe."

The success of *Gorky Park* results in large measure from the
amount of authentic information it conveys—information that is
not tacked on as decoration, or erected like so many freestanding
megaliths on the plain of the novel's plot, but information infused
into the atmosphere of the novel. The information is specifically
Russian and it motivates Smith's characters to think and act as
they do. This effect is all the more interesting because the characters and the story that contains them will not be unfamiliar to
readers of English or American thrillers. The book's hero, for instance—Arkady Renko, chief homicide investigator for the Moscow prosecutor's office—is a Slavic cousin of John le Carré's
George Smiley: decent, seedy, hugely competent, an individualist
at odds with his conspiring superiors and an unfaithful wife. Like
Smiley, Arkady is a doomed man, which, in this kind of fiction, is
not to say that he will necessarily die.

Early on a winter morning, three frozen bodies, mutilated
beyond recognition, are discovered beneath the snow of Gorky
Park. Arkady's usual customers are the victims of quarrels or
drunken rages, but these three—the corpses of two men and a
woman—are exceptional. The method of their murder and disfig-
urement suggests a conspiracy. The KGB, which interests itself
only in crimes involving national security, appears on the scene in
the person of Arkady's old enemy, Major Pribluda, who immediately retreats—which is odd, because one of the victims proves to
be an American who entered the country illegally. Arkady, an obsessive investigator who has never yet been wrong, dreads this
investigation, correctly sensing that any success he encounters
will endanger his career, perhaps even his life. Betrayed by everyone, Arkady the hunter becomes himself the hunted, and is offered his life in exchange for a little betraying of his own. Of
course, he can't do it. As the story makes abundantly clear, Soviet
social theory condones such betrayal, but Arkady proves to be a
Westerner after all.

The mortality rate in *Gorky Park* is as extreme as anything
this side of Dashiell Hammett's *Red Harvest*, but then there are

so many characters suitable for doing in. Curiously, because the book generates a great deal of suspense, there's never much doubt who the victims and the villains are. In the story's most inspired sequence, Arkady brings the severed head of one of the corpses to a paleontologist whose job it is to reconstruct lifelike heads from skulls; the idea is to identify the victim, but before the paleontologist can complete his patient work Arkady knows by other means who the victim is. Smith can afford to reduce the importance of this episode, because, as he revised his story, he translated it from the modest mystery he had originally intended into a full-dress novel. What holds our attention in the final version is not the whodunit aspect of his story, but the deepening entanglement of the characters, the witty insights into Soviet thinking, and the set pieces that put Arkady in a KGB bathhouse, under house arrest in the country, and finally in a New York City that exists nowhere except in the eyes of a Russian.

The author of this novel that so meticulously informs us who uses which of Moscow's train stations, who runs cannabis into the capital, and how the black market in used cars works, speaks no Russian and has visited Moscow for only five days as a tourist in 1973. At thirty-eight, he is a slender, intense man who talks as easily as he writes and finds his real name, Martin William Smith, too dull to use on his books. His mother, part Hopi and part Yaqui Indian, was a jazz singer and his father a jazz saxophonist; lacking any musical talent of his own, the young Smith proceeded on the assumption he could write. "It's very much like breathing," he says, but he quit his first writing job as a local sports editor to make three times the money as a Good Humor salesman in Philadelphia. Later he wrote for the Associated Press, rewording news releases announcing state consideration of bids for constructing a highway exit; later still, at a magazine called *For Men Only,* he edited stories about daring rescues of Belgian nuns from the Congo.

To all such labors he found himself remarkably unsuited. "I did a little writing for science-fiction magazines," he says, distinguishing carefully between "creating things out of whole cloth" and "creating things out of no cloth. With whole cloth there is some relation to reality. When somebody says, I will give you $300 to do a story on the Mysterious 13 who rule the world, can you go to your bedroom [Smith wrote *Gorky Park* in his bedroom] and in the course of the evening write about the Mysterious 13 who rule the world? Well, I *have* that ability. I could, without too much difficulty, imagine the intricate and long history of the Mysterious 13 who rule the world. I was not in the least daunted. I knew exactly who they were and who their agents were. It was a story not designed to gull anyone; it was a story for those born gulled."

In 1970, Smith wrote a novel, *The Indians Won.* "What a waste of research. I see now all the scenes that could be done. I had simply run out of time to write it because I had run out of that commodity with which you pay for the milk and the bread." Other novels followed. He doesn't remember how many, or how many pseudonyms he used ("I didn't want to be associated with those books"), but there were more than thirty, written within seven years. "I knocked out one Nick Carter story in eight days. It was simply a matter of sitting down and taking a deep breath every other page. I had an awful lot of energy."

With the sale of a novel called *Nightwing* to the movies in 1977, he had enough money to concentrate on a story suggested to him by an article in *Newsweek* about a book called *The Face Finder.* The author, M. M. Gerasimov, was a Soviet paleontologist who specialized in restoring lifelike heads from human skulls. "It's the kind of forensic detail that a writer seizes upon," Smith says. "My book began as an easy-to-control detective story with an American cop and a Soviet cop working hand in hand to solve this crime."

Smith sold the idea to Putnam's and went to Russia armed only with a Moscow gazetteer published by Russian emigrés who thought it more important to list addresses for local MVD offices than to discuss the Bolshoi Ballet. He walked about the city, getting lost, taking notes and sketching buildings. A camera, he thought, would have alarmed the natives, but "drawing was like alchemy: something that once was done but probably never worked." He never saw the countryside he describes so well, or the KGB bathhouse where Arkady encounters the villain. "I have no idea whether such a place exists. I *feel* it does. That was enough for me."

On his return, Smith grew dissatisfied with his original con-

ception of the book. "Americans will set a book in Borneo, Baby-
lon, or Byelorussia and use an American detective. It's a dishonest
approach to the world and it teaches us nothing. There came a
point in writing *Gorky Park* where I said to hell with the kind of
writer I was and to hell with the kind of book this is supposed to
be. I saw I was getting close to a good story, a real book, and
something that would bring out the best in me, if I allowed it to.
Gorky Park was a very bright light on all the work I had ever
done." He decided to use a Russian hero, "though for years, still
thinking like an American, I insisted that Arkady could not
possibly be a Party member." Smith read Soviet law. He read
Tolstoy, Solzhenitsyn, Sinyavsky, Voinovich, Zinoviev, and
Goncharov. "And then I went to the Russians. I spent years with
Russians here in New York. I had them read the manuscript.
They'd say, 'It's perfect.' I'd say, 'Perfect?' They'd say, 'Well, it's
really very good.' I'd say, 'Well, if you had to pick one thing,
what would it be?' I pushed and prodded."

His Russian friends persuaded him that Arkady could not be
a chief investigator unless he was a card-carrying Communist.
They could not persuade him that Arkady's father, a Ukrainian
general, would never have cut the ears from his victims. "They'd
say, 'You just can't do that. You don't understand. A German
might do that. An American might do that. A Frenchman very
likely would. Certainly the Japanese and Chinese do it all the
time. But a *Russian* would *never* do such a thing!' What irritated
them was not that it was brutal, but that it was so *uncultured*. So
what I did, I not only kept the ears in, I made a point of using
their objections as well: I made him 'the Butcher of the
Ukraine.' "

Meanwhile, Putnam's was unhappy about his ambitions.
They wanted the story Smith had contracted for, with an American hero up front. For years, Smith tried to buy the book back
from them, worrying the while that his one true book would
never see print. Finally, Putnam's yielded; Smith borrowed $11,-
000 from his family to recover his property. His agent, Knox
Burger, offered the finished book to Norton, which had published
Nightwing, for $200,000. Norton declined. "Every time I looked
at the novel I decided to double the price," Smith says. "When I
wrote the last line, I *knew*; I have never been so excited in my life,

except for the birth of children, as when I wrote the last line of *Gorky*. Because I knew it was just right. I had this marvelous book and I was *damned* if I was going to sell it for anything less than a marvelous price. The words *one million* seemed to come to mind. Mellifluous!"

Marc Jaffe at Random House bought *Gorky Park* for $1 million, an astonishing price for a book by an unknown author. Knox Burger gave Random four days to make up its mind and then, on appeal, ten days more. Why such pressure for a book that took eight years to write? "I think that's how you make a million dollars," Smith says equably. Besides, Jaffe had just come to Random House and there was some thought that he needed to make a big splash there, just to show the size of the new shark who had taken over the pool. Jaffe says that when he first read the manuscript, he felt "like being hit on the head with a mallet—something that doesn't happen often in an editor's life." Every other editor at Random who read it was, it is now said, impressed. No one doubted it would be a great best seller. "It had to be," says Joe Fox, Smith's editor. "We paid a million dollars for it." Advance copies were printed for what is known as the "Big Mouth List": people whose talk supposedly sets the current flowing. Foreign sales to fourteen countries brought in $530,000; film rights were sold to Koch-Kirkwood for $750,000 more—after some difficulty, for producers worried over the novel's complex plot and the problems involved in shooting against a Moscow locale.

As the money rolls in, Martin Cruz Smith seems proud, but unsurprised. Now he will have to find another apartment; not because he's rich but because his wife, Emily, is seven months pregnant. And then there's the next book. "It's going to be one hell of a wonderful book," Smith says. "I believe that."

May 1981

7. George V. Higgins: Early and Late Cases

GEORGE HIGGINS, I submit, is the most hard-boiled of American crime novelists. Hammett, Chandler, and Macdonald stuff their fiction with commendable quantities of death and realism, but their private operators—cynical vigilantes who wearily consider our corrupt species as it sinks into affectlessness and avarice—are essentially romantic, more than a little sentimental. Higgins, by contrast, writes comedies about the peculiar claustrophobia of the life of organized crime in Boston. He foregoes sentimentality, private eyes, and innocent victims to write exclusively of criminals who work on one another in a community where sin is less talked of than are mistakes: presumptuousness, a change of allegiance, a falling off from competence. When his hoods philosophize, as they are ever ready to do, they impress us with the brevity of inarticulateness: "Everything goes to hell if you wait long enough," for example, and "You don't get away with nothing once, it happens again."

Jackie Cogan, of *Cogan's Trade*, rents muscle and guns (preferably not his own) to those who can't very well call upon the police when they need a little private law enforcement. He is a very efficient man. When an independent entrepreneur hires a pair of thugs to knock over a high-stakes card game protected by the Syndicate, Cogan is employed to administer appropriate discipline. First to be dealt with is the man who runs the game, a man who once had the temerity to have his own game raided; though he is clearly innocent this time, his reputation is finished—and therefore so is he. Next come those who actually did the job. Cogan is so adroit that he can persuade a hood who has never seen him before not only to betray his master but to assist in his murder.

It is all very neat. Higgins's novels bear several unmistakable

identifying marks. Attending to his plots as a pot-smoking teenager in a day-care center might attend to her charges, he devotes
his energies to the true matter of his fiction: talk. Higgins is a
master of speech patterns, conveying not only the reality of conversation but an auditory illusion of reality in his monologues. In
these (and there are many, for he prefers not to show us something happening if he can make someone tell us what happened),
his characters do not talk at all as people really do, but so great is
Higgins's art that he induces our belief; we must strain to figure
out what is going on. A grand master of tactical digression, he
allows his narrative, containing the criminal design, to wind
twistingly around a series of set pieces in which the action is sus-
pended, often for chapters at a time, while the gangsters talk
about sex and marriage, who goes out for coffee, their weight and
root-canal work. To these people the banal frustrations of life are
more important than the taking of it. This is a fine comic device,
and Higgins's stylized stories are the most entertaining of their
kind.

March 1974

On page 46 of George Higgins's *The Rat on Fire* something
extraordinary happens. Two of the principal characters actually
step out of a van and approach the front of a building. Exhausted
by this unprecedented burst of physical activity, which takes one
sentence to describe, they stand around for an entire chapter de-
bating whether to *enter* the building. We never see them do it,
but no matter: locomotion is not Higgins's forte. Before his story
is half done we will see our two friends from page 46 trudging
through the woods, and a man walk from his car to a saloon,
but that concludes the bulletins from the aerobic-exercise
front.

The point is worth making because the remarkably seden-
tary quality of Higgins's fiction contributes not only to the claus-
trophobic atmosphere he develops among the Boston lowlife
whose pathetic attempts at crime he chronicles, but to the endless
talk that is the real matter of his stories. Higgins (as I've said before, but the idea has not proved contagious) does not write crime
stories in the way that John D. MacDonald and Ed McBain write
crime stories; he writes comedies of manners about criminals—

and between these two genres there is a world of difference. In a Higgins story the proposed crime tends to be no more than the bond that holds the talk together; while the plot hardens out of sight, the characters sit around in offices and bars discussing more essential matters: women, work, man's general rush to entropy.

Here, the proposed crime is arson. Jerry Fein, a sleazy lawyer with a fourth-rate theatrical clientele, seeks to disencumber himself of some deteriorating apartment buildings. The only way to do this and turn a profit on his investment is to burn them down and pick up the insurance. That the buildings are occupied by poor black families doesn't concern Jerry or the professional arsonist he hires for the occasion—they equate the blacks who won't pay their rent with the rats who swarm through the buildings' walls—but it does bother the fire marshal, who is paid off to deflect investigations. What to do? The matter clearly requires a lot of talk, most of which is overheard by two undercover cops who have been on the case since its inception. The question of whether Jerry and his thugs will succeed never arises; the question is only whether, with so much incompetence afoot, the crime will take place at all.

A reader uninitiated in Higgins's work might be well advised not to begin with *The Rat on Fire*, which lacks the convoluted plotting and deliciously nasty characters that the author gave us in *The Friends of Eddie Coyle* and *The Digger's Game;* nevertheless, those who know his work will certainly want to read this one. Because no one else writes comedies that are anything like these—very funny and very profane—I'm glad that Higgins produces one each year.

February 1981

THE BRIEFER BELLOW

IT'S A PITY Saul Bellow writes so little short fiction: *Him with His Foot in His Mouth* and another collection published sixteen years ago contain only eleven stories between them. The tech-

nique and themes that he has developed in his novels adapt very
well to the shorter form. The restricted space may be an asset too:
it curbs Bellow's natural didacticism, his tendency to lecture his
reader. Not that these stories are particularly short. Two of the
five run to sixty and seventy pages and a third, a novella, is about
as long as *Seize the Day*. The effect is nonetheless one of extreme
compression and fertility. There's nothing laid-back, scaled-
down, or coolly reductionist about anything Bellow writes—certainly not in these well-crafted, thickly textured stories. Bellow
forces us to read him slowly. Funny as his stories are, they're still
as serious as stories can get. Bellow shows us the disorderliness of
daily life in the presence of man's best ideas.

Nowhere is this contrast better displayed than in the novella,
"What Kind of Day Did You Have?" Katrina Goliger's day
begins in Chicago with a summons to meet her lover at the Buffalo airport. Pretty, awkward, a restless divorcée, Katrina has two
small children. Her lover, Victor Wulpy, is "one of the intellectual captains of the modern world," a famous critic whose judg-
ments have helped shape what the world knows about modern art
and poetry. Now in his mid-seventies, Victor nearly died the year
before, when a tumor was removed from his stomach. Trina
knows she won't have him long, but she's drawn to his power, to
the "big light" Victor gives off, even if he has no use for her except to revive his failing physical powers. Victor understands the
real problems of modern life, but he's become so withdrawn into
his egocentricity that he's incapable of behaving humanely. He
chews up people: he wants Trina to fly to Buffalo to accompany
him back to Chicago. A blizzard grounds them in Detroit; in the
ensuing pandemonium, Victor humiliates an admirer who wants
to talk about Marx.

The most visibly erudite of living American fiction writers,
Bellow provides his stories with a ghostly supporting cast: Marx,
Sartre, Dewey, Hegel, Heidegger, and others whose ideas about
reality are more rigorous than the "poor fictions" by which most
of us live. Bellow's protagonists know that modern American life
bears little relation to ideas that were invented in eighteenth-
century France and nineteenth-century Germany. Haunted by
what might be, the intellectual can barely cope with actuality, yet
his dream sustains him. Victor Wulpy, a monster, is reduced to

bluster, but Ijah Brodsky, the hero of "Cousins," acts to ameliorate the desperation of his relatives. Ijah agrees with Hegel that " 'the very bonds of the world' are dissolving and collapsing like a vision in a dream"—which is why he must aid a mobster cousin who mocks him even as he asks for help.

Another of Bellow's intellectuals, Herschel Shawmut, narrates the title story in the form of a letter of apology to a woman he insulted thirty-five years before. She had said, "Oh, Dr. Shawmut, in that cap you look like an archaeologist," and he had, without thinking, replied, "And you look like something I just dug up." A professor of music history, the world's expert on Pergolesi, Shawmut can't resist this destructive banter: he does it for "art's sake, i.e., without perversity or malice. . . . I can't tell you why."

The difficulty of acting decently, the obligation to maintain the bonds that tie people together, the temptation to reinvent oneself—these are Bellow's themes here and in other books. In "A Silver Dish," a sixty-year-old man, "fleshy and big, like a figure for the victory of American materialism," recalls the horror of his forced complicity in a scam his larcenous father devised. But because Bellow's stories always work in counterpoint, we know, before we learn what the story's about, that this man had nursed his father through his death.

The remaining story, "Zetland: By a Character Witness," is less successful, if only because it lacks the structure of the others. It works well until it simply stops—as if it had once been intended as the beginning of a novel. That's a small flaw in an otherwise excellent collection. In these stories, written over the past ten years, Bellow is writing as well as he ever has. For the most part, he's writing about older people; the presence of death, actual or anticipated, is important, and yet his humor has never been sharper, or the dexterity of his imagery, or the playfulness with which he introduces ideas. The short format suits him well: trot an idea of Marx or Hegel onstage, fool with it for a sentence or two, and then—because this is, after all, a short story—move on.

May 1984

BILLY BURROUGHS
BOTTOMS OUT

PERHAPS THE BEST that can be said of *Cities of the Red Night* is
that the shards of a good novel glimmer fitfully within its fevered
pages. Of several novels, in fact: I counted three, plus fragments
of two or three others. Reading a novel by William S. Burroughs
is like poking around on an archaeological dig. By dusting the silt
from an odd-shaped particle, an effective chapter is revealed. Patient work with a thin-bladed knife exposes an elegant sentence
or, more rarely, a joke. But what are we to make of all these
twisted shreds, these incongruous artifacts? What are they doing
in this area at all?

Of Burroughs's talent there has never been any question.
The question is why, since the remarkable *Naked Lunch*, which
seemed to glow, like a nuclear reactor, with an alarming inner
fire, his books seem to dissipate in our hands as we read them. I'll
suggest an answer in a moment, but first a word from our plots.
Everyone will please keep his face straight for the next couple of
paragraphs.

Plot No. 1 satirizes the private-eye novel. A young man's
disappearance leads our investigator to Greece, where he finds a
headless corpse ravaged by some vile disease. Apparently some
modern-day Druids, devotees of a sex-and-death cult, hanged and
decapitated the fellow. The head turns up in New York, to be
used in a South American drug-smuggling scheme. Plot No. 2 is a
sort of boys' historical romance involving pirates, drugs, and a
crew of hearty homosexual lads who, in 1702, plan to liberate
Mexico and South America from the Spanish despotism and es-
tablish enclaves in which a kind of free-form preindustrial communism can be practiced. What force can resist these boy

commandos, particularly when one of them invents the grenade and the exploding cannon shell? Plot No. 3 is trashy science fiction of the most incoherent sort. Here we have six ancient cities in the Gobi Desert, time warps, Venusians, and a pandemic virus that causes fever, rashes, appalling odors, and sexual frenzy. Is it the virus of love, someone asks, or is it the elemental human virus?

By way of organizing his novel, Burroughs allows his characters to make guest appearances in one another's stories and suffuses all three with scenes of reflexive homosexuality and ritual death. Bare-bottomed boys bounce through his pages, mindlessly engaged in buggery and onanistic games. "We often work naked in the Governor's bedroom, seeing the maps with our whole bodies, performing ritual copulations in front of the maps, animating the maps with our sperm." Ritual death takes the form of hanging or strangulation, the idea being for the victim to reach orgasm at the precise instant his neck snaps and his eyes flash fire. Should this kind of thing pale—and these scenes are repeated so often as to become a kind of incantation—Burroughs offers by way of variety scenes of sexual torture that he describes with lip-smacking culinary images: "The tortured captives will be rendered down into the most exquisite condiments and sweetmeats: raw quivering brains served with a piquant sauce, candied testicles, sweet-and-sour penis, rectums boiled in chocolate."

Well, yes, but what are we to make of this stuff? Burroughs means to be perverse, of course, but he seems, in these redundant scenes of sodomy and execution, merely to be going through the motions. Is there somewhere in this tangled narrative a hint that the author may be tipping us off to his joke by means of a wink or a smile? No, he means us to take what he says seriously. But true perversity, of the sort that *Lolita* and *Story of O* afforded, must make the reader shudder in recognition. It requires of its author such an obsessive concentration that all elements of his story are transformed by the corruption at its core: the world must be made new again, just as it is in every good novel.

In *Naked Lunch*, Burroughs gave us just such a vision; not here. The inspiration behind his new novel seems retarded: the masturbatory fantasies of a twelve-year-old boy who dreams, as boys will, of plague and violent death, of hiding out with his

chums in a secret jungle fort and beating up on the adults around
them. For a book that seemed to promise some kind of allegory, or
at least an apocalyptic vision of the world's end, it is a poor dream
to come down to—nothing, certainly, to trouble an adult reader.
Except, perhaps, for the trouble it takes to read it.

March 1981

GORE VIDAL REVISES HISTORY

ONCE UPON A TIME, in some child's guide to American history, I
came across a portrait of the aged Aaron Burr, nodding (as I remember) over his knitting. I thought him a miserable man (anyone that old *had* to be miserable), and the caption to the picture
said that he died old and alone (served him right, the murderer
and traitor). Now comes Gore Vidal, who is to American letters
what, in Burr's time, Thomas Rowlandson was to English painting: a cartoonist, an excellent draftsman, a satirist fond of the
bawdy and perverse. Vidal understands that the best way to revise history without accepting responsibility for one's conclusions is to write a novel. The novelist, certain that few readers
object to seeing the mighty look incompetent, may simply attribute every motive and action of the great to ambition, stupidity,
and malice. These days, cynicism, sharpened by style and research, seems a reasonable approach to political reality.

Present time in *Burr* covers the last four years of its epony-
mous hero's life: 1833–36. The narrator is Charlie Schuyler, an
inefficient law clerk with literary ambitions who works for Burr
in New York. A newspaper editor urges Charlie to write a pamphlet "proving" that Martin Van Buren, soon to run for president, is Burr's illegitimate son. Charlie agrees, and Burr, proving
strangely cooperative, dictates his memoirs to him. The two of

them split the narration, and both are witty. Burr, says Charlie, "is a man of perfect charm and fascination. A monster, in short." Burr prefers the company of women to that of men—"Women have souls, Charlie! They really do"—and in his last years he dances around New York, a short man detested and respected by the multitudes, treating his acquaintances and memories with irony and good humor, an adventurer even now, rather happy about his life in spite of the conspiracies that beat him down, the debts and legal difficulties that beset him still.

The unraveling of Burr's character, his mysterious past and motives, his reasons for killing Hamilton and leading an expeditionary force to conquer Mexico, form the armature of the novel. But its substance is the revision of history. We learn, through Burr's narrative, that Burr was a hero of the Revolution; had Washington listened to him, he would not have lost New York. Washington himself emerges as dull and fat, a worthy but vain man, and "an excellent politician who had no gift for warfare. History, as usual, has got it all backward."

Hamilton and Jefferson emerge from Burr's recollections in even worse shape. "Between the dishonest canting of Jefferson and the poisonous egotism of Hamilton," Burr says, "this state has been no good from the beginning." Jefferson was "a passionate hypocrite" and a writer of bad prose, a ruthless imperialist who betrayed his principles in favor of acquiring land for the Republic and assuring that white farmers might live off the labor of black slaves. Hamilton looked forward to an America dominated by banks, manufacture, taxes, and an army—the institutions that have led us to Bebe Rebozo and the secret bombing of Cambodia.

Burr is an extraordinarily intelligent and entertaining novel, even if Vidal is not above reaching for easy effects. He has done his homework. He has re-created the smells and noises of the time. Vidal's principal triumph, however, is that he has made of Burr more than a political cartoon: he is a man whose wit, bravery, and sanity sustain the collapse of his ambition, and whose exercise in self-justification is plausible. Failing the presidency, he appears more forthright than those who attain it. We have only Burr's word, of course, but this novel is good enough to cause its readers to cock an eyebrow at the history they remember.

November 1973

Does anyone out there believe that the surest way to make a second pot of good coffee is to pass more hot water through the acidifying grounds of the first? Gore Vidal does; this is the second time he's tried to make it work. After the vigorous comic invention of *Myra Breckinridge* came its tedious sequel *Myron*. After the prancing energy of *Burr*, with its deliciously perverse interpretation of our Founding Fathers, comes the flaccid cleverness of *1876*.

The extended novel is fashionable now: Updike, Cheever, Durrell, Powell, and others have managed them, but Vidal's efforts have faltered. His sequels, even one as well intentioned as *1876* (which Vidal now declares to be the middle part of a trilogy that concludes with one of his earlier novels, *Washington, D.C.*), seem gratuitous, principally because they depend upon, but do not extend, the tricks and perspectives of their originals. Something is lost in the dilution. The outrageousness of *Burr*, which empurpled the faces of professional historians, is here reduced to plausibility. With the flavor gone, only an acid taste remains.

Charlie Schuyler, Aaron Burr's illegitimate son, has returned with his daughter, Emma, the widowed Princess d'Agrigente, to New York after thirty-eight years in Europe. Schuyler is sixty-two and thinks of himself now as a European; Emma has never seen America. Their foreignness allows Vidal to talk at length about the curiosities of the city: the telegraph poles, the goats in the street, the Sixth Avenue el, the thirty-three hundred brothels, the Civil War veterans begging everywhere. Emma's nobility gains them access to the social world of Mrs. William Astor and Ward McAllister; Schuyler's modest fame as a writer gains him fees from newspapers in reporting the politics of an election year. Emma is beautiful and needs a husband; Schuyler is cynical and needs money: America's peculiar combination of innocence and corruption in its centennial year renders it vulnerable to their predations.

Vidal's re-creation of New York and Washington as they were one hundred years ago is a pleasant exercise; it's the people and plot that are boring. What's missing is the deceiving, energizing force of Aaron Burr. In *Burr* Vidal offered an engaging, unlikely defense of its subject's tortuous ambitions. In *1876* Vidal plays his history nearly straight. But interesting as the contested election of 1876 was, it is unlikely that anyone can make good fiction of it. Hayes, Blaine, and Tilden, presented as they were, pale before Washington, Jefferson, and Hamilton presented as if before a funhouse mirror. I would guess that Vidal correctly assumes that of every twenty readers of his novel nineteen will have no idea how the election came out. But from ignorance drama cannot be made, and Schuyler's interminable account of waiting for the returns, and for the returns to be reversed, and for Congress to deliberate, is supremely dull.

Dull is the operative word here. To step back from *1876*, and squint at it whole, is to see it clearly as a glossy bore. Vidal is always clever, but this novel, more than most, exposes the limitations of mere cleverness. Fifty pages into the story I thought it witty, but now I cannot find a single witty line to quote. Facile lines, yes ("The look of sincerity in those pale eyes was so perfectly convincing that I knew myself to be in the presence of a truly deceitful man"), and fatuous lines ("In an election year, all politicians dream of glory"). Nothing much to laugh at here, or anywhere else in *1876*, but frequent smirks may be in order.

Here's the difficulty. If a cynical quip taken each day before breakfast tunes up the system, extended cynicism unimproved by narrative energy quickly palls. Vidal's cynicism is democratic, which is to say that it is all-encompassing, but it is not often sharp or varied. The distance between ho ho and ho hum is narrower than it seems and is best maintained by vigor, or brevity, or both.

March 1976

PETER MATTHIESSEN:
HOT AND COLD

I'M OFTEN TOLD that the way to cure a book reviewer is to introduce a thin blade into his prostate and raise it swiftly to his epiglottis. I generally offer a second opinion. Nevertheless, most reviewers owe Peter Matthiessen reparation for the shabby, yawning condescension with which, ten years ago, they greeted his marvelous novel *At Play in the Fields of the Lord.* I hope *Far Tortuga* will be more carefully read, for it seems to me a beautiful and original work, a resonant, symbolical story of nine doomed men who dream of an earthly paradise as the world winds down around them.

Far Tortuga is the name given by West Indian turtle-fishing men to a remote islet south of Cuba that is not found on modern charts. It may have disappeared long ago, or may be no more than a legendary last sanctuary for the great green turtles that are disappearing from the Caribbean. To hunt the last turtles of the season Captain Raib Avers (you can hear the name Ahab rattling about in that) sails from Grand Cayman island with a ragged crew in an even more ragged boat, the *Eden,* whose wheel is placed, significantly, so the helmsman cannot see where he is going. "Two drunkards, one thief and five idiots," Avers rages, but then nothing is as it was in "de back time": the good crew, boat, and captains are all gone and tourists from America are taking over. The crew thinks the captain mad and responds to his fulminations with shrugs and a litany of resignation: "Modern time, mon."

The boat tacks about the cays and reefs off the coast of Nicaragua. It is too late to find more than a few turtles. As discord and desperation mount, the crew talks about better days: the folklore of hurricanes and pirate captains, of shipwrecks, ghosts, and "wild niggers" smuggled into Florida. The men are moved by the mysterious life of the turtles and by their isolation: "You way out on de edge, boy, you out on de edge of de world." Indeed they are: Avers, as a last gamble, strikes out for Far Tortuga. He comes upon it (if he does; the author is deliberately ambiguous) much as Dante's Ulysses came upon Purgatory mountain, and with a similar result.

To convey this haunting story Matthiessen has invented a structure made from the sparest descriptions of time, weather, and place—"Midafternoon. The tide still falling. A mosquito whines"—and blocks of dialogue unencumbered by attribution to specific characters; we come to learn from the dialogue itself who is speaking. The rhythms of these sailors' speech are both colloquial and formal: Matthiessen appears to reproduce the West Indian dialect exactly but often allows the words to fall into lines of about fifteen unstressed syllables—the result is not poetry, but not far from it, either. Then, as if to slow our progress through his narrative, or emphasize its reverberations, Matthiessen introduces unequal amounts of white space between paragraphs and sections of his story.

The effect is rather like that of a film strip, or of a surreal painting: a sharply realistic story that is precise, even informative about details, and yet one in which the figures we observe point symbolically and metaphorically beyond themselves. In sum, this is a moving, impressive book, a difficult yet successful undertaking. I haven't read anything of similar stature for a long time.

May 1975

In my infancy, when I could still be told a thing or two, various female relatives admonished me to the effect that if I could not say something nice about a person, I had better say nothing at all. Ever true to this precept, I must say at once that Peter Matthiessen—novelist, explorer, naturalist with a social conscience— is one of the most interesting of that able generation of American writers who are now between forty-five and fifty-five years old. Over the years he has developed a disciplined yet elegant prose that pleases the ear as well as the mind. In a better world his masterly novels *At Play in the Fields of the Lord* and *Far Tortuga* would be more widely acclaimed. These nice things said,

I must confess disappointment with *The Snow Leopard*. It is Matthiessen's most personal book, and one of his most ambitious. There is fine material in it, and much that does not work well— perhaps because Matthiessen is applying a literary sensibility to an area notoriously resistant to words.

The book is an account of two overlapping and complementary journeys taken at some risk over steep and difficult paths. One of these—the exterior journey—took Matthiessen to the Himalayas, where he hiked for 250 miles over passes covered with snow and ice to the uncharted Land of Dolpo in a remote corner of Nepal bordering on Tibet. His companion, the zoologist George Schaller, wanted a close look at the bharal, a rare animal that is "neither sheep nor goat but a creature perhaps very close to the ancestral goatlike animal of about twenty million years ago" from which both goats and sheep evolved. Matthiessen, a student of Zen Buddhism, wanted to experience freedom of the spirit—"I long to let go, drift free of things, to accumulate less, depend on less, to move more simply"—and he hoped also to catch a glimpse of that "most mysterious of the great cats," the snow leopard, about which nearly nothing is known.

In its external trappings, the story fits firmly in the tradition of narratives written by the great explorers: Burton and Stanley, Bruce and Shackleton. Matthiessen, who kept a diary, is a precise observer, and if we get perhaps too much of frigid nights and "rigid stars," of sunlight on birds' wings and prayer flags snapping in the wind, the hardships and dangers were real enough and are well described. On only the more important journey—the interior journey—does Matthiessen stumble. Since his wife's death from cancer the year before, he had sought, through the Zen discipline, what he calls "the greatest blessing of my life": the experience of being at one with the universe, the security that comes from "the happy realization that *nothing was needed*, nothing missing, all was already, always and forever known, [his wife's] dying, even that, was as it should be."

While describing his progress toward this state of being, Matthiessen tells us less about Buddhism and its Himalayan permutations than we need for understanding, yet more than his narrative can bear. Some of what he says—that Western science, for instance, is accepting the ancient Eastern truths that time is an

illusion and that all being is One—is hardly news; and much
more—the talk about dissolving the ego, the hope for empti-
ness—is curiously uncommunicative. The fault is not entirely
Matthiessen's. Words have traditionally failed the heart of the
Zen experience; even Zen masters are famously reluctant to
apply them. I think *The Snow Leopard* is a brave effort on
Matthiessen's part; he knew the difficulties he faced and elected to
risk the failure that did in fact result.

September 1978

THE DECLINE OF JOHN GARDNER

JOHN GARDNER'S *The Sunlight Dialogues* is not one of your
scrawny little novels, all wordplay and no plot; it's a *big* novel, as
long as *Anna Karenina* and not much harder to read. The packaging is deceptively old-fashioned: chapters with titles, a list of
eighty-two characters, even illustrations. Most of fiction's best
themes converge within these pages: magic, madness, murder, revenge, infidelity, the quest, the search for justice, freedom, and
the law—all developed through labyrinthine flashbacks and passages of drama, satire, poetry, pedantry, and tedium. Not to mention (a trap for the unwary) the scattershot symbolism, the
amputated allegory. I'll bore you with that in a moment, after this
look at the surface of his story.

In 1966, Fred Clumly, age sixty-four, was a stolid, law-and-
order police chief in Batavia, a town in western New York. Law
and order are disrupted by the arrival of a bearded, babbling,
stinking madman, a magician of sorts who paints the word *love*
across one of the town streets. The Sunlight Man, Clumly calls
him for lack of any other name and locks him up. The lunatic
stages a magical escape and then returns to free another prisoner,

who murders a policeman as they leave. The hunt is on, and so is the pressure put on Clumly, who seems to do nothing right, though in fact the best fictional detectives—Inspectors Javert, Porfiry Petrovich, and Maigret, as well as Clumly—know that you catch your man *after* you have understood him.

To understand the Sunlight Man is to learn first that he is Taggart Hodge, son of Batavia's principal family, a man driven from the town by scandal and tragedy. Now, Taggart summons Clumly to remote places where he magically disarms him and subjects him to mad ramblings about Babylonian deities and the nature of freedom and law. In time, through Taggart's words alone, we see that both he and Clumly are equally lacking in charity for men, both a bit demented. Clumly defends order and society as a whole; Taggart preaches freedom and individual anarchism. One, naturally, will die; the other will regain his humanity.

Gardner's violent story is much more complex than this: not only in subplots, digressions, flashbacks, and anecdotes (which both entertain us and impede the narrative), but in its symbolical structure. The symbols begin with the second paragraph: "a weapon—say, X calibur," Gardner writes, and there you have it, if you're awake enough to catch it: this is an allegory of King Arthur. Holy numbers, the mandala, the creation of order (all Arthurian themes), are introduced on the first page, and Clumly is the chief candidate for the king: "Opinion was divided, in fact, over whether he's gone away somewhere or died." Clumly's police station, we learn later, has "toy-castle towers." Later still we have Clumly likening himself to a king whose knights have failed, and misquoting Tennyson in a way to make the rhythm bounce: "The old order changes," he says, "giving way to the new."

Similarly, one can spot Taggart, the Sunlight Man, as Gawain, who, in Celtic legend, was a sun god, later associated with Christ (Taggart spouts Christ's lines all over these pages). And onward, through two quests, a birdbath for the grail and a city built to music that inevitably disintegrates.

The question is: to what use is such heavy symbolizing put? The answer is: nothing worth having, nothing that strengthens the story. In earlier books, Gardner has written brilliantly, melding myth and realism in brief and trenchant stories. *The Sunlight*

Dialogues is more fascinating in its parts than in its whole: the circumlocutions seem self-indulgent, laid on in an archly literary way, as if, perhaps, this were not Gardner's fourth, but his first novel.

January 1973

John Gardner is so talented that he can bring off, at least in part, anything he wants to write. It's what he wants to write that worries me. Six months ago we had *The Sunlight Dialogues*, a huge novel in which a cat-and-mouse game between a police chief and a philosophical lunatic was studded with obscure Arthurian symbolism. Now we have an epic poem, *Jason and Medeia* (as bloody a story as any Greek mythology can afford), a new poem as long as *The Odyssey* and written—save for a few modern references and lines translated from Euripedes's play—as it would have been twenty-five hundred years ago.

"When radiant dawn with her bright eyes gazed at the towering crags"—*that* kind of verse, a kissing cousin of the classical hexameter that Homer used, which has rarely worked satisfactorily in English. "Barbarous experiment, barbarous hexameters," wrote Tennyson, who knew his prosody and gave an example: "When was a harsher sound ever heard, ye Muses, in England?/ When did a frog coarser croak upon our Helicon?"

As the poem begins, Jason and Medeia live in Corinth. Jason is bored: "These are stupid times." Kreon, Corinth's ruler, who opposed Antigone, has arranged for lesser kings to vie for his daughter's hand—and the succession to Corinth's throne. Jason is tempted: if he divorces Medeia, he may regain the crown in Iolkos, which he had to flee when Medeia murdered King Pelias, and Corinth's crown as well. Medeia, the virgin witch who helped him win the Golden Fleece, is worried and summons her prophetic ravens. Jason goes to Kreon's palace and there, for the better part of the poem, recounts his adventures on the Argo: how it was to sail with great warriors on a ship that talked to its crew, to sail through rape and murder and seize the shaggy prize. Kreon's daughter melts before Jason's story, but Medeia plots revenge.

Gardner is adroit at embroidering a myth: the Argonauts' sojourn at Lemnos, for instance, or Orpheus's attempt at rescuing Euridike. But at best his verse is derivative, and at worst it is fruity: a chuckle makes "a sound like spiders waking"; children's voices are as "lazy as the butterflies near my shoes." When fruitiness palls, fatigue takes over: "Exhaustion was the name of the game," Gardner writes, and then a few lines later: "Self-destruction was the name of the game." Gardner simply will not listen to the sound of his own voice: "Knit together in a single mold," indeed! He harrows the Oxford English Dictionary for hundreds of obsolete and archaic words, then invents scores whose meaning cannot be determined: benom, kumry, ultion.

This is indeed a queer performance. Had Gardner recovered *Kypria*, once said to be Homer's lost epic of Cyprus, we would greet it as gladly as we would an unknown vase by Euphronius—but surely we don't need any *new* antique vases, any new epics in the classical style. The debate flourished four hundred years ago: what is the purpose of imitation? The French poet and critic du Bellay said that mere imitation is of little profit, that those who would imitate a form should devour it, absorb it, and then produce something of themselves and of their time. John Barth did this with Greek myths last year in his *Chimera*. Gardner does not: his verse, his story, his language, his characters, are neither of their time nor of ours, but a reflection of forms that poets would have used two and half millennia ago.

                                                            June 1973

Within this great welter of words, symbols, gassy speechifying, and half-hatched allegories there was once, I suspect, a good lean novel, but I can't find it now. Like the mural on Americanism that Miss Applecore coaxed from her sixth grade, *October Light* beamishly reveals a variety of inspiration and tedium, of deft lines nearly crushed by heavy-handed smudges.

The plot is simple. One evening James Page, a seventy-two-year-old Vermont farmer, chases his eighty-year-old sister, Sally, upstairs with a piece of stovewood and locks her in her bedroom. James, part savage and part Green Mountain philosopher, thinks the country has gone to hell—you can see it all on TV, which is why he shoots Sally's TV set to pieces right before her eyes. Sally is a liberal, believing in New York City and amnesty, and amuses herself in captivity with a "trashy" novel about marijuana smugglers. Many of this novel's pages are mercifully missing (like Sally and James, it is not quite "all there"), but Gardner remorselessly quotes the rest. Some of the smugglers quote Bergson and Rousseau, others talk like the Pirates of Penzance. In them Sally sees an allegory of Third World attacks on capitalism, even sees herself as the Third World and her brother as brutish imperialism.

But by now the story has become complicated. At first, James won't let Sally out, then she won't come out. Vermont character *in extremis*. Family and friends gather to preach and cajole. The story grows arch ("I sometimes think we're all characters in some book," Sally says) and offers more messages than I cared to count. Chief among these is that self-imposed isolation is no protection against what others will do to us or we, unwittingly, to them. Okay, but I wish Gardner had trusted the reader to deduce his implications; the stuffy ornamentation, phrases like "the whole progress of man" can prevent us from finishing a book this long, can set us to wondering how Edith Wharton or Willa Cather would have managed it.

November 1976

Postscript: In the fall of 1977, as Gardner was preparing to publish *On Moral Fiction*, a critical essay in which he denounces his fellow novelists for their failure to make a moral commitment to truth telling, I came across an article in *Speculum*, an academic journal devoted to medieval studies, which charged Gardner with misappropriating the words and ideas of other scholars in one of his recent books, a popular life of Chaucer. After checking all the references—which showed that Gardner had indeed helped himself without acknowledgment to whole paragraphs from other books—and after setting up an appointment in advance, letting him know what I was up to, I called Gardner at his Vermont home for comment. He proved unrepentant. "Of course I knew what I was doing," Gardner told me. "It wasn't done by mistake." I reported on the matter in *Newsweek*. I thought it then the saddest business I was ever engaged in; I still think so, and won't reprint the piece here. I have not read Gardner's work since. If I had, I would never have caught, as a reviewer for the *Chicago Tribune* did only two years later, Gardner's attempts to pass off as his own work, in a novel called *Freddy's Book*, passages from two little-known works on Swedish history.

JOHN BARTH'S DIFFICULTIES

WHEN HAWTHORNE rewrote the Greek myths for children, he left out all the good parts: the sex, the compulsive ambition, the failure that overtakes so many bright young men. Everything grotesque or wonderful in the legends is foisted on the monsters—the Gorgon, the Chimera—leaving Perseus an antiseptic lad (we aren't told that his mother made love to gold) and Bellerophon happy to live ever after with his winged horse (nothing from Hawthorne about Bellerophon's fall, his blind and lonely death).

Chimera, John Barth's version of these stories, together with a fable he has invented about Scheherazade, is more eccentric still. Yet it's truer to the spirit of myth, which, however abbreviated it may be, refers to the totality of man's condition. Barth suggests that through myth we may approach "the original springs of narrative" and yet retain a contemporary tone and perspective; perhaps, he says, we ought not to stretch a realistic story over a mythic framework, as Updike and other writers do, but confront the myths directly.

In the first episode, Scheherazade's younger sister tells the story of her more famous sibling. She has sat for a thousand nights at the foot of the bed where Scheherazade has made love to the king and told him stories that she interrupted so she might survive another night, so the king will not resume his practice of "gynocide": raping a virgin every night and murdering her the following morning. The stories, like the lovemaking, share a common structure of "exposition, rising action, climax and dénouement," and yet Scheherazade could not invent the stories herself.

They are fed to her each afternoon by a genie, a writer much like Barth himself, who travels back through time to share with her his enthusiasm for *The Arabian Nights* and to recapture, if he can, his own ability to write.

Like Perseus and Bellerophon, who narrate their own tales, this genie is about forty, balding, gaining weight. All three worry about their careers: what will happen next? Granted what has gone before, what must we do, what must we know, to carry on? "What mythic hero isn't over the hill, as it were, by the time he's forty?" asks Bellerophon's wife.

Perseus, twenty years after he killed Medusa, rescued Andromeda, and turned her enemies into stone, is bored, matched with a shrewish wife, and thinks of setting out again—on a tour of his old battlegrounds. Worse, he feels he is petrifying: old age is turning him to stone. He needs another Gorgon to restore his flesh. Bellerophon, at the same age and in the same condition, remembering how he killed the Chimera and dropped stones from Pegasus's back upon the invading armies, worries about the heroic pattern of his life. "You're self-centered enough to be a hero, at least!" his mistress says, and it is true: Bellerophon is the perfect pedant, a prig who has studied heroes' lives and can think of nothing but his own career. When a queen offers herself to him, he replies with a lecture, complete with Mendelian charts, on the genetic probabilities in the offspring of gods, demigods, and mortals. In time, as Bellerophon becomes woefully aware, his life amounts to no more than the sound of his own voice telling it.

The substance of these enchanting stories make a pleasing progression: from youth and sex in the first to the cares of an aging hero in the second, and then, in the third, to an ironic imitation of a hero's life. Skillfully, deceivingly, the substance becomes inseparable from the narration. "The process is the content," Barth said recently in an interview. Faithful to the myths, but extrapolating from them, he spins dizzily into metaphysical foolery, wordplay, reversals, surprises, excursions to the present. Barth's style is sexy, punning, and alliterative, yet oddly formal: there is in these pages a baroque ordering of words best grasped when read aloud. More important, there's a contagious sense of joy in living, in loving, even in mortality.

October 1972

Make no mistake: *Letters* is a daunting book. Amid the fabulist fictions that have, in the past twenty years, sprouted at every hand, it rises like a monument—a monument being, of course, a construction that demands attention but is not itself alive. Patience, Shakespeare tells us, sat on a monument, and that is one of the things the reader can do with *Letters*, but whatever he does with it, he had better bring Patience along for company. Again, make no mistake: this longest and most complex of John Barth's novels is really an awesome performance. Like Nabokov's *Ada*, Pynchon's *Gravity's Rainbow*, and Gaddis's *JR*—the only contemporary novels other than Barth's own to which it may be fairly compared—*Letters* is brilliant, witty, at times erudite, and damn near unreadable as well. The reader's jaw drops in amazement, then remains locked in the yawn position.

That this is so is due in part to the novel's design. Because Barth is not one of your writers who believes that the best art conceals its art, he tends to write fiction that is *about* its own design: in *Letters* the design becomes a matter of onanistic obsession. Put briefly, Barth's intention here is to write a novel that will serve as a sequel to all five of the books he had written prior to embarking on this one, and to do so in the form of an epistolary novel, a genre he well knows was exhausted nearly two centuries ago but which he will revivify by means of all manner of alphabetical, anagrammatical, and numerological games. The letters themselves, divided among seven parts (one for each letter in *Letters*) and written over a space of seven months by seven correspondents, are presented in such a manner that if each is placed on a calendar according to the day of its composition the resulting design will spell—what else?—"Letters." Moreover: if, in this calendar design, each letter is represented by its opening letter, the result, read horizontally, spells: "An old time epistolary novel by seven fictitious drolls and dreamers, each of which imagines himself actual."

If this sounds simple, wait a minute. Of these seven correspondents, three have been plucked from Barth's previous fictions, two are descendants of characters in the earlier novels, one is original (because the five sequels are yoked into a new story), and one is the author himself. As for the letters through which these stories are advanced, Barth offers prodigious variety: letters to the dead, to oneself, to the unborn; letters unopened, unanswered, and unmailed; letters in bottles, letters in summary, letters delayed in the mail; anonymous letters, posthumous letters, love letters, forged letters, official letters, historical letters, newsy letters, even carbon copies of letters. The writers are aware of what Barth has done with their lives in the past, yet they write anyway, and as they do Barth develops his familiar themes: the revision of history, the recycling of lives, the restructuring of sexual liaisons.

In increasing order of interest, the seven correspondents are these: Barth himself, cool organizer of the whole. Todd Andrews, the lawyer from Barth's first novel, *The Floating Opera*, who has brooded for fifty years on his father's suicide. Jacob Horner, protagonist of *The End of the Road*, who tries, in the face of a death threat, to reassemble his immobilized life in a quack therapeutic community. Ambrose Mensch, resurrected from *Lost in the Funhouse;* an author himself, he writes love letters and reveals at unilluminating length Barth's debt to him for several earlier stories. Jerome Bonaparte Bray, descendant of the Grand Tutor in *Giles Goat-Boy*, a madman who thinks at times that he is Napoleon, about to launch his second empire in the American West, and at times that he is a bug (most likely a bee, Napoleon's symbol) in charge of a computer that will launch a "Novel Revolution"— that is to say, the novel to end all novels.

Then there's Andrew Burlingame Cook VI, descendant of both Ebeneezer Cooke and Henry Burlingame of *The Sot-Weed Factor;* like all his ancestors, he seeks the truth about his slippery and innocent relatives who, through conspiracies and betrayals, tried to reverse our country's history. To this end, he offers the letters of A. B. Cook IV (that translates as ABCD, if you can think as Barth does). To admit that *Letters* sports eight narrators would be to spoil Barth's rigid design, but we need Cook's correspondence to learn rather more than we can bear about the secrets of the French and Indian Wars, the Revolution, the War of 1812, and the plot to free Napoleon from Saint Helena. Finally, and most engagingly, Germaine Pitt, a.k.a. Lady Amherst, a randy Englishwoman of fifty, scholar and provost of Marshyhope State University in Maryland, who regales the author with intimate details of her developing affair with Ambrose.

Such a condensed overview cannot begin to suggest the wealth of stories and wordplay, the complications and correspondences that *Letters* affords. Barth cannot write a dull page and there is much here that is delightful, but by writing a great many very similar pages, and drawing so heavily on material he has exhausted before, he becomes very quickly dull. Germaine, I think, entertains us so vigorously precisely because she has been invented for this occasion. The others do not fare as well. Long ago, before (as he says) he "turned his professional back on literary realism in favor of the fabulous irreal," Barth gave us all that Todd and Jacob can offer. Ambrose's reshaping of three earlier stories reads like the first draft it may once have been. Bray's computer foolery is funny only until it sinks altogether into insanity. The Cook-Burlingame duplicities, endlessly elaborated, are simply a baroque extension of what, when fresh, seemed so ingenious in an earlier story.

And yet, and yet: it is impossible to dislike the book. Perhaps, given the perspective a reviewer can never immediately enjoy, I'll look upon it with more affection. Barth is as inventive and as muscular a writer as we have just now. Faint-headed readers may not finish *Letters*, but no one who cares for contemporary fiction can ignore it altogether.

October 1979

Brilliance in a novelist is like fire in a house: a tool useful to man, but troublesome if not restrained. Very likely, John Barth is the most brilliant American novelist now at work, but his new novel, like some of its predecessors, is more than audacious—it is rash. We've come to expect an arch self-consciousness in his narratives; often, even when the author is clearly enchanted by the eccentricity of his adopted tone of voice, that self-consciousness works very well. We expect a certain repetitiveness, too; Barth rarely knows when to let go. But in *Sabbatical* (which for all its faults is shorter, more pleasant and accessible than his last novel, *Letters*) Barth for the first time seems persuaded that any amount of slipshoddiness may be allowed a writer who invents a sufficiently dazzling container to put it in.

Fenwick Turner, fifty, a former member of the CIA's Clandestine Services division, and his thirty-five-year-old wife, Susan Seckler, a professor of American literature, have taken a sabbatical year to beat about the Caribbean in a small sailboat. They have decisions to make: shall Susan take a more demanding teaching position? Have a baby? Shall Fenn find the impetus to write a novel? Or shall they just go on sailing around the world? Fenn and Susan are more than married; they are pals, so intimately connected that they share each other's dreams. Their families are not so happy: Fenn's twin brother, a CIA spook so devious he is called "the Prince of Darkness," has disappeared at sea. This man's son is reported to have been murdered by the Chilean police. Susan's twin sister has survived a gang rape and sexual torture by SAVAK. We first meet them on the last leg of their journey, sailing up Chesapeake Bay, coping with storms and family visits, mooring at an uncharted island that may be a CIA training center. Fenn's old employers try to bribe him back to the spookery trade and Susan undergoes an abortion.

That's most of what *happens* in the story, but of course the novel is *about* something else: like much of Barth's fiction, it is about itself. Once upon a time, an author didn't openly discuss his story's architecture or his literary and mythical allusions; Barth talks of little else. Fenn and Susan are acutely aware of the significance of the journey in literature and the stages of the hero's progress: Homer, Virgil, Byron, and Poe are much discussed. So is the metamorphosis of their journey into a novel: "So what else needs doing in this chapter?" Fenn asks. And later: "We speak desultorily, as if waiting for the plots of our lives to get on with it." Perhaps because Susan is a scholar, the novel is heavily footnoted; the notes often lead to footnotes on other pages.

Less tolerable, because they seem ill considered, are the great wads of undigested matter that Barth heaves into his story's wake. An essay on Vietnamese folk songs, for instance, and twenty pages of actual news reports about a real CIA agent who was murdered, even as Fenn's brother may have been. Barth also allows the reader to savor, for seven pages, details of Susan's sister's sequence of rapes. The point of this, I suppose, is to suggest the evil of the world from which our lovers have taken their sabbatical; even so, to write such a scene in these affectless times seems an act of collaboration with the enemy. So much for the slipshod; as for the rash, I find it odd that Barth should place at his story's core a happy marriage, an almost unworkable device in

fiction. So much of happiness in marriage is mired in homely details that are comfortably boring to the principals (the tedious
family phone calls that Barth gives us verbatim), but unspeak-
ably boring to outsiders. In so doing, he allows the spy-story aspect of his plot—a reliably workable device—to dwindle away.

May 1982

A NOVEL NOT FOR LIKING

PAULA FOX'S *The Widow's Children* is so good a novel that one
wants to go out in the street to hustle up a big audience for it.

"Here. Read this novel. Please."

"Is it any good?"

"First rate."

"Will I like it?"

"Not a chance. It's for admiring, not liking."

"Oh. Well, I like to like a book."

There's the problem. Most readers of novels want to be en-
tertained, not subjected to art. For them, art and entertainment
are incompatible commodities—the former is difficult and the
more you have of it the less you have of the latter. They know
very well that novelists long ago agreed that marriage is hell and
families something worse, that characters in fiction come in vary-
ing degrees of pathos and despicability. All this they will accept if
the novel is *likable*. Paula Fox does not indulge such weakness.
She makes difficulties for herself in writing fiction, approaches a
novel like a spelunker. Hunching slowly over real rocks, the
searchlight on her forehead describing delicate arcs in the darkness, her beam makes pleasing patterns, but there's not much
room for an audience. Story being of little use to her, she focuses
on a situation that darkens and intensifies. Her characters play

against one another, but none is a whole person; each reveals only that edge of his personality which can be wedged tight into the scene that occupies his author at the moment.

Desmond and Laura Clapper, about to embark on a boat for Africa, throw a tiny party the night before the sailing. Laura knows, but tells no one, that her aged mother died that afternoon in a nursing home. It is this concealed event that charges the evening with electricity. Desmond, who through Laura's intervention has inherited a business that he does not understand, drinks himself into a truculent stupor. Laura's daughter, Clara, who describes herself as a boarder in the house of Atreus, succumbs to a chronic ache of self-disgust. Also present are Laura's brother, Carlos, a homosexual, and Laura's friend Peter, an editor who no longer likes to read, for whom "the sight of a printed page filled him with a faint but persistent nausea."

Drinks flow, cigarettes burn. Laura, feared by everyone, forgives everyone his fear. The guests speak but no one listens; each falls into his private reveries. Such a freeze-frame approach to narrative is detrimental to an orderly story, yet Fox's purpose is not to move from here to somewhere else, but to turn each scene into a compression chamber: "Clara had trouble breathing—the air was leaking out of the room, draining color from everyone's flesh, faces, and hands and the room furnishings had gone the same ashen color, nothing left to live on but a sweated smoky heat. They were all dying to the vigorous sound of the rain outside."

Mortification, humiliation, unattended gasps for recognition—Fox spares her characters no distress. Peter, who recognizes that the terrible grip of the family must be broken, protests only in "prig's squeaks." A mother's smile at her daughter is translated into the language of pathology: "Clara could see the three plump cushions of her lips, the large, somewhat dingy teeth, and behind them, the quivering mucosity of her tongue." Just so, no doubt, but how is a reader to rise to this story? Fox's brilliance has a masochistic aspect: I will do this so well, she seems to say, that you will hardly be able to read it. And so she does, and so do I, who admire her work, find myself muttering in the street—"admirable, not likable."

September 1976

A SURVIVOR OF OUR TIMES

NO ONE, I hope, will be surprised to hear that in his new novel—his first in a dozen years—William Styron again employs his great gift for dramatic narrative to serve a tragic view of life. Nor is it surprising to find him probing once again at a social evil so extreme that it resists rational explanation. What may at first seem surprising is that the author of *The Confessions of Nat Turner* has again taken slavery for his theme—but then, as Styron reminded us in an essay published last year, slavery is embedded in the cultural tradition of the West; it is "the sleeping virus in the bloodstream of civilization," which we ignore at the risk of our future. In *Sophie's Choice*, Styron examines the slave world that the Nazis created at Auschwitz and the permanently disabling effect that this "world of the living dead" had upon its survivors.

I don't mean to suggest that his story is unremittingly grim; it is not. By means of a particularly felicitous construction, Styron manages to offset some of the horror with moments of levity, sensuality, good humor. His narrator, a Virginian much like Styron himself, looks back to 1947, when he was twenty-two and poor, an uneasy virgin translated from the South to a Brooklyn rooming house where he begins the novel that will become *Lie Down in Darkness*. From the room above comes an ecstatic racket: the noise of two of his fellow boarders at play in a single bed. Stingo, as he was then called, is drawn into their lives. The woman, Sophie, is a beautiful, golden-haired Polish gentile, about thirty, with a number tattooed on her arm. The man, Nathan, is Jewish and not her husband; kindly and generous much of the time, he succumbs to dark rages, which end with poor Sophie being beaten.

Stingo is immediately smitten with love for Sophie and grieves for her infatuation with a man who uses her so cruelly. As the summer passes, and Nathan's fits grow worse, Sophie begins to release to Stingo, in disordered fashion, chapters of her past history. One of the millions of Poles and Russians, Serbs and gypsies, who were sent to concentration camps to die beside the Jews, Sophie survived, but only barely so. Released from Auschwitz at the brink of death, she recovered her physical health, but not her spirit. Her father and her husband had been murdered by the Nazis, her daughter had been killed on the first day in the camp, and her son is lost—probably he is dead as well. Sophie is haunted by that peculiar guilt that can afflict survivors: the suspicion that she should not have lived, the wish that she had not.

The search for the sources of Sophie's guilt is the real matter of this novel, just as Sophie's masochistic love for Nathan, who offers her release from the discomfort of living, provides the considerable suspense that propels the story along. Like Simone Weil and Hannah Arendt before him, Styron believes that real evil is bureaucratic, monotonous, boring—perhaps even a function of failed religion. Without dwelling on the horrors of the gas chambers and crematoriums, he develops the other, lesser-known side of Auschwitz: the slave society of "human beings continually replenished and expendable" in which gentile prisoners were expected to work and starve for three months, then die. Sophie survived in part because, as a skilled linguist, typist, and stenographer, she was coerced into the camp's administration, thereby becoming an accomplice to, as well as a victim of, her captors' crimes.

Sophie's confessions, as I've said, do not emerge in chronological sequence, but rather in a moral sequence: she begins with some self-serving lies and reveals what she feels to be the worst about herself only at the end. Far from loving her father and husband, she despised them for the vicious anti-Semites they were. She even attempted to seduce the camp commandant—first with her mind, by pretending an anti-Semitism that would have made Julius Streicher blush, and then with her body. A writer less artful than Styron would have let her succeed in one or the other enterprise, but Styron lets her fail and live with the shame of the bungled seductions. Although we do not know it at the time, Sophie's spirit has already been destroyed by an atrocity so simple, so cruel, that it took my breath away: it is the event to which the novel's title refers, and in good conscience I cannot say more about it than that.*

By concentrating on the main thrust of this story, I've necessarily distorted the whole. For all the austerity of its theme, much of the book is quite funny—particularly Stingo's bootless attempts to get two apparently available girls into bed. Clearly, Styron seems to suggest, there are differing levels of suffering to be reckoned with in this story—and differing levels of guilt, too, for Nathan, in his uglier moods, tries to associate Stingo with southern racism: the lynchings, Senator Bilbo, and all.

But surely the most appealing quality of the book is the presence of Sophie herself, as complex and as plausible a heroine as any in recent fiction. Victimized about as thoroughly as a person can be (assuming you grant, as I do, Styron's thesis that the torturer's ultimate victory lies in his ability to afflict his victim with the need to continue torturing himself), she remains a loving, lovable being. Even after Auschwitz, even as her love propels her toward destruction, she is somehow triumphant: a force of life that has been wrested from death, just as Nathan, the Jew who has been spared Auschwitz and cannot forgive Sophie for surviving, is a man who has been dead from the start.

May 1979

FRAUDULENT LIVES

A WEEK AGO I would have insisted that although a good novel may be ragged and lumpy, a good short story may not. Tidiness, a certain coherence, is part of what we expect from short fiction.

*Except to say that Camus uses the identical incident in his novella *The Fall*. There, however, the event is merely referred to in passing and therefore lacks the devastating effect that Styron, by his emphasis, achieves.

But Cynthia Ozick has convinced me that exceptions can be made. So great is the energy that animates her stories, so concentrated the art, that I would rather read a flawed one by her than a perfect one by most of her contemporaries.

For example: in the title story of her new collection, *Bloodshed and Three Novellas,* an unbelieving Jew visits a Hasidic community. He seeks something—perhaps the challenge to his skepticism that is thrown at him by a rabbi who forces him to bring from his pockets two pistols: one a toy, one real. As symbols, the pistols work beautifully in the story's structure; at narrative level, they are not explained. Never mind that the story is about sacrifice and its symbol, what's this fellow doing with these things? In a preface to the collection, Ozick admits that a problem exists, but diagnoses it incorrectly. Many fine prefaces have been written to fiction, but no fiction has ever been improved by a preface.

In this same preface Ozick worries that her novella "Usurpation" has been misunderstood. It's a nervy, convoluted story about writers' envy—of publication, of talent, of fame—and about the curse of getting what you want. Its form resembles nesting boxes: stories told within stories. "Magic—I admit it—is what I lust after," the narrator says, but the story is skeptical about magic, the imagination, even about storytelling itself. Ozick suggests that the story's perspective is so essentially Jewish that it should not have been written in that Christian language, English. Again her diagnosis fails: "Usurpation" is marvelous—audacious and witty but so compressed that the whole of what its author means to convey is not made quite coherent. No wonder the artist is anxious, wishes to explain: properly, she reaches for perfection; understandably, she won't settle for what she's written: a fine, flawed story.

The remaining novellas are indeed perfect and quite different from one another. "An Education," written in a plain, satirical style, tells of a girl's willing bondage to a selfish, parasitical couple who seem to be smart, as well as an incarnation of the life force. "A Mercenary" I think a small masterpiece: it is a story about uprootedness and fraudulent identity. Lushinski, having survived the Nazis, the Russians, and his fellow Poles, serves as a diplomat for an African nation. His bags and false passports are

packed against his need to escape. Lushinksi belongs nowhere; he
makes money lecturing and in television, re-creating as an art
form his compelling and possibly spurious past. In time he becomes again a victim—Ozick is as tough with her survivors as she
is with writers. "I believe that stories ought to judge and interpret
the world," she says. It is a good dictum and hers do: severely,
but with wit and a sensuous appreciation of language.

April 1976

Three slim volumes in eleven years do not a prolific writer
make, which is perhaps why, when the conversation in the bar
car turns to contemporary masters of the short story form,
Cynthia Ozick isn't mentioned as quickly as John Cheever, John
Updike, or Joyce Carol Oates. Yet I fearlessly predict that when
the chroniclers of our literary age catch up to what has been going
on (may Ozick live to see it), some of her stories will be reckoned
among the best written in our time.

Ozick's stories vary in length, but all are endowed with great
energy and wit—and with a sense of playfulness that, just now, is
rare; Mark Helprin shares it, perhaps no one else. The unexpected intrusion of religion—specifically the more irrational aspects of antique Judaic tradition—into her characters' placidly
secular lives invigorates her work. Her stories have a discomfort-
ing, enchanting way of changing gears in mid-career: what began
as a cheerful satire becomes suddenly a fantasy, with every element assuming new significance. Only a masterly technician can
manage such a trick. To see her do it must cause teachers of creative writing palpitations of the heart—it is precisely what they
tell their dull, ambitious students never to attempt.

In the title story of her new collection, *Levitation: Five
Fictions*, a young gentile woman is married to a Jew. Both are
unknown novelists, "anonymous mediocrities." We see them engaged in pleasant banter. What happens then is simple: this
woman must recognize the unbridgeable gulf between them.
That gulf is the Holocaust; her recognition is brought about during a party. A survivor speaks of the Holocaust in a room where
there are only Jews—and this woman, a convert to Judaism—to
attend him. So far, so realistic. Then the room, with its birthright
Jews, suddenly begins to rise, leaving the wife below. The story
doesn't end here, but I mustn't give away all of Ozick's reversals.

Excellent as that story is, it only hints at what Ozick can do. In another, comprising two seemingly dissimilar parts, a narrator who claims to have "nothing to do with make-believe" muses over photographs of Freud's studio in Vienna, a cluttered room filled with little prehistoric stone figures that seem to be goose-stepping into the Nazi future. The scene changes. We are now on the planet Acirema (a name that may be held before a mirror), where women congregate in Sewing Harems, committed, by use of thread and needle, to "the closure of the passage leading to the womb." Pleasure without responsibility; some children are never-theless born, interrupting these women's careers; a degenerate race ensues. By means of an inspired metaphor, Ozick manages a sendup of the women's movement. But she has more on her mind: both parts of her story hint at a final victory of irrationality. To deny the role that the primitive plays in our lives is to see it come back at us in a dangerous and degraded form.

Not all of Ozick's stories are so complex. The longest here is also the most pleasing: a story of an idealistic civil servant un-justly dismissed who dreams of a New York City in a prelap-sarian state. Inadvertently, she creates a golem. The golem, a kind of Frankenstein monster, achieves her mistress's dream—and then destroys it, as golems do. A pity, because this golem—the first girl golem—has from the moment of her incarnation an en-gaging personality.

Which brings me to my final point. In her previous collec-tions, Ozick wrote stories about men. Here she writes about women. Has she been biding her time, girding her loins? An ir-relevant question; the results are equally delightful.

February 1982

AFTER MARRIAGE

A MEN'S CLUB conjures up images of leather and decorum, cigars and anachronistic service—not at all what Leonard Michaels, hitherto known for his short stories, offers in his first work of

longer fiction. In *The Men's Club,* seven men in California, for
the most part strangers, meet one night in the home of one of
them to swap sexual autobiographies. This club, "a regular social
possibility," is, the narrator observes, designed "to make women
cry." Why should women, with their anger and politics, have all
the fun? The premise of this consciousness-lowering group is that
men are equally adept at self-pity. "Can I tell this story?" one
man asks. "Only if it's miserable" is the reply. As the night wears
into morning, the men drink and shout a lot, throw knives at the
woodwork and, at their host's invitation, rape a refrigerator that
his wife has stocked for her women's group.

Michaels endows his men with unlikely professions. The
host, for instance, is a psychotherapist who sports tattoos and a
trunk of obsessively collected memorabilia; at thirty-eight, he has
slept with 622 women. Grant him twenty-two before his eigh-
teenth birthday, that leaves him a new one every twelve days for
the next twenty years, with no time out to visit his urologist. Michaels's sad comedy might have been more affecting had his con-
fessors been more complexly conceived; unfortunately, he is
satisfied with largely undifferentiated dolts. And yet, the stories
these men tell are moving and adroitly wrought. The novella's
frame may be coarse and the men unmemorable, but Michaels's
book deserves to be read for the brief tales it contains.

Men are not the offended gender in our society, and these
stories of unhappily resolved marriages and sexual encounters
show their narrators to be primarily at fault, even when (rarely)
the men are used by women. It is this curious, credible slant to an
otherwise bald and unconvincing narrative that lends to *The
Men's Club* a distinctly feminist cast that is far more appealing
than what we find in most novels written by angry women today.

April 1981

In 1962, when *Who's Afraid of Virginia Woolf?* opened on
Broadway, some jester remarked that the best show in town could
be seen free by standing outside the Billy Rose Theatre, watching
the marriages break up as the audience filed out. The world
would be a more interesting place if art could so affect us; if it
could, I suspect that Raymond Carver's readers might be moved
to similar reassessments. His short stories convey images of loss,

of rupture, and of loneliness within and just after marriage that are both cautionary and chillingly resonant. Like most good writers, he works with themes and characters that are far from original: burnt-out, inarticulate people who are just leaving, or who have just been left, who cannot manage to communicate through speech. And like most good writers, he manages to translate such familiar materials into something newly strange, distinctively his own.

He achieves some of his special effects through a severely ascetic prose. Carver uses words as if he had to withdraw each one from the bank and was concerned for the size of his balance. As we see in his new collection, *What We Talk about When We Talk about Love*, such rigorous economy enables him to develop an instant momentum. One story begins: "In the kitchen he poured another drink and looked at the bedroom suite in his front yard." Here we get, besides a lot of information, a look at another of Carver's special tricks: the odd displacement of the baggage of ordinary life. What is this man's furniture doing outside his house? We are never told precisely but are left to infer that it stands for the end of something. Once there was a woman attached to that furniture, but she is not here now, so he is willing to sell it or give it to an eager young couple who will surely be no happier with it.

Carver is concerned here—as he was in his previous collection, *Will You Please Be Quiet, Please?*—with the collapse of human relationships. Some of his stories take place at the moment things fall apart; others, after the damage has been done, while the shock waves still reverberate. Alcohol and violence are rarely far removed from what happens, but sometimes, in another characteristic maneuver, Carver will nudge the drama that triggers a crisis aside to show that his story has really been about something else all along. A boy is hit by a car. His anguished parents sit by his bed in the hospital, waiting for him to emerge from his coma. Will he recover? We're never told. The point is the exquisite degree to which the parents' distress is increased by repeated phone calls from the local baker, who asks why the boy's birthday cake has not been picked up and paid for.

There are seventeen stories in this slim collection. All are excellent and each gives the impression that it could not have been written more forcefully, or with fewer words. My own favorite is the title story, armed with symbols and little arrows pointing toward classical literature, in which two couples sit around a kitchen table drinking gin in the afternoon and talking about love. As the anesthesia sets in, and the light drains out of the room, and relationships among the four alter subtly, it becomes clear that no one in this room is going anywhere, certainly not to the "new place" for dinner—and yet curiously, against all odds, something significant about love in its several varieties has actually been revealed.

April 1981

SOUTHERN MOLASSES

JUST WHEN I thought the southern Gothic novel had been declared extinct and its best specimens put away safely under glass, Reynolds Price offers this slablike vestige, a novel about repeating patterns of search, failure, and rejection among three generations of North Carolina white folk and their guardian Negroes. True to tradition, the whites are lonely, ill of mind and body; lacerating themselves and their kin, they nurse for decades festering family grudges. Meanwhile, the blacks work, watch, accommodate, endure. Can these bones live? Well, no, but because novels of comparable ambition are rare, I raise my knuckle to my forehead. If *The Surface of Earth* fails, it fails nobly, victim of its author's determination to make it unendurable.

One evening in 1903, a schoolgirl tries to escape her parents by eloping with her teacher. All her life Eva will make people need her and then repudiate them, seeming to affirm her affection while actually dismissing the claims of her husband, and later of her son. "She cared for herself, the small dry room in the front of her skull where her bare self lived." Eva returns home to care for her interminably ailing father; her husband seeks another life and finds in time another woman and happiness. Their son, ignored by both parents, combining the hunger of his father and the mean spirit of his mother, looks for his own life. Later still, Eva's grandson must repeat the pattern. The flight to self-indulgence, the grief of love denied, the evasion of responsibility, and the need for a firm attachment to another human being make a stuttering design afflicting the generations of Eva's family and its black retainers for four decades.

Price's fourth novel is a huge one, longer than all his preceding novels put together. In its lumbering course there are many good effects: the complexity of its characters, white and black, their delicate and shifting relationships, their unpredictable destinies. Any given part of this novel is impressive, and yet there is a cumulative overbearingness to the whole that makes it finally difficult to finish. Too many dreams told in full; too many letters unabridged; too many monologues in which people tax one another for their failures or burden them with more personal history than they (or we) can bear to hear.

Price's story relies too much on compulsive explanations. Mother and son have only to sit on a porch on a pleasant evening and it's once more into the metaphysical molasses: the uses of life and death, the nature of happiness and of one's debts to others. The Greek tragedians knew how to do this—they kept the action offstage, but they didn't run on for so long. If Sophocles had fitted the chorus of *Oedipus at Colonus* with sixty more statements on the human condition, we all would have fled the theater. Price, in his long book, has no sense of proportion. Less is more—that kind of thing.

July 1975

THE DE VRIESIAN
FIELDS

FASTER THAN a speeding Cuisinart, the reviewer's memory slices through produce pushed into his tube over many years until from the resulting julienne a salient fact emerges. Peter De Vries has now written two novels narrated by furniture movers—another first for American letters. What does De Vries see in a man with a sofa on his shoulders that he should make of him an oracle who discourses wittily on matters spiritual, sexual, and literary? A continuity of incongruity, perhaps; one De Vries novel is much like another. In *Let Me Count the Ways*, a philosophical mover in Indiana survives too many women and a breakdown while quoting Mencken and Sidney Hook. In *Consenting Adults, or The Duchess Will Be Furious*, a moving philosopher in Illinois survives a breakdown and too many women while quoting Proust and Schopenhauer.

I don't mean to imply that if you read the earlier story you are excused from reading this one. *Let Me Count the Ways* belongs to De Vries's middle period, in which his books, funny as they were, ran to fat, didacticism, and the search for God; there is none of that in the new one. Ted Peachum's ontological shudders, brought about when he is told at sixteen that he must wait for the ten-year-old girl across the street to grow up, result in a sexual, not a religious, awakening. Carrier of chairs and hauler of highboys, Ted is into drawers in both senses of the word. He takes a mistress; when she marries his best friend, he joins them both in bed; later he takes on the indistinguishable Peppermint sisters— all three at once. Ted describes himself as a self-pitying Stoic and a jilted Narcissus, but like all of De Vries's narrators he is a master of the *bon mot* ("The road to good intentions is paved with hell") and, as he staggers down the sidewalk with a chair on his head, he is trailed by a group of disciples.

Consenting Adults shows De Vries performing close to peak efficiency. His story may end sentimentally, but his stories are not what one remembers: his aphorisms and his inventive way with a character are. Moreover, De Vries manages to be both witty and funny at the same time. These two qualities are often mistaken for each other, but few writers have been able to manage both.

September 1980

KOSINSKI'S DEVILTRY

THE DEVIL TREE is a difficult, impressive novel. If it is read carefully, it should confirm Jerzy Kosinski's position as one of our most significant writers, but it is Kosinski's style to imitate simplicity, to tease the reader to mistake his purpose. I suspect that Kosinski is contemptuous of the generality of readers: if the disingenuous and seemingly detached anecdotes that compose his novels invite our inattention, so much the worse for us. There is another reason for the unwary to dismiss Kosinski as hastily as possible: his fiction and essays are all of a part, developing and exhibiting a rigorous and coherent philosophy that is not pretty, not comforting, that opposes what most of us were brought up to believe. Moreover, Kosinski, in his fiction, does not lecture us on his philosophy, as other novelists do, but leaves us to infer it if we can. To understand, even to admire, Kosinski's fiction is to recoil from it.

The antihero of this fable is Jonathan Whalen, young heir to a legendary fortune of American industry. Jonathan's father died of a swimming accident, his mother perhaps by suicide; now, as principal stockholder in the company, Jonathan's physical existence is a matter of concern: "People have always been employed to make sure of my existence," he says early on. But his existence is the principal concern of the novel: at first he seems a man whose actuality and potential are defined only by others. He is dressed like a bum, which infuriates the police until they find that he carries $2,000; when they make a call to his bank, they become sycophants. So far, so puerile, but Kosinski has more on his mind. Jonathan tells us that he has "many selves," that he is defensive and concealing of his emotions, is preoccupied with examining himself, that he tends toward self-repression, cannot let go, resists his impulses, cannot explain himself to the girl he loves.

Jonathan has been a drug addict; now, feeling dead, unable to react, he attempts self-definition. He will not succeed: his impulses oppose it. By withholding his feelings from his girl, he exercises power over her: love is a matter of someone winning, someone losing. Creeps sidle up to Jonathan, proposing ways to use his power to their mutual benefit; the company from which he derives his income has him trailed by bodyguards because, for the company, he has no useful existence except by continuing to survive. "Sin," Kosinski has written elsewhere, "is an act which prevents the self from functioning freely," and so sin and freedom are Jonathan's problems. Freedom, he explains to a minor character, "means not being afraid, not disguising myself and not performing, not structuring my feelings to gain another's approval. I could see he wasn't interested."

No. Other people's freedom is never much honored by Kosinski's characters. "The basis of horror," he wrote some years ago, "is often the theft of the self, the fear of having one's own identity overshadowed." Today we face a mechanized society that seeks to enforce its own collective values. We live, he says, in an indifferent universe; before we ourselves become indifferent, we may strike back. "The only possible creative act . . . seems to be the destructive act." Other novelists—de Sade, George Bataille, and Jean Genet—have said much the same. Jonathan sets out to destroy his oppressors, but perhaps it is too late. The book, in a marvelous close, returns to the surface of people, voices, and things with which it began, to a retreat into the silence that is the central image of impotence in all of Kosinski's work.

Novelists enjoy posing as philosophers; for the most part, they don't do it very well, but by tradition readers humor them. Kosinski's cold-blooded egocentricity is no more or less palatable

than Hardy's harrumphing pessimism or Tolstoy's fanatical vision of a new Christianity, in which the promised bliss is distrib-
uted now, and evenly about the earth. Still, reviewers are a pious
lot: Tolstoy posing as a religious leader looks only fatuous, but
what Kosinski says he believes gives reviewers the vapors. We
can't endorse *that*, they seem to say, forgetting that no one has
asked them to endorse his ideas, but to inquire whether Kosinski's ideas are central to his art. I think they are, and this is
what differentiates them from, say, the deplorable ideas Kurt
Vonnegut tacks on to his novels, as if he had no other intention
than to cater to the underdeveloped expectations of his adolescent
readers.

Other difficulties: Kosinski ignores conventional narrative
structure in favor of a theme-and-variations effect, a montage of
images that stresses the importance of pattern. This, Kosinski has
written, is the structure of film, of psychoanalysis. Each episode,
whether a flashback or symbolic emendation, seems to float
within the structure of a loosely defined narrative. Some are
funny, some grim. Perverse sex and gratuitous violence figure
largely—because in such episodes we can quickly see some people defining others in terms of their own requirements. A color-
less diction—plain, declarative sentences—pervades the whole,
but it is nonetheless precise and economical. In each episode we
can find something that reflects obliquely the overall design. We
are not used to books written in this manner, which is why I fear
that this novel may be misread by many, but once we grasp Kosinski's purpose, the effect is most impressive.

February 1973

Lurking at the center of Jerzy Kosinski's recent fiction is an
adolescent's daydream—part erotic fantasy, part myth of psychological dominion. His humorless heroes, contemptuous of convention and the unindividuated lives of ordinary men, move at
their will about the world. Solitary, jealous of their freedom, yet
courted by the powerful, they pause from time to time for a spot
of baroque revenge or to break a rich young virgin into the joys of
sexual submission. Such images make many readers recoil, but I
can vouch for the truth of them. I was, at seventeen, just such a
hero for a time—that time being the interval between turning out
my light and falling asleep.

In *Passion Play*, Kosinski explicitly confronts this dreamlike quality. Fabian, his protagonist, is a maverick polo player; in his helmet and spurs, holding his whip like a lance, he seems a "sudden apparition from a realm of fantasy and early memory." Living with his two horses in a spectacular van, this knight errant drives about the country in search of a game, a one-on-one duel with another polo player (very dangerous these duels can be), an occasional job as a riding instructor, and perhaps a brief affair with the kind of young girl who hangs about polo stables. Passion spurs Fabian on his quests—and the need to master his own life, to impose his will on his horses, his rivals, the virgins on whom he is determined to imprint his brand.

This is portentous stuff, to be sure. Dreams and myth may be the building blocks of fiction, but they impose upon the writer who openly employs them problems of tone and credibility that Kosinski has not quite resolved. Kosinski deals in fantasies—some innocent enough, others deeply disturbing—that can be combined more readily within an individual's psyche than in a novel. Toward the end, for example, Fabian takes over at the last minute for a rider who has fallen ill, and performs with dazzling skill in a hazardous jumping competition. The scene, expertly realized, is as romantic as any in *National Velvet*. Yet a few pages earlier, Fabian has lured an aristocratic virgin to a squalid sex club where, amid the gross and public exercises, she has yielded herself with a will. Would not such a girl have been repelled by what she saw? Perhaps not. Do two such dissimilar fantasies belong in the same novel? Perhaps. But Kosinski's conjunctions are not altogether convincing, and the burden of proof lies with him.

I don't mean to belabor the point. Uninterested in conventional narrative and in what E. M. Forster called rounded characters, Kosinski is willing to take large risks and has rarely troubled to be so pleasing as he is here. *Passion Play*, the most accessible and sensuous of his recent fables, may be the only novel about horses that is suitable for adults. Clearly, Kosinski knows them intimately: the fusion of horse and man into a single instrument of force and will, the excitement of the contests, the sheer excitement of the rider's life—these connections and episodes are vivid and effective. So, too, are some of Fabian's dismounted encounters, particularly a remarkable sequence in which, amid a clutter of bridles and bits and saddle blankets, Fabian trains one of his young girls to delight—even to find her freedom—in the demands of her rider.

September 1979

CREATING LIFE ANEW

LIKE MANY GOOD NOVELISTS, Bernard Malamud has essentially but one story to tell. We mustn't be distracted by surface variations—that one of his novels, for instance, seems to be about baseball, while another is set in a wretched grocery store and a third in czarist Russia—or by the fluctuating amounts of wit, metaphor, fantasy, and violence with which he invests his fiction. Malamud's theme, best put as a question, is ever the same: how shall a man create for himself a new life?

Nor does the answer vary: one is reborn to life, and to one's life's work, by discovering passion, and by learning how to balance the conflicting demands of passion and commitment. It is at best an edgy business. "What stays with me most," says the protagonist of *Dubin's Lives*, Malamud's new, most mellow and expansive novel, "is that life is forever fleeting, our fates juggled heart-breakingly by events we can't foresee or control and we are always pitifully vulnerable to what happens next." The heroes of Malamud's other novels have cause to know this well.

William Dubin, fifty-six, is a transplanted city boy who lives with his wife, Kitty, in rural New York. He is a biographer, and apparently a good one; for his life of Thoreau, President Johnson gave him a medal. To Dubin, a biography is a map of human life; it teaches the conduct of life: "Those who write about life reflect about life . . . you see in others who you are." Perhaps, but Dubin isn't living much. He can't begin his biography of D. H. Lawrence, that complexly primitive, blood-haunted man. He can't really love Kitty, a widow he married by arrangement, out of their mutual need. Dubin constantly modifies his pronounce-

ments on life with the words of the famous dead; Kitty, equally
estranged from the present, broods about her first husband and
grieves for her absent children, who seem to have fallen into
cheerless lives. Sleepless Dubin, anxiously dieting, seeks in nature an antidote to sorrow by jogging relentlessly about the countryside (among other things, *Dubin's Lives* is the only intelligent
fiction yet written about this modish mortification of the flesh).

Dubin's problems with the flesh are augmented by the arrival of Fanny, a sexy girl of twenty-two, who is briefly the
Dubins' "cleaning person" and presently the biographer's obsession. Sexually talented Fanny brings Dubin to life again—
even his book begins to stir—but the deceit that the affair involves further debilitates the marriage that he and Kitty so
endlessly analyze. "One may be able to mask dishonesty," he
thinks, "but not its effects: the diminution of libido, ebb of feeling
for a woman, love for her. Deceit distances." Kitty is instinctive
and knows roughly what is happening; Dubin, given to talking to
himself in the mirror, is a poor liar. "We live side by side but not
together," Kitty protests. Dubin agrees, but he wants them both:
Kitty for their past, for what he owes her; Fanny for his last
chance at erotic love.

What a lovely story this is: anxious and thoughtful, comic
and wise. Even the countryside, with its smells and vapors, its
colors and betrayals, comes alive; the seasons, in their rotation
and deceptions, complement Dubin's inner weather. Dubin himself, who talks like a biographer but sees the world and the people
around him with a novelist's eyes, could not have been so convincing were his author not so widely read. We bleed for him in
his autumnal mode, even as we grieve for Kitty, so unable to be of
use, and for Fanny, who manages to outgrow her sluttishness, to
become sensitive to feelings and ideas. There is a lot of talk in this
novel, and much of that is about marriage; if *Dubin's Lives* is to
be faulted, it would be for running on too long. Malamud makes
his points and then makes them again and perhaps a third time.
Yet it is the nature of this book that, awash with wry humor, it
must circle back (as Dubin does while jogging) to burrow ever
deeper into the problems of writing, the problems of a long and
weary marriage.

I suggested at the start that in *Dubin's Lives* Malamud has written his one story once again, and so he has, but this time he has forsaken the violence and crime that have supported the earlier versions. *Dubin's Lives* may not be better than its predecessors—it contains some stilted dialogue—but in its evocation of the sere and yellow leaf, it seems more mature. I hope I will not be misunderstood if I say that I think Malamud a marvelous writer. I intend the compliment that that poor, misused adjective must carry these days, but I mean more precisely that Malamud's fiction, like John Cheever's, is full of marvels. And it is by apprehending these marvels that his heroes arrive at understanding.

February 1979

Fantasy is a refuge for the bad writer, a challenge to the good one. The temptation is to pile the marvelous on the implausible, yet good fantasy requires an exquisite tension: maximum imagination must be played against minimum distortion. The more a writer violates reality, the more difficulty he encounters in suspending his reader's disbelief. Fantasy accommodates narrative easily enough, and is especially helpful to allegory, but it tends to stumble over that other element of interesting fiction: character. For these reasons, I think, the serious writer contemplating fantasy finds himself hard pressed to keep an intelligent reader engaged, to make him care. Still, properly conceived, fantasy proves an efficient truth compactor—which may be why so many good writers try it on. Bernard Malamud has often done so, never more effectively than in *God's Grace*.

He is still, of course, concerned with the question that lurks at the core of each of his novels: how shall a man create for himself a new life? For Calvin Cohn, the paleologist, the question is particularly urgent. His old life—everybody's life—has been extinguished by nuclear holocaust. Cohn survived through God's oversight; he was, just then, at work at the bottom of the sea. God condemns Cohn to death through a rent in a cloud: "Live quickly—a few deep breaths and go your way." That this is the only certain admonition any of us has from God does not occur to Cohn. Accompanied by another survivor, a chimpanzee, Cohn arrives at an idyllic island in the Indian Ocean; there he sets up housekeeping and civilization. The chimp, fitted with an artificial larynx by a German doctor, begins to talk in a German accent.

Moreover, he wants to talk about Jesus, which leads Cohn to wonder whether an island populated by one Christian and one Jew can indeed be Paradise.

Other chimps appear; Cohn's surviving shipmate teaches them to talk as well. How can such miracles occur? Malamud is silent; his concern with plausibility lies elsewhere. "If explanation was needed," Cohn concludes, "the world was different from once it was; and what might happen, and what could not, he was not as sure of as he used to be." Presently Cohn finds himself lecturing the assembled apes on man's history, science, and literature in the hope that they, the world's inheritors, can avoid his fate. He revises the Ten Commandments to suit present circumstances. He prepares a seder, using available materials, so that the chimps, like the Jews of Exodus, may celebrate their deliverance. All, for a time, is well—Cohn conceives that God may again come to love his creation—until the matter of sex arises. And then, in rapid order, come murder, betrayal, degeneracy, and an apocalypse that is both tragic and appropriate to what has gone before.

What began as wry comedy concludes very darkly indeed. Not the least of Malamud's accomplishments here is his graceful, inexorable transition from one extreme to the other, though I must say he takes his time getting fully under way. A third of his novel is gone before he closes in on the issues: what it is to be human, why man invented stories ("Man began to tell them to keep his life from washing away"). Like all good allegories, *God's Grace* hints at essential questions: how like man is his cousin the ape? What role does language play in civilization? If other primates are genetically nearly indistinguishable from us, must they sin as we do? One question is confronted directly: "Why hadn't [God] created men equal to whom He imagined?" To this, God provides an answer: He created man to perfect himself.

Malamud intends us, I think, to grasp the parallels between Cohn and the protagonists of other stories: he is (in order of publication) part Moses, part Prospero, part Robinson Crusoe—and perhaps part Dr. Moreau and Ralph (of *Lord of the Flies*) as well. That is to say, Cohn is a decent, competent man who tinkers with evolution; a leader, he is angered by his tribe's relapses. The apes with which he is matched are distinctive individuals; though they imitate Cohn, Malamud never allows us to forget their otherness. In short, *God's Grace* is precisely what a fantasy for adults ought to be: at first charming, then affecting, and finally deeply moving.

September 1982

DOCTOROW'S AMBITION

RELUCTANT AS I AM to admit that reviewing is anything less than an exact science, I suspect that the dithyrambs with which E. L. Doctorow's *Ragtime* was greeted five years ago were largely misdirected. The man's politics may be to the left, but his fiction is surely to the right, swimming securely in the main current of American literature. It should have been possible to praise his clever and engaging novel without advancing fatuous claims for its supposed inventions. Nevertheless, Doctorow was applauded for inventing a gimmick that has been around since Dante's day and made wildly popular by Walter Scott: the introduction of historical persons into a fictional narrative. Those who were determined to find something new in *Ragtime* failed utterly to notice something old: that the story of Coalhouse Walker's revenge, which occupies the novel's second half, was adopted from a nineteenth-century novella, Heinrich von Kleist's *Michael Kohlhaas.*

Doctorow's novels may differ in form and tone, but (and this is what makes him a traditional writer) his experiments with split narration and parallel stories are less consequential than is the consistency of his concern with American history, American myths, and the Great American Plot. You remember the G.A.P. An innocent, lonely, ambitious (or proud) hero (or heroine) is corrupted by a callous, hypocritical society. He (she) would have to be nuts to have known better. Expiation is possible, though usually unpleasant. These three sentences may be as easily applied to Hester Prynne, Isabel Archer, Huck Finn, Jay Gatsby, Jake Barnes, and Quentin Compson as to the narrator of *Loon Lake.*

The narrator's name is Joe, but we are not told as much until page 71 because Doctorow has been saving it for an appropriately dramatic moment. Until then, he gives us Joe's story in both first- and third-person forms, blending it confusingly with the first- and third-person narration of another principal, a derelict poet named Warren Penfield, to whose dismal verse we are given ample introduction. If I make the book sound difficult so far, it is, yet it is worth pushing through these briars to reach the fields beyond.

The year is 1936, the depth of the Depression. Joe, eighteen, runs away from his miserable working-class parents in New Jersey. He joins a carnival, but when his friend, the fat lady, is raped to death, he flees again to the redeeming Adirondack forest. There, at night, he sees a private train go by: in the back car a naked young woman holds a dress before her. (There is a lot of night in this book; its most luminous scenes take place at night.) Joe follows the track to its end: an isolated, fifty-thousand-acre mountain retreat overlooking a lake owned by a mysterious industrialist with gangster connections. Attacked by a pack of wild dogs, Joe becomes an uninvited guest; in time, he befriends Penfield, who had come to Loon Lake to kill the murderous industrialist but remained as resident poet, and in time, with Penfield's help, Joe steals the naked young woman away.

So far, so romantic. Doctorow, a connoisseur of American literary myth, draws deeply from Thomas Wolfe and Scott Fitzgerald. *Loon Lake* is neither as angry as *The Book of Daniel* nor as affectless as *Ragtime*, but it is as much concerned with our American myths of guilt, celebrity, power, and loneliness as they. Penfield, for instance, escapes from Loon Lake in a seaplane with the industrialist's wife, an aviatrix much like Amelia Earhart; their plane disappears, just as Earhart's did. Joe escapes with his girl, an apprentice gangster moll, in a Mercedes-Benz, hoping to lose himself "doing the life" as an assembly-line worker in one of the industrialist's auto-body factories.

Imperceptibly, romance yields to realism and then to melodrama. Joe's work in the factory and for an underground union, his fear that he and his girl have been followed by gangsters working for their former host, his friendship for an ambiguous co-worker and his child bride, transform him briefly from a "calculating, heedless" desperado into a creature nearly too human to look after himself. But not for long, of course: "The desolate chance of real destiny" reclaims him. Joe returns to Loon Lake on a mission of revenge. The form of this revenge is revealed only on the novel's final page and then it is not shown but only stated. Far be it from me to reveal it, though an alert reader should be able to guess something of this sort was up. Penfield, the disintegrating poet, provides a clue in a letter to Joe: "Perhaps we all reappear," he writes, "perhaps all our lives are impositions one on another." Perhaps, but in the end, Doctorow's kicker is unsatisfactory.

This is an irritating book and an engrossing one. It's difficult to keep Joe's story separate from Penfield's and alarming to see how easily Doctorow slips from really elegant writing into pretentious, even purple prose. Apparently someone suggested to him that his shifting narrations and sequences in time resemble the surface of a lake, but that's nonsense: the reflections and refractions from water never show us what happened after and before. Still, Doctorow *is* a storyteller, a mythmaker. The scenes he develops have hooks that catch and hold.

September 1980

The distinguishing characteristic of E. L. Doctorow's work is its double vision. In each of his books he experiments with the forms of fiction, working for effects that others haven't already achieved; in each, he develops a tone, a structure, a texture, that he hasn't used before. At the same time, he's a deeply traditional writer, reworking American history, American literary archetypes, even exhausted subliterary genres. It's an astonishing performance, really; about the only thing a reader approaching one of his books can be sure of is that Doctorow won't give him quite what he expects.

Lives of the Poets works in a way I've never seen attempted before. It can be read as a collection of short stories, or as a novel, or as both at once. Again, Doctorow embraces one of the hoariest of literary themes: the peculiar vulnerability of a writer transmuting fragments of his own experience into fiction. It's hard to imagine how anything new can be wrought from such material; half the unpublishable novels rejected by editors today—and too many of those published—deal with just this subject. Yet Doctorow brings it off triumphantly—in part because he never shows us his writer writing, and in part because he says nothing directly about the process of writing fiction. Instead, he shows us how a writer's mind works.

Six short stories precede the novella from which the collection takes its name. The novella should be read last, but it may be useful to consider it first, for it invites us to infer that its narrator, known only as Jonathan, is the author of the other stories. Jonathan is a husband and a father; he has two houses and yet he has taken an apartment for himself in SoHo. There perhaps he will write, or welcome his mistress, should she return from roaming the world. "I am doing this," he says, "to find out why I am doing it." At fifty, Jonathan is undergoing a full-dress midlife crisis; he's concerned now with matters that never trouble the young. He's thinking about the *zeitgeist*, entropy, and "the doom of commitment . . . this drift through the blood of my obsolescence." Everything seems to be winding down: his body succumbs to bumps and stiffness, his friends are falling out of marriage and talking too much about it. "Whatever happened to discretion? Where is pride? What has caused this decline in tact and duplicity?" Yet Jonathan is far from despair. He senses in the city around him signs of renewal. Though Jonathan never comments on his work, the reader can recognize certain phrases, images, and turns of thought that Jonathan has already altered to serve the six preceding stories. In creating the fictional Jonathan, Doctorow creates the fiction that he has made art out of his life; the truth is, he has created a life to account for the fiction.

If the novella is Doctorow's *Odyssey*, an epic voyage through its narrator's sensibility, full of unplanned detours and moral dangers, the stories, too, are about migrations of different sorts. Each has its own style, its own place, its own time, yet there's a unity as well. Each is written with the utmost economy and restraint; in each, Doctorow is looking for open wounds in the heart—he takes us where the hurt is. Against his will, a boy is obliged by his aunt to forge letters from his dead father to his grandmother, who is unaware of her son's death. Another boy (which is to say another fragment of Jonathan's experience put to use in fiction) discovers his mother making love to his tutor; unable to cope with the experience, the boy betrays his mother to his father. In a third story, reminiscent of those in *Winesburg, Ohio*, Doctorow exposes the loneliness of a seemingly vivacious young woman on the verge of a nervous breakdown.

One of Doctorow's narrators observes that Houdini had a routine: "getting out of the kind of straitjacket to break the heart." The image serves a precise purpose in the story, but it's a metaphor, too: all these stories are about straitjackets to break the heart. Better than any fiction I know, *Lives of the Poets* illuminates the sources from which fiction springs.

November 1984

THE DECIBEL LEVELS OF PHILIP ROTH

LISTEN! The sound of buffalo hooves thundering on the horizon. Angry readers are swarming with brooms and bicycle chains. This time they'll *really* wallop Philip Roth, stomp him for his dirty mind, his grotesquerie, but mostly for all that money—a fortune, really—that lured him from one publishing conglomerate to another, and for what? A long novel is finished, but we must wait till spring to see it, and so as a teaser, an example of how really successful writers work, we have ... a short story about a man who turns into a female breast.

Something to appeal to that vestigial freak-show addict in us all? Perhaps, but don't go away yet. Most of Roth's best work is at least partly aimed at some arrested area of our development. Excess, obsession, perversion (in the broadest sense of vectors deflected from their proper courses), the self-enclosed universes that we build around ourselves and our efforts to escape them: these are Roth's themes. Humor teetering on hysteria, the shriek deflated by self-conscious irony, the narcissistic maundering of the analysand: these are his tones of voice. What upsets many people is Roth's delight in outrageousness—about sex, about politics, about Jewishness. What he writes is not only disliked by many intelligent readers, it is detested or dismissed contemptuously. And that is a shame because Roth is not only a skillful craftsman, but a serious one. At the end of *The Breast* he pauses to remind us: you must take this seriously.

Something happened to David Kepesh one night: an "endocrinopathic catastrophe." David turned into a detached mammary gland, "an organism with the general shape of a football, or a dirigible," with a nipple at one end. David may now be a six-foot, 155-pound lump of fatty tissue, but he is still hung up on sex. The nipple now, which was once his penis, is the center of David's performance: he speaks and hears through it, receives sexual stimulation through it. (I'm sorry, but no summary will make this story sound in any way tolerable; the story is not tolerable anyway, nor was it meant to be.) David is in a hospital, fearful that his dilemma may be televised. His father and mistress come to console him; even his psychiatrist keeps up his visits.

"You want me to be *ordinary—you* expect me to be *ordinary* in this condition!" David yells. "What do any of you know about grotesque!" And yet it is hard not to be ordinary. David, the professor of literature, listens to recordings of Shakespeare and memorizes long passages. He runs through a list of alternatives to being a breast: he is dreaming; he is mad; perhaps he is a blind quadriplegic. What has happened to him happened in the stories he once taught: Kafka's "The Metamorphosis," Gogol's "The Nose."

Roth's sure-handed craftsmanship is evident here; the story is entertaining and often funny, but finally it doesn't work. Roth suggests themes he doesn't pursue—is the story, for instance, meant to parody the oral phase of sexual development, with David on the giving, rather than the receiving end?—and yet I would not have wished the story longer. Perhaps what's wrong with it is that Roth did not decide whether it was to be a buoyant farce like Gogol's story, or a dark parable like Kafka's. And there is probably no middle ground to choose, not if one wants, after all the comedy, to be serious, to leave something that will work at some root level of the reader's unconscious.

September 1972

The Great American Novel is as elusive as the Loch Ness monster. (When was the last confirmed sighting? In 1885, when it looked like *Huckleberry Finn?*) Mythical beasts, the both of them, but that won't stop us from setting up our telescopes and yardsticks, or from speculating: *where* will it surface? What will it look like? Baseball is another vortex for men's fantasies. The most *discussable* of sports, it is in fact two very different games that point toward a third. One deals with measurable reality (baseball's familiar obsession with statistics); another with our memories of games and players past (fact yields to fiction here), and the third with possibilities: the performances yet to come (though they probably won't), which will reaffirm our childhood faith that baseball is about something important.

Philip Roth knows we need such beliefs—and in *The Great American Novel* he tramples all over them. Smitty, his narrator, is eighty-seven and loopy; he insists he was once a famous sports columnist, and he improves his time in a state institution by writing the Great American Novel about the Ruppert Mundys, a major-league team that, with the rest of the Patriot League, fell victim to scandal and corruption. The league was dismantled at the end of World War II and erased from the record books. Smitty is incensed by the conspiracy—nobody will admit to having heard of the Mundys, of Luke Gofannon, who hit sixty-three home runs in 1928, or even of Smitty—and so he puts it all down, the tall tales, the sex, the Communist infiltration: a definite addition to our mythology, this story of how baseball should have been.

Once (Smitty tells us) the Mundys dominated the league, but in 1943 few players were available and the club lost its stadium to the government. The homeless Mundys became a permanent visiting team, staffed by a one-legged catcher, a one-armed right fielder, and a fifty-two-year-old third baseman who falls asleep in the field. Smitty interrupts his account of the Mundys' decline (they will lose 120 games in 1943) to tell us how the most promising rookie pitcher in history lost a game in which he pitched seventy-eight consecutive strikes; how the Christian gentleman who managed the Mundys (but never on Sunday) brought baseball to darkest Africa; how a seven-year-old genius with managerial ambitions caused "Jewish Wheaties" to be served to the Mundys (thereafter they won all their games), and how a player named Spit Baal invented "a pitch so juicy that by the end of an inning the catcher had to shake himself off like a dog come in from romping in the rain."

And that, fans, is only the beginning. This kind of story could go on forever and nearly does—restraint and just generally knowing when to stop not being among Roth's strong points. In fact, Roth's strongest skill, his ability to show how people become unhinged as they respond to the demands made upon them by the narrow worlds in which they live—"people living beyond their psychological and moral means," as Roth said in an interview last year—is missing from this novel. Intensity has been abandoned for a story ideally suited to Roth's lesser, more eclectic skills: his talent for parody and caricature; his inclination to extend and complicate a situation rather than to plunge very deeply into it; his fondness for excess; his energy; his unflagging (if conventional) imagination.

He has pulled off some remarkable set pieces here (most notably a scene in which Roth parodies Hemingway parodying Melville) and solved some touchy technical problems (how, in our sensitive generation, to be funny about blacks, Jews, and women while exploiting their most offensive stereotypes). Five years ago, in *The Universal Baseball Association, Inc.*, Robert Coover told a marvelous story about a madman who invented a baseball league and played all the games in his head. His is the more intense and unified vision, but Roth's, inclining to slapstick and cartoon figures, is the funnier. The book is, for all its limitations, simply hilarious: I laughed aloud for two days.

May 1973

No writer alive can sustain a full-length novel at as high a decibel level as Philip Roth, though Joyce Carol Oates, working without Roth's humor, comes close. *Portnoy's Complaint*, the novel that made him rich as well as famous, was about as noisy as a novel can get. *Our Gang* and *The Breast*, though lesser efforts, were not noticeably less clangorous. People living on the brink of collapse, unable to function because they have overextended themselves, lacerated themselves, locked themselves into obsessions and other prisons of their own construction—these are Roth's creatures, whom he treats with affection and wit. More than most of his contemporaries, Roth takes big risks with his fiction, working through different modes for effects and scenes considerably larger than life. In *My Life as a Man*, for instance, he must surely have intended to create the most intolerable marriage ever seen in American fiction, complete with a wife-beating scene unequaled in all literature. Yet even with such a mission, Roth's stridency seemed more contained, a function of his characters rather than of the author himself. I must confess I liked the din, but for the present Roth has turned quiet, more artful, and *The Ghost Writer* is his best novel yet.

There's plenty of emotional disorder here—from Roth we expect nothing less—but in this story the anguish exists to serve the manner in which it is revealed. On the surface, nothing very dramatic occurs. Nathan Zuckerman, a twenty-three-year-old writer who has published four promising short stories, arrives one evening at the home of a much older and distinguished author, E. I. Lonoff. There he encounters—and conceives a calflike infatuation for—Lonoff's protégée, Amy Bellette, a lovely young woman of vaguely European background. Nathan pays homage to his host; Lonoff proposes a toast "to a wonderful new writer." Late that night, Nathan overhears Amy making sexual overtures to Lonoff. Lonoff's wife quarrels with her husband and stalks out the door the next morning; the old writer goes stumbling after her.

From such bare events emerges a complex story of fathers and children, the artist's responsibility, the deceptive line between what a writer knows and what he imagines. Nathan narrates the story from a remove of twenty years. He knows, now, that when he arrived at Lonoff's house that evening, he was seeking a surrogate father; his own had recently quarreled with him over a story Nathan had written about his family—a story his father insists will confirm in gentile readers the contempt they reserve for the Jews. Believing that art mustn't knuckle under to social obligations, Nathan turns to Lonoff, who confirms his theory by the example of his own reclusive existence. "Fantasy for thirty years," says Lonoff of his life, but his wife knows better: her famous husband's modesty and fussiness mask his intolerable selfishness.

Amy, too, must be pressed into Nathan's service before this night is over. Eavesdropping, he grasps the erotic potential of her relationship with Lonoff and responds as any beginning writer must: "Oh, if only I could have imagined the scene I'd overheard! If only I could invent as presumptuously as real life!" Immediately, he sets about to do so, endowing the elusive Amy with more mystery still. Just suppose Amy were a Jewish girl who had survived the concentration camps ... suppose she were Anne Frank, or thought she was. Arriving in this country as a young woman, she finds that her childhood diary has become famous. She is a writer! But for her testament to be effective (the artist's responsibility again), she must maintain the fiction of her death, must deny her father the news of her survival. Nathan might marry her. Who then would dare to criticize a Jewish writer who had married ... Anne Frank?

As if such complexities, such nifty footwork with a theme and variations, were not enough for a novella, Roth throws in a clever bit of sleight of hand. *The Ghost Writer*, as he makes emphatically clear, is a kind of homage to Henry James, just as *The Breast* was intended as a kind of homage to Kafka. That night at Lonoff's Nathan reads James's *The Middle Years*, a story about an ailing writer who yearns for a second chance at life but must content himself with the devotion of a young admirer of his work. This writer knows there is no such second chance; so does Lonoff, as he rejects Amy's proposals. Master and disciple, young America confronting old Europe, ambiguous ancestry, art as a dubious balm for the wounds of life—these are James's themes, and now Roth, in this warm and witty story, has made them his as well. James's writer, ending his career, speaks of "the madness of art." Nathan, at the brink of his, offers what may be the contemporary equivalent: "What *do* I know," he asks, "other than what I can imagine?"

September 1979

Philip Roth's new novel is more necessary than satisfactory.

I'm glad he wrote it, but I'm also glad to hear he's finished now with his alter ego, that notorious and embattled Jewish writer Nathan Zuckerman. The discomforts of great commercial success has been a popular theme in American fiction since Howells wrote *The Rise of Silas Lapham*, but in assessing the grief that assails a popular writer, Roth has enlisted three novels to do the work of perhaps two and a half. *The Anatomy Lesson* offers an important variation on the theme of the trilogy, and a few grand comic scenes, but signs of strain have begun to intrude. Roth is overworking his material, stretching it too thin, repeating himself. There's an irony here: in this story, Zuckerman has exhausted his writer's capital; having used up his life in his books, he's unable to write at all.

To recapitulate as briefly as possible: the central theme of the Zuckerman trilogy is "the unreckoned consequences of art." In *The Ghost Writer*, which remains Roth's best novel to date, the young Nathan Zuckerman is exposed to the perils of the life of a literary recluse. In *Zuckerman Unbound*, he must endure the perils of literary celebrity. In *The Anatomy Lesson*, Zuckerman confronts the perils of being a famous writer who is finished with writing. Forget fame and wealth, Roth seems to say, forget the women who pull up their skirts as soon as they enter a writer's room: the writer's life is not a happy one. It is, quite literally, a pain in the neck.

The new book begins with pain and sex—topics any reader can relate to—as if Roth meant to hook us into his story before veering off into the literary wars. Zuckerman, at forty, is at the end of his tether. Since he published *Carnovsky*, the novel that made him famous four years ago, he can't write at all. Writing is not just impossible, it hurts. For eighteen months, Zuckerman has been afflicted with an undiagnosed pain "that ran from behind his right ear into his neck, then branched downward beneath the scapula like a menorah held bottom side up." Work at the typewriter has become "ten talons clawing at twenty-six letters. Some animal carrying on in the zoo like that and you'd think it was horrifying." The medical men are full of suggestions: the pain is expiation for the life he has led, for the novel he wrote that caused his parents such grief, for his accumulated hostility, for making "a Jewish comedy out of genital life." Three times di-

vorced, Zuckerman has four women attending to his comfort, but
what really keeps him going is a mixture of marijuana, Percodan,
and vodka, "the best pain suppressor of all."

Zuckerman has other problems. He's losing his hair. Milton
Appel, the country's most influential Jewish critic, has attacked
Zuckerman's work in terms as irritating and persistent as the pain
lodged in his neck. But what bothers Zuckerman most is his recognition that he's exhausted himself as a subject for his writing.
"My life as cud, that's what I'm running out of. Swallow as experience, then up from the gut for a second go as art." Zuckerman,
the writer as patient who needs to be cured, decides to become a
medical student. Doctoring will release him from the prison of
himself. Listen to other people's stories for a change. "Other people. Somebody should have told me about them long ago."

The good stuff in *The Anatomy Lesson* survives a second
reading. I've read it twice now—with a long interval between—
and both times I've found myself pressing toward the end. Over
the years, Roth has refined his tone of voice, his comedy, and his
mastery of fictional techniques, but if he's now incapable of con-
juring up a dull scene, he's still fully capable of running a good
idea into the ground. Flying high on Percodan, Zuckerman en-
gages a limousine with a young woman driver. He says he's Milton Appel, a publisher of pornography. Talking nonstop—a
consequence of the drug—Zuckerman translates himself into another life. It's a marvelous scene until Roth carries it too long;
Zuckerman has the details, even the rationale, of this pornographer's business just right. The episode reminds us of Zuckerman's persuasiveness in translating the enigmatic Amy Bellette
into Anne Frank in *The Ghost Writer*.

Roth's reviewers have for decades confused the author with
his protagonists, even as Zuckerman's fiction is assumed by his
family and other Jews to be a libel upon them. It's an imperti-
nence, really: art is what one makes from life; it is not life itself.
Zuckerman is not Roth, though he shares some of his biography.
Roth (I hope) never stewed at such an interminable boil over
Irving Howe's rejection of his work as Zuckerman does over
Appel's. As Updike does with his two alter egos, Rabbit Ang-
strom and Henry Bech, Roth uses Zuckerman as a safety valve:
Zuckerman can spout all the bile and undifferentiated anger that

Roth, a most mannerly man, cannot. Useful as he is to his author, can his ghost have been exorcized with this novel? I hope so, but it's hard to shake the image of Sherlock Holmes crawling back from the brink of the Reichenbach Falls.

October 1983

THE LAST OF THORNTON WILDER

FOR SEVERAL REASONS we should try to like *Theophilus North.* Thornton Wilder is one of our most decorated writers, but he is seventy-six now and without plans for another book, so we must take seriously the valedictory tone of this one. Themes previously explored are here recapitulated. The hero's past is very nearly Wilder's own. Beyond the author's fondness for a youth that might have been, there is some talk of Shakespeare's plays, and perhaps Wilder means this story to be his *Tempest:* a tale in which some magic is worked, some wrongs righted, a match made, and the relation of master and man redefined before the sorcerer's wand is broken. Perhaps—but something is missing.

In the summer of 1926, a thirty-year-old teacher named Theophilus North comes to Newport, Rhode Island, to tutor the children of the fashionable rich and to read out loud to the rich themselves. He is well educated and has at various times aspired to nine different careers, ranging from saint to scoundrel. In Newport he discovers nine separate cities differing in the age and social class of their inhabitants. In the stories of which this novel is composed, North marches through them all—careers and cities—healing the sick, repairing marriages, rescuing a damsel from injustice, restoring life and health to the old and frail, and freedom to the confined.

Why should the socially secure—or even the poor, for that matter—turn to this junior guru for salvation? His ambiguous social standing gains him entry by both the front and back doors of any house; he will lie for a greater good but never betray a trust; he will even go to bed with a woman if there's some reason to do so other than whatever fun might attend the sex. His success, his ability to trap people into virtuous conduct, derives from his practice of what was recently called "situation ethics," which can be defined as action based on invincible confidence in one's own moral perspective. "I seldom offer advice," North says, but in fact both he and his author are intolerably didactic, endlessly thrusting admonitions and vague aphorisms at wan lovers, eccentric millionaires, high-spirited servants—not to mention the suffering reader.

An antique heartiness pervades the dialogue: "Zounds! Holy cabooses!" says Theophilus North, and then: "How could a decent American boy like you get mixed up with a gang like that? ... What would your mother think, if she knew what you were doing?" North, thank goodness, is on the receiving end of some of this guff himself: "May I ask your promise as a Yale man and a Christian . . . ?" For these and other sufficient reasons, we want to steady the hand of the villain who, early in the story, crouches in the bushes with a pistol aimed at North. Gently now: *squeeze* the trigger.

Goldarn it, he misses. Wilder, of course, rejoices in his young hero—and his refashioning of his own experience. But his tale is mannered, romantic, and sentimental—qualities that would not be so disabling had they been controlled by the irony that Wilder introduced into his first novel, *The Cabala* (a novel, by the way, that has much in common with this, its fatter sibling), or the wit that informed his best book, *The Ides of March*. As it is, the loosely connected episodes of *Theophilus North* offer only comic-opera scenes, a pallid playfulness. Something is missing: Sheridan's wit, perhaps, or Mozart's music.

October 1973

TWO STORIES FOR THE EAR

BEWARE THE ADVOCATES of speedy reading. Good writing must be heard in the ear and any novel that is well written takes longer to read than one that is not. Occasionally we who believe in a kind of Pythagorean perfection of prose find ourselves like so many second-graders mutely moving our lips, testing whether a writer's arrangement of phrases, words, and syllables is indeed harmonious, is sufficiently deceitful in its seeming lack of effort. Both Toni Morrison's *Sula* and Cormac McCarthy's *Child of God* are a pleasure to the ear, and the former seems to me an exemplary fable, its brevity belied by its surprising scope and depth.

The story is set in a Negro district outside a small Ohio city; most of the events take place in the years between the two world wars. Here, as anywhere in America, the blacks have created a world of their own and know, given whatever circumstances, what to expect. "They did not believe death was accidental—life might be, but death was deliberate. . . . The purpose of evil was to survive it. . . ." Sula Peace, an attractive black girl, becomes for this community a dangerous and finally evil person, accomplice or witness to the harm or death of those who had a claim upon her care. Combining her grandmother's arrogance and her mother's self-indulgence, Sula grows to be a hollow person, a slave of her fears and whims who in time betrays her only childhood friend.

Sula's moral and spiritual entropy is set against the essential mysteries of death and sex, friendship and poverty, and the desperation and vulnerability of man that one encounters in many stories, but rarely so economically expressed. Toni Morrison's narrative contains symbolical and fabulous elements and is laid out in small set pieces, snapshots arranged in a pattern that cannot be anticipated until the author is done with her surprises. There is a great deal of humor here, and a sense of celebration, in spite of deaths by water and fire, of all there is that a man or a woman can lose—husbands, lovers, children, even misery—and all of it is beautifully wrought.

Child of God, like *Sula*, demands its reader's attention from its opening sentence and is also composed in brief fragments, but Cormac McCarthy's skill as a writer is not supported by a grasp of his narrative as a whole. Lester Ballard, his central character, is an entirely numb man, a man of few words, only barely alive. "A man much for himself," McCarthy writes, who lives in a deteriorating shack and slouches with his rifle down roads by night. The scene is ostensibly Tennessee, but more nearly a caricature of a Faulknerian landscape: a place that lends itself to incest, murder, necrophilia.

McCarthy is a brilliant writer who can, in a page or two, create a blacksmith Kipling would admire, a man who explains in words close to poetry how to beat and hammer an old ax to make it new again. McCarthy can, in a few paragraphs, write about a boar pursued by hounds as if the subject were fresh, and yet against the brightness of these scenes his protagonist lumbers in silhouette. "Goddam frozen bitch," he says of the female corpse he has kept preserved to sleep with; rarely was the epithet more accurately applied. Lester's numbness would not have been so appalling had not his author seemed willing to make do with it himself.

This novel, according to its jacket blurb, "explores the limits of human degradation." Unfortunately, it explores nothing at all. Certain acts—a brain-damaged child, for instance, chewing the leg off a robin—are presented to us in McCarthy's admirably distilled prose from which all emotion has been pared away. But there is no resonance, no perspective in attendance, and these isolated episodes, left unconnected on our laps, fade from our memory even before the book is finished. Cormac McCarthy is a good writer confronted with a difficult subject; the pity is that he retired from the field before he engaged his narrative.

January 1974

JOHN UPDIKE'S DOUBLE SET OF MAPS

TWO-THIRDS CLOSET drama and one-third lumpy essay, the whole once intended to coalesce into a novel—no wonder John Updike presents *Buchanan Dying* to us much as a father would introduce an ill-formed child: affectionately, and with a parent's commitment, but a little nervous, too, about how it looks to us. And the sorry truth is, it doesn't look very good. I'll summon a few kind words in a moment, but from any realistic perspective, Updike's first attempt at a play must be considered the runt of his otherwise impressive litter.

First, the form. It is a play meant to be read, which is another way of saying it is not a good *play*. For two of its three acts, our fifteenth president lies immobile on his deathbed, attended by various characters from his present and his past. "Dying," James Buchanan tells us, "I discover, is rather like dancing, and not un-like diplomacy; legerity and tact are paramount. I was a fair coun-try dancer in my time." Perhaps, but there is little dancing on *this* stage. Buchanan, perforce supine and elderly, must replay parts of his past with characters who will be seen and heard to be much younger; what this masochistic approach to staging does to a courtship scene with a twenty-three-year-old woman is better left unimagined.

To further encumber himself, Updike attempts to re-create the diction of Buchanan's times. Virtually every writer of histori-cal fictions from Shakespeare to Anthony Burgess has made con-temporaries of his characters; for the sake of vitality, it is only sensible to have Caesar speak as an Elizabethan or a sardonic American statesman. But Updike has gone to speeches and letters for his phrases and the result lies thick in the ear: "Then cast off this prothonotarial tether," cries one of Buchanan's drinking buddies. Buchanan's own speech frequently presses against the rhythms of blank verse.

Buchanan himself is hardly a leavening agent. A Democrat who preceded Lincoln in office, he is little known today. Said to be cool, hard, and ambitious, even treacherous to his friends and associates, Buchanan exemplified the antithesis of Jacksonian activism. Fearing that "firm action meant the abyss. Inaction was the one last hope," and convinced that the Constitution did not provide for forcible maintenance of the Union, Buchanan hoped the nation's troubles might dissolve if left to simmer unprovoked. Updike presents him as a haunted, self-conscious man, aware of his own "impotent detachment and cool fatality." Buchanan's difficulty, in Updike's view, is his determination to step back from the abyss, whatever that abyss may be: a commitment to love or faith, fear of a forest or civil war. Far-sighted in one eye and near-sighted in the other, Buchanan's ambiguity of vision impaired his life—hence, Buchanan dying.

Updike's portrait of the man is sympathetic, intelligent, concerned. There are scenes in this play, and sections in the long concluding essay, that are felicitous and interesting—but not enough to redeem this wordy, ungainly, and ultimately ill-advised attempt at theater.

June 1974

Let's hope the institution of marriage survives its detractors, for without it there would be no more adultery and without adultery two-thirds of our novelists would have to go into air-traffic control or data processing. Adultery as a form of human anguish is the central theme of most of John Updike's fiction; indeed, it has proven fiction's most trusty, least exhaustible theme since the days of medieval romances. *Romance* is the word that Updike applies to *Marry Me:* clearly he is aware of the continuity. Like Chrétien de Troyes, he uses the narrow confines of an illicit affair to explore problems of choice, will, and responsibility, the problem of a kind of love that is mostly pain, that precludes rational thought and, by becoming an obsession, threatens social order.

The time is spring and summer 1962, the place coastal Connecticut. Jerry is married to Ruth and Richard to Sally; they are all about thirty and have lots of young kids. Jerry and Sally are having an affair. They meet on beaches, fly separately to meet in Washington, tell a lot of lies. They want to get married. Sally feels she is already Jerry's wife and "this strange fact, unknown to the world but known to them, made whatever looked wrong right, whatever seemed foolish wise."

Jerry is more perceptive: "What we have, sweet Sally, is an ideal love. It's ideal because it can't be realized. As far as the world goes, we don't exist ... any attempt to start existing, to move out of this pain, will kill us." In calm moments, Jerry knows that if they were to get married, they'd lose the kind of love they have; he also knows they'll lose it anyway. Love is not enough: it must become relaxed and right in the world's eyes or it will be lost.

Ruth discovers the affair before Richard does. In fact, she and Richard had had their own brief affair a few months earlier—an adventure that lacked the passion that breaks up families, that went unnoticed, that left Ruth feeling wiser and a better wife. Her discovery of Jerry and Sally's involvement strips it at once of its adolescent, idyllic character—not because of Ruth, who remains stoically sensible, but because of Jerry, who is a coward and smug in his grief and cannot decide what to do. He can't bring himself to leave his family; he can't live without Sally; he wants Ruth to advise him, to tell him to go. "I'm not happy," Ruth tells him, "and I don't want a divorce." The summer dissolves in quarrels, discussions, confrontations, decisions made and then abandoned.

Updike shows us with appalling clarity the exact course of the disintegration of these two families. He manages to convey—for me, at least—a kind of spiritual fear, and he does it without resorting to violence or melodrama—no children die, there are no great drunken rows, not even much shouting. These are educated, civilized people and although Sally is greedy and Jerry spoiled, the four of them mean to behave sensibly, mean to do the least amount of damage. They worry about the children, about money, about destroying marriages that everyone admits are basically sound—about knowing what's right and doing what's wrong anyway.

This understatement, this unwavering vision fixed on only

four characters, are part of what makes the story so effective. Updike's best fiction has always been his most narrowly focused; in
this novel the plot is direct—complex without becoming complicated by symbols thrashing obtrusively just behind the canvas—
and refreshingly free from the portentousness that has marred
several of his most ambitious novels. *Marry Me* is the best-
written and least self-conscious of Updike's longer fiction; it contains his most sophisticated and sympathetic portraits of women.
There are, I suppose, married and divorced couples who will read
it without being moved, but I wouldn't want to know them.

November 1976

The cliché has it that life imitates art, but the sorrier truth is
that life more often imitates satire. Witness Andrew Young, our
U.N. ambassador, speculating recently on African ambition: "If
they had a chance to get what we have in Atlanta," he told a
crowd at Stanford, "I think all Africans would buy it. It just so
happens that we Americans do things better than anyone else on
earth." Would he have said the same in Kampala? Never mind:
his point is precisely the point that John Updike makes in *The
Coup*, a novel about the last African to resist the Americanization
of his continent.

The story is told by Colonel Hakim Felix Ellelloû, the de-
posed dictator of a former French colony now called Kush, an
immense, barren, drought-stricken land that comprises part of the
Sahara and some fever forests as well. Not even the most optimistic of Third World propagandists could call Kush a developing country—it is all but dead, which suits its former ruler
well. Like his author, Ellelloû is something of a poet, advancing
his narrative by chains of simile and metaphor; he is a mystic, too,
mixing the austerity of Islam with muddied Marxism. Educated
in America, he hates our country's obscenity and glut. When the
Americans try to relieve starvation in Kush by piling a mountain
of junk food on its border, Ellelloû sets fire to it—and to the official who brought it. Better to tolerate the Russians with their
"torpid monism" and their missiles implanted beneath the soil of
Kush than to endure a return to "bourgeois feudalism."

An engaging demagogue with a reactionary dream, Ellelloû
wrought a revolution in a country where there were no factories

to nationalize, no land holdings to seize. "There was poverty but not oppression; how could this be?" Nevertheless, he tries to be a good dictator, executing the old king in public and traveling about his wasteland in disguise. It does no good. His bemused subjects lust after the whorish luxuries of capitalism, and in his absence his ministers intrigue with the Americans. To remove such a man in the most ironic possible way proves no problem at all. Ellelloû recognizes that he is a man whose time has passed. "Great fanatics can no longer arise," he says. "They are swamped by distractions."

The Coup is one of Updike's boldest and most imaginative performances. If at first glance it seems far removed from his usual concern with the American suburban malaise, a second glance should perceive it is not: in this, his African novel, Updike has simply reflected his satire of American culture in the mirror of his invented African black man. Only a few years ago, such a novel by an important white writer would have been inconceivable; even today, I fear, it may draw the kind of harassing fire that William Styron took when he published *The Confessions of Nat Turner.* Yet objections that Updike has not accurately represented the African mind are irrelevant. The business of a novelist is to create a world that is true only to whatever purpose he intended—and this is what Updike (who warns us that he has drawn his geography only from suspect literary sources) has gleefully, joyously accomplished.

I must add that in doing so he has indulged in some of his most rococo prose. The minaret that is a "friable phallus" and the dome that is "a blue-tiled breast" can become oppressive, and one of his sentences, by no means his longest, offers twenty-five adjectives, two adverbs, five metaphors, and three similes. Yet for the most part this ornamentation works—some of it arrestingly well. Besides—and I hope this will persuade you to read it—*The Coup* is Updike's wittiest fiction since *Bech: A Book.*

November 1978

John Updike's tenth novel, *Rabbit Is Rich,* is one of his very best, yet I suspect it will gain him no new admirers. Whatever it is about his longer work that offends the unconverted blossoms wildly here: the rich prose coiled in serpentine sentences, the spiritual anemia of his characters, the insistence on geographical precision in describing the wilder shores of sex. This is not, I suppose I should say at once, the kind of book you would want your parents to read. Nevertheless, Updike has matured as an artist in the past ten years and if in his new novel he is again concerned with themes and techniques that he has previously explored, he brings to them an assurance, a complexity of response, even a kind of serenity that was lacking before.

Once more, Updike's hero is Harry (Rabbit) Angstrom, whom we first met as a frightened young man attempting to flee his marriage in *Rabbit, Run*, and met again ten years later as a blue-collar worker, thicker in his girth and sensibilities, in *Rabbit Redux*. Ten more years have passed. It is 1979 and as the world seems to wind down about him—there are Soviet tanks in Kabul and hostages in Iran, the pope is in America and the gasoline lines extend for blocks—Harry finds himself fat, forty-six, and finally middle class. He lives with his wife and mother-in-law in Brewer, Pennsylvania, and runs with reasonable efficiency the Toyota dealership that the two women have inherited. Harry has joined the Rotary and the newest country club in town; he feels for the first time almost happy. "He sees his life as just beginning, on clear ground at last, now that he has a margin of resources, and the stifled terror that always made him restless has dulled down."

His euphoria can't last, of course. Harry is one of literature's most consistent losers. A man more acted upon than acting, he hopes only to find a rut to wallow in, and yet there is a part of Harry that welcomes disaster. Events conspire against him. A leggy girl shows up at the Toyota shop, prodding Harry's memory and desire: the girl, he imagines, may be the illegitimate daughter he has never seen. Harry's son, Nelson, quits college and, with a pregnant girl in tow, resumes living at home. Bitter, fearful, loathing his father and "tired of being young. There's so much wasted energy to it," Nelson imposes his useless presence on Harry's used-car division. And then there's the woman in a string bikini by the country club pool, the new young wife of one of Harry's golfing buddies and the focus of Harry's rejuvenated lust.

From such midlife, middle-class banality, Updike has crafted an intense, yet delicate comedy suffused with a melancholy recognition of mortality. Images of death and the flesh's frailty abound; even on the golf course "green seems a shade of black. Every blade of grass at his feet is an individual life that will die, that has flourished to no purpose. The fairway springy beneath his feet blankets the dead." Harry, so often cowardly, so reliably loutish, is himself the source of much of this novel's negative thinking because much of what happens in this novel takes place within Harry's head. Were he not so complexly conceived, so sensitive to what others cannot bear to say about themselves, we could not endure his reappearances. Harry stands, I suspect, as Updike's alter ego: the instinctive bigot that neither he nor we would ever dare let loose. What Harry says is what the rest of us hear occasionally chattering away inside our skulls, but which (of course) we do not really think—and would never permit ourselves to say aloud.

How, then, can he not be appealing? Particularly when Harry, reflecting on his sorry condition, is allowed such elegant prose? "When Harry was little God used to spread in the dark above his bed . . . and then when the bed became strange and the girl in the next aisle grew armpit hair He entered into the blood and muscle and nerve as an odd command and now He had withdrawn, giving Harry the respect due from one well-off gentleman to another, but for a calling card left in the pit of the stomach, a bit of lead true as a plumb bob pulling Harry down to all those leaden dead in the hollow earth below." In passages like that— and there are many such here—Updike seems less engaged in writing modern fiction than a meditative essay in the manner of Montaigne or Thomas Browne.

Updike hasn't done with Rabbit. The next decade, I expect, will see him felled by a coronary. Ten years from now, look for *Rabbit Recovers*, or even *Rabbit Resurgens*.

September 1981

In his extended exploration through our suburban malaise— the contradictions of marriage, the anguish of adultery, and the frustrating search for one's self—John Updike has used two sets of maps. One of these, surely, was assembled by John Bartholomew & Son, the Edinburgh firm that designed the great atlas for the *Times* of London: it accounts for the precise, even relentless realism that informs Updike's *Rabbit* novels and his short stories about the Maples. The other, I suspect, is the work of a medieval cartographer: a man who wrote "Here be dragons" in the blank spaces, who knew that topographical features may have moral significance. This is the map Updike followed when he wrote *The Centaur, Couples,* and *The Coup;* it's the map he uses in *The Witches of Eastwick.*

The witches, of course, are feminists. Updike didn't invent the metaphor—feminists have applied it to themselves—but he expands it. His three witches, divorced women in their thirties who live in a tourist town on Rhode Island's coast, really do have occult powers, powers they acquired when they shed their husbands. "So many of Alexandra's remarkable powers had flowed from this mere reappropriation of her assigned self, achieved not until midlife. Not until midlife did she truly believe that she had a right to exist, that the forces of nature had created her not as an afterthought and companion . . . but as the mainstay of the continuing Creation." Alexandra makes figurines for sale in gift shops; she's the leader of the coven. Jane plays the cello and gives piano lessons. Sukie reports for the Eastwick paper. All three are involved in serial affairs with unattractive married men: "Being a divorcée in a small town is a little like playing Monopoly; eventually you land on all the properties." Thursday evenings, however, are sacred: then the coven meets to drink too much, to form "the infrangible triangle, the cone of power."

Power, that infamous agent of corruption! When the Devil comes to Eastwick to take over a dilapidated estate, he finds this liberated, if disordered, trio ripe for temptation. Updike's Devil is exactly what we would want him to be. Pushy and foul-mouthed, he plays good tennis and collects pop art. Being the Devil, he wants everybody: Alexandra, Jane, and Sukie all at once. When a fourth woman, not a witch, arrives in town, he wants her, too. At that point, the witches turn their talents from girlish tricks— summoning a thunderstorm to empty a crowded beach, turning a tennis ball into a toad—to the genuine black stuff.

The Witches of Eastwick is an attractive comedy, but a cold one. Updike's witches are interesting; they wear their necromancy lightly, yet remain unsympathetic. What can they see in the dreary men they go to bed with? And why, if they've decided that "men aren't the answer," are they so perpetually in heat? It's long been a hallmark of Updike's fiction that his characters are obsessed with sex without ever seeming to enjoy it. Sex and wit are by no means incompatible, but as soon as Updike trundles a big sex scene in through one door, his humor and charm flee through another. Thus what may be this novel's most elaborate scene—a Halloween orgy in which the four principals cavort around the Devil's hot tub—succumbs to heavy breathing. Orgies, admittedly, present difficulties for the literary artist, but Updike keeps trying; he's been writing them for years.

I don't mean to make too much of this—the novel does have humor and charm and a general aura of restraint. Wisely, Updike has refused to make his witches excessively spooky. The story also contains some of Updike's most elegant prose: there's a memorable description of autumn coming to New England and another, even more arresting passage in which Jane plays one of Bach's transcendently difficult suites for cello. Thinking of the music, Jane seems to sum up much of what this novel has to say: "The outside of things was sunshine and scatter; the inside of everything was death."

May 1984

GOODBYE TO JOHN CHEEVER

> *The fleetness he felt on skates seemed to have the depth of an ancient experience.*
>
> —*Oh What a Paradise It Seems*

JOHN CHEEVER died of cancer last Friday at his home in Ossining, New York. He was seventy years old, a much decorated writer of episodic novels and luminous short stories who achieved at the end of his career, commercial success as well. The phrase

"Cheever country" was never his but has nonetheless entered the language, denoting a loosely defined area populated by middle-class WASPs that extends from New York City to the suburbs of Westchester and Connecticut and to that "ingenuous town" called St. Botolphs, somewhere outside Boston.

In such novels as *Falconer* and *Bullet Park* and stories like "The Country Husband" and "The Housebreaker of Shadey Hill," Cheever examined the disappointments and fears of contemporary urban and suburban men and women, as well as their intimations of redemption. More precisely than his fellow writers, he observed and gave voice to the inarticulate agonies that lie just beneath the surface of ordinary lives. Not ideas but the ordinary stuff of humanity is the matter of Cheever's fiction; he wrote of fleeting figures in a landscape, their senses and emotions, their panics and desires, the furtive demands of the libido made plain, the ungovernable impulse translated into action. His affluent characters are much the same, beset by that numbness of the heart which has no name in English.

That they are aware of their affliction is everywhere made clear. In a story called "The Bus to St. James" a man watches his daughter in dancing school: ". . . It struck him that he and the company that crowded around him were all cut out of the same cloth. They were bewildered and confused in principle, too selfish or too unlucky to abide by the forms that guarantee the permanence of a society, as their fathers and mothers had done. Instead, they put the burden of order onto their children and filled their days with specious rites and ceremonies." Again, in his last published work, a novella called *Oh What a Paradise It Seems*, a minor character muses while driving: "Then he seemed lost. He was lost. He had lost his crown, his kingdom, his heirs and armies, his court, his harem, his queen and his fleet. He had, of course, never possessed any of these. He was not in any way emotionally dishonest and so why should he feel as if he had been cruelly and physically stripped of what he had never claimed to possess? He seemed to have been hurled bodily from the sanctuary of some church, although he had never committed himself to anything that could be called serious prayer."

That sense of loss and being lost that is central to Cheever's writing appears to have touched his life as well. Born in 1912 in

Quincy, Massachusetts, where he was raised, the young Cheever was expelled from Thayer Academy for smoking. A year later, his father lost his money in the Crash of 1929. Cheever did not go to college; he became a writer instead, after promising his parents he would not seek vulgar fame or fortune. His early stories, including some of his best—"The Enormous Radio" and "Goodbye, My Brother"—were written in confined quarters but published in the expansive pages of the *New Yorker*. His first collection, *The Way Some People Live*, appeared in 1943. Critics praised his work from the beginning, though his novels, beginning with *The Wapshot Chronicle* in 1957, were often said to be infirm of structure, really little more than assemblages of stories. Cheever, who claimed to pay no attention to reviews, bridled at this judgment: his critics, he said, had no sense of the history of the novel. Nevertheless, *The Wapshot Chronicle* won him the National Book Award; his collected stories, published in 1978, received the Pulitzer Prize.

The vulgar success that he had forsworn, however, eluded him, except in Russia, where *Bullet Park*, the first of his two dark novels, sold one hundred thousand copies in a single day. At home, his books slipped out of print. An alcoholic, Cheever suffered a heart attack in 1973; later, after confinement in an alcoholic rehabilitation center, he drank nothing stronger than tea. *Falconer*, published in 1977, became a best seller, as did his collected stories the following year. Last April, he received the National Medal for Literature for his "distinguished and continuing contribution to American letters."

Despite the praise that *Falconer* received, Cheever will very likely be remembered for his stories, of which half a dozen are already American classics. Reviewers tend to call these stories realistic, yet they have a disconcerting habit of slipping into the surreal or supernatural, as if fantasy were the most efficient means to deal with a world we do not control, a world not susceptible to definition in rational terms. We have made our lives, Cheever seems to say, and insulated them with split-level ranches and country clubs, wrapped them around with automobiles and martinis on the patio, but the center will not hold—we lack love and conviction—and the whole elaborate structure may presently implode. Out of touch with themselves and their environment, his afflicted men and women become furtive creatures—thieves, voyeurs, addicts, alcoholics, lechers, and night crawlers—but somehow maintain their purity. Cheever knew that out there in a world that most people envy there are people who are bravely enduring. He saw their banality, yet he saw within that banality the persistence of ancient myths, archetypes, and patterns, and that is why the fleet man on skates senses an ancient experience. That is why a story of the most banal lust can conclude with a marvelous sentence: "Then it is dark; it is a night where kings in golden suits ride elephants over the mountains."

Writers may remember Cheever for other elements in his work. One is his mastery of narrative form. Relying little on the strenuous dialogue common to much contemporary fiction, Cheever concentrated on subtle variations of the storyteller's voice. By altering his distance from his mute and desperate characters, he endowed them with a wry eloquence; their passions and frustrations bubble up as if it were never customary for such to be concealed. Another is his prose: unmatched in subtlety and precision by that of any of his contemporaries, it is simply beautiful to read, to hear in the inner ear—and it got better all the time.

Cheever moves us because he held out to his characters the possibility of redemption through the sense of being alive, "the great benefice of living here and renewing ourselves with love." His death impoverishes the immediate prospects of our literature, but then, as one of his characters noted, "The dead are not, God knows, a minority. . . . How can a people who do not mean to understand death hope to understand love, and who will sound the alarm?"

June 1982

TWO

Further Perplexities of Everyday Life

PLEASE DON'T COME IN THE GARDEN, MAUDE

IN A MORE PERFECT WORLD, we'd have a right to expect pornography to resist the demands of fashion. After all, the product affects components that are beyond our power to change, and as for the packaging, who cares for the length of a hemline that will presently be trampled underfoot? And yet fashion does its busy work here as everywhere else, and for the same reasons: to improve the product, to make it seem more necessary, and (a perennial problem for pornographers) to make it look respectable. Two recent developments in the genre are particularly intriguing.

Sex is being made into a religion again. Always, in the suburbs of Benin and Beverly Hills, there have been covens of night people who jump up and down in the buff and impale virgins on stone phalli, but these believers have lacked access to a printing press. That's not Alex Comfort's problem. A prudent man reading *The Joy of Sex* will feel like a Mohammedan in Saint Peter's: it's all very impressive, intricate, even humbling, but it's overexcited—an idolatrous construction. The Angelus strikes early here—"Orgasm is the most religious moment of our lives, of which all other mystical kicks are a mere translation"—and then Comfort reveals the other holy trappings: the proselytizing, the definition of obligations, the prescriptions and proscriptions, and the promise that sex, like any good religion, will set us free.

Beds, we are told, must be a certain height, twin beds are forbidden, there is a time for washing and a time to refrain from washing, deodorants are "banned absolutely" and a woman's armpits "should on no account be shaved." Some freedom, this: *The Joy of Sex* makes the Talmud look like a manual for libertines. This particular bible, I suspect, is like most bibles—more bought than read. Certainly there's nothing in its perfervid text that has not been explained in other, uglier how-to-do-it books. The devoted, surely, buy it for its religious art: for the drawings of a handsome young couple (he wears a beard; she, inexplicably, a shirt with French cuffs), drawings that are both relatively taste- ful and relatively explicit—and more than a little romantic, for the human rump has never looked as cute as here depicted.

A more important trend has been toward condensation, a sweeping away of the dross. Older readers may remember a phrase that has virtually disappeared from the language: "Show me the good parts." The problem of pornography in days of yore was that it felt obliged to go through the motions of propelling the reader from one sex scene to another over some kind of recog- nizable track. The ground had to be laid, if that's the word I want, for the lecherous curate with his closet full of whips and the spinster aunt who has a key to the remote gazebo. No one was expected to dwell on these transitions, just as, in my generation, no teenager was expected to read *all* of *God's Little Acre* or *The Amboy Dukes*. We knew what we wanted and we knew that the good parts, for reasons best known to their authors, had to be iso- lated for examination on sterile slides. It was all very scientific, you see, and it still is, except that the nifty scientific thing to do now is to produce a book that consists of nothing but good parts. That's much more scientific, suggesting, as it does, *research*.

And so Nancy Friday, a woman with no credentials for this kind of thing, presents us with *My Secret Garden*, a groaning board of female sexual fantasies. Ignorant of clinical experience and distrusting statistical method, yet armed with the objectivity of innocence, Friday first asked her friends for information about their erotic daydreams and then advertised for more. She draws a few conclusions: that men are (a) ignorant of women's capacity for sexual fantasy and (b) afraid of it. She assumes, too, that only women have responded to her appeal, that women novelists like Doris Lessing and Edna O'Brien would not write fiction if they dared to tell us the truth about their sex, and that women by up- bringing nervous about their fantasies will, in reading the hun- dreds of capsule dreams included in these pages, become somewhat freer spirits.

Well, these condensed summaries of imagined sexual experi- ences should have some effect. The Alka-Seltzer syndrome, for one. Reading through this book, as a reviewer must, is like eating one's way through a Chinese menu: the entries are exotic, yes, and sometimes hot; all the fat has been pared away. I suspect that Nancy Friday, who keeps trying to say something significant about these fantasies, is not a fraud. Probably she did not write them herself, though she has edited them to the point where all but one or two sound as if they had been written by a couple of imaginative alumnae of, say, Bennington College, who got together for a fifth reunion and six daiquiris.

Her publishers* are more realistic. *They* know, even if she doesn't, that this is cryptoporn—which is to say, pornography that claims to be something other than itself—and it will be sold as such. No need to trouble such authorities as Seymour Fisher (author of *The Female Orgasm*) or Leah Cahan Schaefer (*Women and Sex*) for their evaluations of Friday's research—get "J," who wrote *The Sensuous Woman* instead. Then put running heads at the top of each page—EN MASSE IN THE SHOWERS; SAM IS WATCHING US; HE THOUGHT HE WAS PERVERTED—to seize the bookstore browser in an electric grip.

Needless to say, all our favorite actors are featured. Here we find women who favor *this* arrangement; there, women who are aroused by *that*; the other thing is not neglected, and in time we come to dogs, black men, even a giant octopus. Exhibitionism and masochism, as well as bondage and gang rape, are very big with Friday's volunteers. Her book is shocking, yes; not because women have such dreams but because their fantasies are so banal, so like those that male pornographers have endowed them with for at least three hundred years.

I confess I approached this book with an innocence of my own. I had written once that the reason most women are indifferent to pornography's allure is that the male authors of these books, men who pretend to write from the female point of view, ascribe to women only those responses that some men hope most women have—responses that few women recognize at all. Shattered illusions! I had hoisted my consciousness to the level where my respect for women required that they create for themselves fantasies that I could not imagine for them, and what does Friday offer me? "I am at a convention. I am the only woman there. I

---

* Trident, a now defunct imprint of Simon and Schuster. Delacorte publishes the Friday farragoes now. It's important that these names be remembered for what they did and do.

have no choice: I bend over a chair," etc. The women in Friday's harem rejoice in being sex objects, in being *used,* and in using men as sex objects. The news these confessions offer us is precisely the news that we get from the "confessions" in *Penthouse,* minus (of course) the gynecological photography. For these reasons, I take the publication of this book to be bad news for women's lib.

The bad news extends further still. A sadness hangs over these brief narratives, a sadness of husbands deceived by what their wives are thinking when they are with them, and of wives who are disappointed: ". . . Many of which I've never done before, and often wish my husband would ask me to do." Some of these women insist that *they're* okay—"I am not crackers. I am very normal but sex interests me enormously." Others simply assume their normality: the apprentice nun, for instance, who made love to another, and now associates with four men—"We are all broad-minded and at times have a small sex party." Indeed. Where does the fantasy begin? This is only one of the questions that Friday is disinclined to ask. Many of these women are not revealing what they dream of, but what they say happened to them—which they may dream of at another time. The pornophile will not mind: dream and reality are all one to him. And Friday comes across with what pornophiles want: she packs it all in, very close and with oil, like sardines.

To accomplish this, she must refuse to disbelieve whatever her informants tell her in their testimonies to various agitated states of mind. Moreover, Friday betrays her frame of reference through her own language: not just the random dirty words that she drops here and there, but her foolishness, phrases like the "layable ladies," as she calls men's wives, and her pretensions to method—"it is scientifically known." She has some sense of the value of privacy in fantasy, but little interest in whether fantasy is rehearsal or compensation for missed opportunity. These fantasies are above all thin stuff, reducing women to the tingle of their nerve ends, with never a thought to whether their emotions are engaged. Commitment, passion, an involvement with something other than the epidermis, have no part in Friday's vision of the enlightenment: Iseult, for her, would have nothing more to offer Tristan than the suggestion that he "rub a little higher here."

Jung's opinion that the man in a woman's erotic fantasy may be in fact her animus, the masculine aspect of herself, is not an idea with which Friday is prepared to cope. Nor can she cope with Jung's conception of a woman's complexity, in which the mother, the virgin, and the witch are combined with the hetaira—the sexual creature and the only aspect of woman with which Friday feels at home. And so I come back to my theme: the essence of pornography is its reductiveness—of both the nature of women and the relation between the sexes—which is why *My Secret Garden* is the real goods, fashionable, exquisite pornography.

On her very last page, Friday announces a sequel and offers an address to which we may send our own pathetic contributions. My fantasies in this area tend to be of the kind of thing that Fred Astaire did with Ginger Rogers as an invisible orchestra played "Night and Day," but in the interests of science I have thought of something more baroque, and have written it from a woman's point of view, and have sent it along to Miss Friday. I can't wait to see if she prints it.

August 1973

THE FURTHER SHORES OF SEX

FEMALE EROTICISM IS literature's undiscovered country, and from the evidence of these books* a traveler ambitious of returning had better stay at home. Pain, anarchy, death, or disability— these are the attractions offered the unwary tourist. No wonder women writers have been traditionally discreet about these matters—or hypocritical, pretending in what they wrote that women's sexual responses were indeed what their male readers

---

* *Nine and a Half Weeks*, by Elizabeth McNeill; and *Story of the Eye*, by Georges Bataille.

had always hoped they were. A man wrote one of these books, but the concern of each is woman's sexuality pushed to an extreme that exists, for most women, only in fantasy. They explore, as Georges Bataille once wrote in his essay *Death and Sensuality*, "the need for disorder, violence and indignity that lies at the root of love," in a realm where "joy is the same thing as pain, the same thing as death."

Elizabeth McNeill's *Nine and a Half Weeks* purports to be a woman's memoir of a season spent in masochistic thralldom. The pseudonymous narrator is in her twenties; her unnamed lover may be a little older. They could have been your typical upper-middle-class couple in New York with little more on their minds than cold cuts from Zabar's and a bed from Bloomingdale's—except that he beats her, degrades her, and forces her to carry out their games in public. Yet there at "the oneness of extreme pleasure and extreme pain" (Bataille's phrase again) she finds herself more alive, more in love than she could have imagined. It never occurred to her that their arrangement was pathological; instead, "for weeks on end I was flooded by an overwhelming sense of relief at being unburdened by adulthood.... There was only the voluptuous luxury of being a bystander to one's own life; an absolute relinquishing of individuality; an abandoned reveling in the abdication of selfhood."

I won't wallow in details—not for reasons of delicacy but because it is the nature of such stories that they cannot be excerpted or summarized without appearing preposterous. What counts here is careful architecture and a deftly supple style; the reader must be propelled, by the elbows if necessary, through a brief and intense narrative, and not allowed to pause and look around. (This is not, by the way, what happens in pornography, which, with its machinery of increasingly complex stimulation, invites dawdling.) Elizabeth McNeill fixes her story with a laser-like regard, calmly incinerating such irrelevant detail as characterization and news about what her lovers do in working hours. This couple has no reality except as sexual energies smoldering among the detritus of Saks and Bendel's, Tender Vittles and outmoded Gucci bags. Dismay rising to exultation is the narrator's only emotion; as readers, we are allowed behind her eyes and skin but never into her mind.

McNeill's story is so artfully shaped, so unnervingly assured, that it's hard to believe that the woman who wrote it is the woman who so recently writhed in such helpless subjugation. Perhaps it's a novel after all—and yet none the less true for that, for time and again the author tells us something about herself that is not only alarming but convincing, something that makes the reader think: ah, she couldn't have *invented* that.

If McNeill approaches what is finally unsayable—an area that, like religious mystery, is singularly resistant to verbal definition—Bataille plunges in head first and kicks his feet about. Bataille, who died in 1962, was a librarian employed by the French civil service, and a critic and novelist who attracted the admiration of Sartre and Michel Foucault. He argued (as did de Sade) that the ultimate expression of sexuality is death. *Story of the Eye*, first published half a century ago, is a novel whose time will probably never come.

A boy, sixteen, tells of his obsession with a girl of his age, a girl for whom sex is not only overpowering but depersonalizing; sexual ecstasy possesses her in the form of epileptic fits, evoking "blood, suffocation, sudden terror, crime; things indefinitely destroying human bliss and honesty." At surface level, the story, with its triangular liaisons and antique blasphemies, is absurd; at a submerged level, where ovoid symbols of eggs, eyes, and testicles become objects of sexual play, it acquires an appalling coherence that Delvaux or Dali might applaud. What should, however, most trouble the liberal imagination is the clarity of those passages, so frequently intruded into the story, in which Bataille implies that we are never so alone as we are when sexually engaged, and declares that the only relief from the curse of sexuality is death.

Not many people want to entertain such ideas, and those who are willing to grapple with them find they have few words with which to do so. "In the end," as Bataille wrote elsewhere, "the articulate man confesses his own impotence."

April 1978

HERSTORY

No one who has read Adrienne Rich's remarkable poetry should be surprised by the themes and directions she explores in her first book of prose, or by the courage and intensity with which she writes.* Her study of motherhood, whether actual or potential, as the experience by which women are expected to define themselves (and largely do), and as an institution by which a male-dominated society controls and diminishes them, is highly serious, incautious and, for men, as bleak as a basilisk's stare.

Rich surveys motherhood simultaneously from three perspectives. She is most affecting when most personal; herself the estranged wife of a man who committed suicide and the mother of three sons, she writes explicitly of the anger, guilt, and frustration (as well as joy) that their clamorous dependence imposed upon her. With history she fares indifferently—badly when relying on inadequate and outdated texts to support her anthropological fantasies about women's exalted status in prehistory; more interesting, but perhaps not always accurate, when relating the history of obstetrics: the coming of anesthetized passivity and the removal of childbirth from women's presumably loving hands to the cold forceps that were the exclusive and, she says, cruel province of the male. She is most provoking when most political, developing her thesis that the social institution of motherhood was invented by men as a means to keep women under their control.

This last, which relies heavily on political rhetoric and a reductive view of the present condition of male humanity, is volatile stuff. "Motherhood has been penal servitude," Rich writes, no doubt intending a pun. "*It need not be.*" Motherhood, as an insti-

---

* *Of Woman Born: Motherhood as Experience and Institutions,* by Adrienne Rich.

tution invented by patriarchal societies, withholds from women the right to make decisions essential to their lives—decisions about contraception, childbirth, careers—and operates on the assumption that a woman is ignorant, best fit to cater to a man's emotional needs and to work all her days isolated in the home raising, in a manner determined by him, children (preferably male) that are certifiably his. "Under patriarchy, female possibility has been massacred on the site of motherhood. . . . I have lived under the power of the fathers, and I have access only to so much privilege or influence as the patriarchy is willing to accede to me, and only for so long as I will pay the price for male approval."

Essential to her view of a male conspiracy to enslave and demean females is the notion that men will of course deny it. A sincere denial is especially contemptible: "Power seems to engender a kind of willed ignorance, a moral stupidity, about the inwardness of others, hence of oneself." All men are deficient in humanity and undeveloped in affection; fearful and resentful of women, they turn to a "supernaturalizing of the penis"—though she doesn't mention the equally fanciful attempt to "supernaturalize" the womb in the form of the Holy Grail. Men jettison human relationships and emotional values in favor of "bloody struggles for power over other men." Men are flops as fathers, too, because they shirk the early nurture a child needs: "Most of our sons are—in the most profound sense—virtually fatherless."

I don't intend to criticize Rich's thesis of motherhood as an oppressive institution—partly because to do so would confirm me in my unwonted role of male oppressor, partly because the reconsideration of history by qualified women is now a task of exceptional importance, and partly because I agree with some of what she says about the *effects* of the institution, if not her fantasy of a male conspiracy. I have news, however, for Adrienne Rich about matters that have concerned me at least as much as they have her. Fathering, for instance: it's a far more complex and multifaceted enterprise than mere physical nurture during a child's early years. And male bonding, a central theme in this country's literature, is far too varied to be dismissed as "defensive" and only "skin-deep"—particularly if Rich is going to promote female bonding for the sake of self-knowledge and enrichment. I wish, too, she had left men more than a gram of humanity, if only so men could believe what she says about women. No one can write truly about one sex while maligning the other.

It's a pity that Rich so often falls into awkward and cliché-ridden prose—a falling-off from the poet's precise use of words to the sloppy rhetoric of revolution. Let no one doubt that this book is meant to be a catalyst to revolution, or that revolutions encourage bad prose, bad history, and a scapegoat class that is perceived to be inordinately powerful (royalists, Jews, kulaks, men). Nevertheless, the book is valuable in several of its parts, most particularly its prolonged, complex attempt at defining "the great unwritten story of mothers and daughters"—of the solace that women can find in each other, of the intimate relation that women unavoidably share early in their lives and can regain. Beyond the politics and rhetoric stands a brave, bitter, abstract yet still inquiring sensibility.

October 1976

DUKE: *And what's her history?*
VIOLA: *A blank, my Lord. . . .*

The words are from *Twelfth Night*, but feminists today will nod in recognition; women have always been allotted little history. Your odd queen, of course, some whores and writers, will always get their notices—the business of history is exceptions. Still, generally to ignore half the human race suggests imprudence if not willful falsification. "History is part of the way in which we have been defined by men," writes Sheila Rowbotham.* Men's performance, Ann Oakley says, is the standard by which women are measured. History, therefore, is a weapon that these women mean to use. But the weapon is double-edged: "The pursuit of the past," Rowbotham writes, "can become a substitute for trying to change the present." She might have added that a determination to change the present can betray history; it is harder to say accurately what is or was when one is a devout advocate of what ought to be.

---

* *Hidden from History*, by Sheila Rowbotham; *Woman's Work*, by Ann Oakley; and *Herstory*, by June Sochen.

These books, smitten by ideology and foundering on generalizations, are not good, but their publication is evidence of a real need, and suggests that better books will follow. All three cover roughly the same period of time—from the seventeenth century to the near present. Rowbotham and Oakley deal exclusively with England. They show (I think convincingly) that the idea of working women as pitiable objects is a Victorian invention; in preindustrial England, women were productive workers—they were surgeons, pawnbrokers, army contractors—and no line was drawn between housework and income-producing labor. The Industrial Revolution, demanding increased production, defined a sexual division of labor by moving men into factories, leaving women to manage the homes. Some women did go into the factories, but the Victorian lawmakers—men, of course—got them out by insisting that factory work made women immoral. The unemployed wife became a status image, first for the rich and, after 1840, for all classes.

Rowbotham's book—the best of the three—is a serious attempt to marshal from secondary sources little-reported details of women's efforts to act as free people. She traces early attempts by women to achieve political and sexual equality, to form unions, to be informed about contraception and abortion. A Marxist, she blames capitalism for many of women's woes, makes much of "man's property in woman," but can sketch delicate distinctions among women's lot according to class. Hers is a history that derives from politics: in the twin movements of feminism and socialism she sees a future in which all people control every aspect of their lives.

Oakley attempts too much: she wants to combine history with sociology, an anthropological manifesto with a polemic. The data, which show how women came to their obligatory idleness, are adequate. Of these authors, Oakley alone has done original research, giving us four inconclusive interviews with housewives who explain why they mind/don't mind housework. If they don't mind, says Oakley, they're suspect. "Women abdicate their personhood for the sake of their maternity. . . . Housework is directly opposed to the possibility of human self-actualization." Nuns, teachers, and book reviewers are used to being told they don't know what "real life" is; let us welcome housewives to our underdeveloped ranks. "There is no such thing as the maternal instinct," Oakley reports; she wants to abolish housewives, the family, gender roles. Unfortunately, such a falling-off from reason mars many recent ambitious feminist tracts.

The less said of *Herstory* the better. Intended as a history of women in America, it is instead an anthology of ignorance; the drivel fairly leaks from every page. What are we to think of an author who says that pioneer women knew little about the facts of conception, that the Puritans thought the Indian to be "a son of Satan," that one of Christ's "feminine" virtues was "cooperation," or that Americans "are required to dress alike, eat the same breakfast cereal"? Like most of what June Sochen sets forth as fact in this dismal book, these assertions are simply wrong. She commits what I take to be the ultimate feminist sin: overlooking a woman's greatness to make a political point. Anne Bradstreet's poetry, she says, was "acceptable" because her subjects were "approved." Approved by whom? Like Shakespeare, Bradstreet (the first American poet) wrote good poetry on common themes.

All history is suspect because all history is partisan, which is not to say that it is not useful, particularly when it deals with an obscure or neglected subject. But the present women's movement defaults when it leaves to its angry or half-educated adherents the critical task of setting history straight. Reading these books made me wish for books unwritten: Barbara Tuchman's history of the early League of Women Voters, Cecil Woodham Smith's account of Victorian women's unions.

January 1975

THE MACHO MYSTIQUE

CURIOUS NEWS: macho fiction lives. What with the current fashion for novels of feminist sensibility the wonder is it hasn't handed in its mess kit. By definition, macho fiction is fiction women won't readily enjoy—not because it is pornographic (on the contrary, it is resolutely antierotic), but because it celebrates a fantasy of masculine self-sufficiency. It is, above all, solemn stuff. "There are men," James Salter intones in *Solo Faces*, "who seem destined to always go first, to lead the way. They are confident in life, they are the first to go beyond it. Whatever there is to know, they learn before others. Their very existence gives strength and drives one onward. Love and jealousy were mingled there in the darkness, love and despair." Surely these are sentiments to set a man's pulse racing, but women, I fear, may see in them no more than a couple of lame assertions propped up by some crippled syntax.

Nevertheless, women are essential to macho fiction. A woman is a smooth-skinned primate who, by virtue of her domesticity and enervating sexuality, is incapable of understanding a man's need to blaze his solitary path in a senseless world. A woman is something a man must leave behind, preferably pregnant, with the suggestion that he may return in a year or two; the woman, of course, waits. A woman is particularly useful if she can be killed in a baroque manner ("She sat there as if built of stone," Jim Harrison writes in *Legends of the Fall*, "with a ricocheted bullet from the canyon wall neatly piercing her forehead like a red dime") so that her man may be ennobled by his grief. A woman, however, is useless on a mountainside. "What's he bringing her up for?" Salter's hero asks. "To milk her," his companion replies. "One woman," Salter writes later, "is like another. Two are like another two. Once you begin there is no end."

Heady stuff, this, but as you will have gathered, macho fiction fairly bristles with ideas. Whenever he eases up on his knife-and-bullet work, Harrison pitches in a brief editorial: "Only rarely did a man occur on earth bad enough to die." That impressed me (particularly the suggestion that what we do here on earth is "occur") until I came across what he has to say about the social problem of children encountering bullets. "Nothing," Harrison writes, "is quite so grotesque as the meeting of a child and a bullet"—because, I presume, neither knows how to introduce itself. Harrison's previous novels, like Salter's, have been taken seriously by critics. It's easy to see why.

Part of the esteem these writers enjoy must result from the care they take to prevent their philosophical nuggets from rattling about unattended on the page. Like all good macho writers, their primary concern is for plot, for stories of fear and obsession, of death and mutilation. In macho fiction the body counts tend to be inflationary, yet the stories end serenely, with a certain rough justice achieved. Take, for instance, "Revenge," one of the three novellas in Harrison's book. An American pilot falls in love with a Mexican gangster's lady friend. No good can come of this. The lady is disfigured with a razor, then tortured with snakes, drugs, and compulsory prostitution before being immured in a convent. There the pilot, recovered from a near-fatal beating, finds her. The finale reminded me of that in *Cyrano de Bergerac*, except that in keeping with macho law it is the woman who dies, leaving her two lovers to become best buddies again.

Because the other novellas in Harrison's collection are even busier than "Revenge," I'll pass on to Salter's novel, which, by comparison, seems restful. His hero is a rock climber, Vernon Rand, who walks away from a succession of compliant women to find his manhood in the mountains near Chamonix. For his daring rescues of less manly climbers and his hazardous solo forays over treacherous ice and snow, Rand becomes a legend, which suits him well enough until his skill and nerve desert him. Like Harrison, Salter affects a pseudosimplicity of style which is (when he doesn't lapse into preachiness) adequate to what he requires of it: the climbing scenes are really quite effective.

Make no mistake: these are determinedly literary works. To emphasize the point, Harrison has one of his heroes, just before he chucks a man out of a window, refer admiringly to certain meditations in E. M. Cioran's *A Short History of Decay*. He does not go so far as to quote or paraphrase or in any way describe these meditations, nor does he explain how such a remarkable and obscure book has found its way into his bloody story. For fans of macho fiction who may be unfamiliar with Cioran's work, I thought I'd pass on an example of what Harrison's tough guy found to admire. "Courage and fear," Cioran writes, "two poles of the same disease . . . the subtlest and cruelest crimes are perpetrated by those who take things seriously." Indeed, but how strange! Nothing could be further removed from the macho mystique.

July 1979

THIS TRAIN'S LONG
GONE

A COUNTRY IS NOT WITHOUT HONOR, save among its own prophets. *No Name in the Street* is James Baldwin's angriest book, his most sclerotic. Turning the pages, one can actually perceive the thickening of thought, the coarsening of argument, and the deterioration of language until, toward the end, Martin Luther King's funeral is described as Sheilah Graham might have done it, had she had difficulty getting in. It is all very embarrassing, at least for one who admires Baldwin's early work and the skill with which he assembled the component parts of English syntax. I am sure that this ramble toward digressions, self-pitying asides, and truculent belligerence will presently become embarrassing to Baldwin, too, because he must soon realize that one who calls himself a "public witness to the situation of black people" need not clutch so uneasily at the rigid postures and rhetoric of a younger generation.

Baldwin's distress at his absorption by white America has been evident for several books. Now, apparently paying his dues to Eldridge Cleaver, who accused him of a "shameful, fanatical, sycophantic love of the whites," Baldwin wants us to know that he's a bad man, too. Using arguments and phrases that are between two and five years out of date (there was apparently some delay in completing this book), he tells us that there is no justice for the poor, that black people don't like cops, that whites are monsters, unredeemable, past pity. Baldwin is obviously doing here what Cleaver told him to do: "in spite of the universality of human experience" (Cleaver's phrase), he is to avoid "white-minded" thought and look for "an additional dimension" of blackness.

Dutifully, Baldwin goes through the motions: the white man is a conscious liar, cannot readily distinguish between joy and sin; his civilization is built on hypocrisy and therefore has no moral force; we live in the Fourth Reich, which will plow under the flower children, then the blacks, then the world; and the Panthers can't get a fair trial. At the end, Baldwin justifies the propriety of *discussing* killing whitey, though here, as in his last novel, he falls just short of advocating it. "I then have no compassion whatever for this country," Baldwin writes, "or my countrymen." The key, again, to the new bad Baldwin is Cleaver's phrase—"in spite of the universality of human experience"—which contrasts with a younger Baldwin who, in *Nobody Knows My Name*, wrote, "It is a terrible, an inexorable law that one cannot deny the humanity of another without diminishing one's own."

But heck, folks, denying one's own humanity by diminishing others' is the theme song of our times and Baldwin wants us to know that he can sing along. In this essay, he worries about the unease of fame and his former chauffeur's problems with a murder charge, but he is mostly worried about persuading us that he, the expatriate, the northern Negro, the famous man, the only black in the Beverly Hills Hotel, knows "what black Americans endure—know it in my own flesh and spirit." Whoever would have doubted it until this special pleading? Baldwin shows us a good scene (and there are several good scenes in this book) in which he tells us how, once famous, he went south to be called "boy" and be directed to the back of the restaurant.

He wants us to know that in spite of fame and limousines he shares the experience of the young, tough blacks who have denounced him, although when he goes incognito to Martin Luther King's funeral he is not happy about being choked off by the people—no brothers, these blacks, just people who don't know him. He waves at Jim Brown, gets pulled into the church. "The church was packed, of course, incredibly so," he observes in his new Sheilah Graham prose style. "I saw Harry Belafonte sitting next to Coretta King. I had interviewed Coretta years ago. . . . We had got on very well. . . . Ralph David Abernathy sat in the pulpit. I remembered him from years ago. . . . In the pew directly before me sat Marlon Brando, Sammy Davis, Eartha Kitt—covered in black, looking like a lost ten-year-old girl—and Sidney

Poitier.... Marlon saw me and nodded.... At last, we were standing and filing out, to walk behind Martin home. I found myself between Marlon and Sammy."

This is embarrassing enough, but it is not as sad as Baldwin's limp acquiescence in the projection upon America of fundamental problems that have always beset human beings. Baldwin writes, " 'Only connect,' Henry James has said." Well, it was E. M. Forster who said it. The point would not be important if Baldwin didn't blunder on: "Perhaps only an American writer could have been driven to say it, his very existence being so threatened by the failure," and so on, and it really doesn't matter, this time, what failure Baldwin is laying on Americans. For Forster, the important thing was to "connect the prose in us with passion," to "connect without bitterness until all men are brothers," and there is nothing particularly American, or even particularly British, about that. Even Baldwin wrote about it once.

May 1972

WITHOUT THE LAW

EXTRACTS FROM *the trial of Louis Nizer, Esq., Mr. Justice Prescott presiding:*

DEFENSE ATTORNEY: Now, sir, you are charged with conspiracy to write, publish, and sell copies of *The Implosion Conspiracy*, an account of the trial of Julius and Ethel Rosenberg, the atom spies. How would you characterize your book?

PROSECUTOR: Objection to "characterizing," your honor.

COURT: Sustained.

DEFENSE: The book may speak for itself. Use only words drawn from the book, please, Mr. Nizer.

NIZER: *The Rosenberg trial is not only the most extraordinary spy story of the century, it is a love story.*

DEFENSE: Spy stories are dead these days, but a "love story" sells books? Is that what you're trying to say?*

PROSECUTOR: I object!

COURT: So do I!

DEFENSE: Your honor, we have exhibits that will prove the emotional quality of the Rosenberg case.

COURT: Very well.

NIZER: *The horror of execution was juxtaposed against sentiment, like Wagnerian thunder counterpointed by idyllic music. . . . Hopes and fears mingled in the torment of uncertainty.*

COURT: I don't understand.

NIZER: *Incarnate villainy. . . . A heart-pounding moment. . . . Punished to die.*

DEFENSE: Please raise your voice so his honor may hear you.

NIZER: *Fear of doom swelled the senses. . . . Fears were like nails. . . .*

DEFENSE: To make clear to the Court the romantic nature of that case, did you say that Ruth Greenglass "had literally been through the fires of hell"?

COURT: The Court has some fear for the future of metaphor.

PROSECUTOR: Your honor, everyone knows the defendant writes as if he were jumping on a secondhand bladder. Squeaks, wheezes, and other predictably vulgar noises invariably result.

COURT: His rhetoric may be more effective before a jury than in the pages of a book. There are no peremptory challenges of readers. Has the book any substance?

NIZER: *Pulsating life. . . . Abreaction. . . .*

---

* Time has dulled this reference. I was alluding to Erich Segal's smarmy novel *Love Story.*

DEFENSE: He means, your honor, that he has studied the emotion of the case. He knows everything there is to know about it.

PROSECUTOR: Objection! The book has no notes, no index, no bibliography!

DEFENSE: Still, Nizer knows. You must take his word for it, just as you must accept his more pretentious pronouncements on the law, on philosophy, even on the cure of stuttering.

COURT: Substance, dammit! Substance!

DEFENSE: Very well. The book begins in 1951, with the opening of the trial of Julius and Ethel Rosenberg, and Morton Sobell. The title comes from the nature of an atomic blast, which is an implosion, and applies also the rancor and accusations within the Rosenberg family. According to the government, David Greenglass, a machinist working with the Los Alamos Project, was persuaded by his sister and brother-in-law, the Rosenbergs, to steal the secret of the atomic bomb and, through Harry Gold, another spy, to give it to the Russians. Greenglass admitted his role, but not the Rosenbergs. They claimed Greenglass was bitter over a business dispute. Still, Nizer believes the evidence brought forward in the trial conclusively proved the Rosenbergs' guilt.

NIZER: *Yes. . . . However, the death penalty was unfortunate.*

DEFENSE: Because the Rosenbergs never admitted their guilt, even when they might have saved their lives by doing so. And because their execution left orphans. Because they were convicted on the evidence of confessed traitors, which is always suspect, and in a climate of hysteria against communism. The description of their deaths by electrocution should deter any reader from advocating the death penalty again.

COURT: Fat chance.

DEFENSE: Nevertheless, the real drama of the Rosenberg case had nothing to do with passwords or torn Jell-O boxes, but began *after* their conviction. The appeals: 23 courts and 112 judges ruled on their guilt. The case came before the Supreme Court seven times. There were riots, and marches all over the world: President Eisenhower ignored fifty thousand letters advocating clemency.

COURT: Mr. District Attorney?

PROSECUTOR: Mr. Nizer does not present the testimony in order. He advances defense rebuttals immediately to follow the claims of government witnesses.

DEFENSE: Does he not write much of his book in this readable form of a trial transcript?

PROSECUTOR: Yes, but not enough. Sometimes he summarizes what was said or rewrites it for dramatic effect. The reader can't tell what he is reading.

NIZER: *No fortress is less impenetrable than a closed mind.*

PROSECUTOR: See! He means just the opposite! Your honor, the defendant is clearly guilty.

COURT: No. It takes unmistakable innocence to produce a book like this. Case dismissed.

February 1973

For weeks I've been babbling about this book* to people who politely ask, "Who's Arthur Bremer?" I don't say anything dumb—"He's us, he's Everyman, America"—but in my mind's eye I see Bremer wincing in his prison cell. He meant his name to be known. Sartre, and before him Thomas Browne, reminded us that no one knows who built the temple at Ephesus, but Erostratus is remembered for having burnt it down. The easy route to reputation: "a little something to be remmered by," Bremer says as he thinks how calm he'll be when he shoots President Nixon. Let us now praise famous men: Booth, Oswald, Sirhan. Into the history books with a fusillade of shots. But Bremer misses his chances, even the chance for his own death, which he had so carefully rehearsed. Failing to kill Nixon, he goes after Governor Wallace—and fails again. While Wallace chats on television,

---

* *An Assassin's Diary*, by Arthur H. Bremer.

Bremer is tried, jailed, and (although this happened only a year ago) forgotten.

His course toward becoming an archtypical American loser is patiently recorded in his diary, which he thought would be studied as carefully as the Dead Sea Scrolls. The first part is lost—Bremer buried it somewhere—so we begin, as epics do, in the middle of the course. Like a character in a television crime show, Bremer is constantly in motion, driving to Milwaukee, Ottawa, Detroit, flying to New York and Washington. He is out of work but he has some money, wants to be noticed. He hires the same kind of limousine Nixon uses—"I really felt good being stared at by the poor people"—and scorns a police photographer who is distracted by demonstrators: "He should of photographed the quiet ones. He never pointed his camera at me."

The wonder is that Bremer did anything at all. Frustration fairly steams from these pages. This twenty-one-year-old virgin represses his dreams and is made "woozy" by even one drink. He forgets his guns at an airport, loses one pistol in the bowels of his car, and fires another accidentally in a motel room. He gets lost in Ottawa, can't follow directions repeated to him three times, can't find a hotel and, when he does, can't find a bellhop for his luggage. Never mind that he has to stand in crowds for hours, waiting for Nixon to flash by "like a snap of the fingers. A dark shillowet"; the details of everyday life conspire against him. He even loses his belt. Failure, he seems to think, is something that can be done to you by others. This is the stuff of comedy, a Jerry Lewis film script—but it isn't funny. "Must have begun to cry 8 distint times yesterday night," Bremer writes. "ALL MY EFFORTS & NOTHING CHANGED." The words sprawl over two pages. "Just another god Damn failure."

Indeed. Even some weeds are taller than he is. He notices that kind of thing. His failures are so consistent that he suggests he needs a vacation. In the early pages of this diary Bremer describes at length his frustrating trip to a massage parlor in New York. Though the girl kept her panties on—house rules—she tries (and fails) to do for Bremer what he needs to have done. A pathetic scene: Bremer is reminded of it when the words he uses to describe his failure to kill Nixon prove an unconscious metaphor: "I just need the little opening & a second of time."

"I Am A Hamlet," Bremer writes. He is conscious of being an actor who needs a suitable costume: "Dressed in my vested conservative bussiness suit," he writes, "& overcoat with a gun & a tie that was just rediculus for anyone my age." The satisfaction of his role comes from proximity to the famous: "Call me Ismal," he writes, and then of Nixon, "I wanted to be close to him & live it up my last few days." When he turns his attention to Wallace he asks, "What would he have done without *me?*" Or Ahab without his whale, let alone Ishmael to tell the story. Reality—news of the candidates' itineraries—is for Bremer something to be checked out on TV or peered at through another lens: his binoculars, with which he studies a naked woman and then Milwaukee, "this cold peopled place," where "Down town is barely visible . . . being a good 12 miles off on the horizon."

Our familiar world so strangely, despairingly perceived. It is a place where innocence and violence converge, just as we have been told they do. Like many of our best writers—Donald Barthelme, say, or Bernard Malamud—Bremer senses the madness, the absurdity of our world, and resorts to fantasy to bring about some order. This is a small book, written with the economy of desperation; we don't have to read far into it to be chilled by its author's determination to destroy himself.

April 1973

Okay, gang, I don't care how bored you are with it, we're going to run through the Patty Hearst song again.* And this time put some *feeling* into it. You know how it goes. Flute solo: a young, empty-headed newspaper heiress about to be married. Now drums, trumpets: kidnapped by the Symbionese Liberation Army! Sighing strings: locked in a closet for two months. Pizzicato strings: Patty's conversion to terrorism—did she jump or was she pushed? Growl trumpet: ransom demands, denunciations (a little cello here) of mourning parents and fiancé. Snare drum, castanets: Tania, as she is now called, and the SLA rob a bank. Oboe interlude for twenty minutes: her twenty months in hiding. Bass drum: arrested by the FBI! Cacaphonous finale: the trial. F. Lee Bailey's saxophone against the psychiatrists' tuba obbli-

---

* *Anyone's Daughter: The Times and Trials of Patty Hearst,* by Shana Alexander.

gato. Throughout the piece, of course, the klaxon of the press is heard.

Clearly, if we are to endure this story again, it needs orchestration. If my musical metaphor won't do, then perhaps Shana Alexander's aquarium metaphor will: for her, Patty's courtroom was a tank and the principals so many blackfin, pipefish, eels, and sheepshead bass. By profession, Alexander comments on the news, so at the outset of her epic-size account of Patty's trial for bank robbery she warns us that the story may be read three ways: as a media event, as a metaphor for America, as an extension of her own personal problems as a mother and a daughter.

Impartiality and objectivity have no place in Alexander's kit of reportorial tools. Instantly possessive, she declares "Patty was my story"; she had been on Patty's "side" from the start, believes her to be a "handy whipping boy [sic] for [our] society's own errors and failures." Even before it began, she determined to use Patty's trial as a "device" to ventilate her opinions on American attitudes today. For her, Patty was a victim, cruelly used by her captors, psychiatrists, and the law, so the question of her possible legal guilt is irrelevant; she should never have been tried at all.

From this perspective (which will be broadened when Alexander tells us that she sees in Patty her own adopted daughter, with whom she has been having difficulties), it's not surprising to find the pale and tearful defendant described as a mermaid, Ondine, a Borgia queen, Sleeping Beauty, queen of the underworld, and Our Lady of the Sorrows. As for those deficient in their support of the girl, let them beware. The judge, we learn, is deaf, ill, about to die, may have seen a psychiatrist, looks like an elderly shoe clerk, and sleeps in court. Before she can explain why Patty's famous lawyer will emerge as her villain-in-chief, Alexander deplores his suits, his shaking hand, his "festering and rufous" ego, the unflushed toilet in his suite.

Partisan and emotional as all this is, it detracts little from the drama of the trial. With a good reporter's sense of pace and detail, Alexander arranges and abridges the great slag heap of expert testimony, most of it from psychiatrists whose conflicting speculations should never have been allowed in court. Those who argue that Patty's terrorist behavior was voluntary are as convincing as those who insist that she was either brainwashed or in fear for her life. To Alexander's credit, she pursued the psychiatrists, after Patty was found guilty, to arrive at her own plausible conclusion that Patty's life had left her unprepared for the victimization she encountered. She *was* brainwashed, coerced into playing a role that she could not sustain after her arrest; Patty should have been sent to a rest home, not to jail.

I find Alexander equally convincing that F. Lee Bailey, for reasons of ambition, ego, and declining powers, mismanaged a case that need never have been tried. What is unpersuasive is her attempt to take the case out of doors. Patty was not, I think, a surrogate daughter for many of us; we did not see her as a witch who threatened society. Many of us thought the case somewhat ridiculous—particularly the FBI's prolonged failure to catch a pathetic girl of twenty.

Surely Patty's trial did not, as Alexander insists, overturn our myths about good guys and bad guys, about the jury system and family life (do we really have such myths?), nor did it represent the Vietnam War brought home to California. Moreover, Alexander's meditations on Patty as a Persephone figure and the prehistorical existence of matriarchal societies are downright embarrassing, based on bad anthropology and an overhasty appropriation of myth. (If she needed a metaphor for Patty, she might better have chosen the Armed Maiden—Diana the Huntress, Venus in a helmet—an image that can truly threaten a culture of masculine values.) This is bad thinking—but then intelligent observers like Alexander are often unsound thinkers.

May 1979

OPERATION SOW'S EAR

SOME WHO KNOW ME will tell you the contrary, but I want to make it clear at once that I'm in favor of manners. Manners are so interesting and elusive that books have been written about them ever since books were invented. The boy George Washington scribbled homilies on manners in his copybook, and the ancient Chinese, no laggards in protocol, distilled their wisdom into a proverb: "Never pick your nose or your ear save with your elbow."

Lately I have been sitting at home alone, temporarily unable to offend anyone, reading books on manners* and trying to clutch at the essence of the thing. Fear is part of it: if people can't be made to worry about which fork to use, can't be persuaded that good manners are not instinctive, they won't buy millions of etiquette books. Dullness is even more essential: whether it is the prophylactic dullness that prevents men and women from falling on each other's jugulars, or the dullness that eschews individuality, the precise expression of human feeling, or even interesting conversation, it is dullness to which the hucksters of manners aspire. Do you doubt it? Listen to Amy Vanderbilt on how to reply to that troublesome salutation, "Hello, how are you?" "The other should answer, 'Fine, thanks, and how are you?' (Variations are: 'And how are things with you?' or 'How are things going?' or 'It's so nice to see you.')"

I may be doing Miss Vanderbilt an injustice. Like her rival, Emily Post, she has passed through the great receiving line in the sky and is doubtless pleased to have found that the angels and archangels of her acquaintance maintain a strict order of precedence. But if the ladies are gone, their books live still, brought down to date by other ladies, and sometimes it's difficult to tell just who is mangling the language or coarsening the sensibilities of bygone years. Is it Emily or Elizabeth Post, for instance, who repeatedly misuses the word *hopefully*? Which of them felt obliged to tell us that handicapped people are "unfortunate persons"? Is it Amy Vanderbilt or Letitia (Tish) Baldridge who tells alarming stories about herself? One of them, on her return from Rome, went around saying *"piano, piano"* until an American colleague told her to knock it off. For simplicity's sake, then, if not for manners', I will call one team of ladies Amy, the other Emily.

---

* *The New Emily Post's Etiquette,* by Elizabeth L. Post; and *The Amy Vanderbilt Complete Book of Etiquette,* revised and expanded by Letitia Baldridge.

Amy and Emily agree on many matters: that weddings, for instance, are more important than anything—Amy devotes thirteen chapters to them; Emily scrapes by with ten. For both, certain rules remain inviolable: never hang a fur coat on a rack in a cafeteria, Amy says, and Emily adds, "Don't leave half of the food on your spoon or fork to be waved about during conversation." Amy, particularly, tries to accommodate our declining standards. Doggy bags in restaurants now meet with both ladies' approval, but Amy tells me that my child's character will be strengthened if I clean off the mustard container in a fast-food joint. It is Amy who endorses the unspeakable "Ms." and entertains the bizarre idea that "martinis can be mixed a day or two ahead of the party."

Authorities as great as Amy and Emily must take care to change their views slowly, so I was comforted to see that the women's movement has left Emily unaffected: "When a *girl* is meeting a *man* at a restaurant" (my emphasis), she may not "assume the responsibility of choosing the table." Amy is way ahead of her, devoting six chapters to manners in the office. The modern woman tells the man who's just been fired to keep a "stiff upper," and to the man who took her to lunch she writes a note: "I enjoyed the introduction to that corned beef you are always extolling." (I think Amy is wrong here; the writer is presumably the social superior of the corned beef, so the corned beef should be introduced to *her*.)

And so it goes, no page in either thick volume without its practical counsel. Amy tells me what to take to the beach; Emily tells me, "keep your hearing aid turned on and gain the admiration of your friends." Emily may have not a word to say on how to send an offending dish or wine back at a restaurant, but she tells me what to do at a dinner when I find hair in my butter. Amy tells me how to write an apology after I've slandered someone's race or religion; Emily warns me not to cut on my first wife's tombstone the words *greatest love* for fear of offending her successor. Its reassuring to see that the well-mannered fictional characters in both books all have proper Anglo-Saxon names, and that when Amy kills off a man for her chapter on funerals he sounds suspiciously Germanic (Emily's victim, in her corresponding section, is a Jew). And yet (how dismaying!) the ladies differ violently on some fine points. Amy thinks wedding gifts in the form of checks should never be displayed; Emily tells me how to show them. "The family itself is often represented among the pallbearers," Amy decrees, but Emily bridles: "members of the immediate family are never chosen." That *never* is a strong word: where now is authority?

I believe the true authority here is dullness magnified by size. No one who would buy these books needs to learn much of anything in either. How can these ladies not be dull when they think they must write both for the boor who needs to learn that "semiformal" means no T-shirts, no jeans, and for the lady who invites the College of Cardinals for dinner? How can they not be insufferable as they exhort us to march (with our shoulders squared) toward that comatose state in which no one can be offended because nothing has been risked? Onward to entropy, with Emily and Amy.

November 1978

AFTER THE GAME IS OVER

THERE ARE MANY WAYS to waste one's youth; I wasted mine rooting for the Yankees and the Republicans. They were my teams, not because they won but because they were near: Yankee Stadium was an hour's drive from my home; the Democrats a little farther. Brooklyn was *terra incognita*—no one I knew had ventured there—though when my radio wandered off-course I could hear Red Barber speaking a nearly familiar language from a place called Ebbets Field. Not everyone, I knew, worshiped Heinrich and Keller, though it would take time for me to learn the inevitability, the necessity, of defeat, the kind of defeat that makes men endure. My Yankees would presently exhibit it;

Roger Kahn's *The Boys of Summer*, a book about the Brooklyn Dodgers, investigates and celebrates it.

Part of Kahn's book is a memoir of growing up in Brooklyn and dreaming of playing with the Dodgers, of working later as a sportswriter covering the team. There is good copy here: Kahn tells us how his father played ball with him while his mother, seeking to quell the incipient philistine, objected; how he could see part of the playing field by squinting under the outfield gate; how he became a writer for the *Herald Tribune* the way everybody becomes a writer—by doing a lot of underpaid extra work. Along the way he drops clues as to the shape of the larger book emerging. Baseball, we see, can be a metaphor, a sanctuary from life's harassments, a "point where vectors converged," an alternative world. "Yessuh," Red Barber said, "baseball is more than a little bit like life."

So far, so standard. The personal stuff is but the armature for the real substance of the book, for Kahn's concern with ball players as "baseball-playing men." Kahn first shows us the Brooklyn team as heroes whom he idolized, then—in 1952 and 1953, when they were at their best—as athletes whom he knew and wrote about, and finally the same men, much later, when the spectacular glory is gone and only the men are left, living in Indiana and Ohio, selling clothes and cars, working in the Post Office and installing elevator doors. Kahn wanted to look again at these stars who became "old men" at thirty-five, men now in their late forties with arms and legs that hurt.

Carl Erskine has overcome the pain of pitching 335 games by an operation that has left him with a limp; much of his life is devoted to the care of his Mongoloid son. George Shuba, a clerk-typist in the Post Office, still cannot laugh about baseball, though he thinks it unimportant; his "natural" swing, he explains, was developed by swinging "a 44-ounce bat 600 times a night, 4,200 times a week, 47,200 swings every winter." Preacher Roe runs a supermarket and talks about his spitball—Beech-Nut gum gives slicker saliva. Clem Labine sells sports clothes and blames himself for failing to understand his son, who joined the marines and had his leg blown off in Vietnam. Jackie Robinson's son takes drugs and dies in a car crash; Roy Campanella is a quadriplegic. Age and fortune have run all over these men and the others on the

Dodger team whom Kahn visited, but they are not down. They endure. Some, like Erskine and Duke Snider, who, when he was hitting over .300, dreamed of growing avocados in California, are happier with baseball behind them.

The Boys of Summer invites us to remember what we once knew of these men—breaking curves, fast moves to the right, balls rising into the upper deck—and to recognize that our memories are not of men but of figures in a landscape. The men come through in this book, not as fallen angels—the perspective on ball players that Jim Bouton adopted in *Ball Four*—but as whole men seen in the totality of their lives so far. Kahn not only shows us what they are, he looks at how they began. A sense of awe, picked up as a child, persists as he reports on their present condition.

Kahn's book is knowledgeable, leisurely, and anecdotal, as good informal baseball writing must be. But it is more: Kahn never forgets that he is writing about men in relation to a certain discipline, a certain level of achievement, a certain process of decline. Because of this, his book acquires a cumulative power. It is not just another book about baseball or a boy growing up to like baseball, but a book about pain and defeat and endurance, about how men anywhere must live. I fear that people who are bored by baseball will not read it, which would be, for them, as bright a decision as for those who disapprove of adultery to overlook *Madame Bovary*.

March 1972

INTERPRETING DISEASE TO MAN

THIS BOOK IS LIKE AN OTTER: as Falstaff said of Mistress Quickly, it is neither fish nor flesh, and a man knows not where to have it. The publisher calls *Ward 402* alternatively Ronald J.

Glasser's "new volume" and a "dramatic narrative," which means he will not say whether it is fact or fiction. Dr. Glasser clearly intends to claim the license of both modes. "Everything actually happened," he writes, but "the events did not all occur in the same sequence, or in the same hospital, or to the same people; some I witnessed, others I heard of."

It is an extraordinary disclaimer. For fiction it is superfluous; we expect novelists to rearrange reality. For nonfiction it won't do: we expect the writer, even within the amorphous confines of the "nonfiction novel," to assume responsibility for the integrity of the events he reports—which is to say that he may select, condense, and emphasize at will, but he may not redistribute, without regard to time and space, facts and rumors of which he is aware; he may not in short create collages.

Despite its sins, *Ward 402* is good red herring. It *is* a "dramatic narrative"—intern stories, of which we have recently had many, usually are. The narrator of this one (Dr. Glasser, I presume?) is serving time on a children's ward in a huge, distinguished, anonymous research hospital. The schedule is grueling and interns, dulled by fatigue, become sloppy, even callous. The children are terribly ill: some are wasted by diarrhea or diabetes, others lack kidneys or the clotting factor that stops bleeding. For sheer melodramatic effect nothing beats a medical emergency—knives and needles, pumps and fumbling fingers plunged into bodies turning black and purple, lungs filling with water. "This is what it's all about," the intern thinks. With children it is worse; we rarely imagine children in desperate pain. We know intellectually that a certain number of children must die—it is the only way to run a universe—but why not snuff them out at birth? Why wait for them to develop as individuals and then torture them? Glasser does not explore the question, that is not a doctor's business, but he exploits the poignancy of the situation.

To the age-old drama, he adds a new one, the drama of technology. Listen to the sounds; you don't have to understand them: "And then, of course, there is multiple sclerosis, amyotrophic lateral sclerosis, metachromatic leucodystrophy; the agammaglobulemias, Aldrich Syndrome, the fatal granulomatosis diseases." A witch doctor mumbling in Zulu would sound less ominous. This appeal to incantation in books designed for a popular audience is a phenomenon peculiar to our time: "the creatinine clearances, the BUNs, the alkaline phosphatases, phosphates, sodium, potassium, magnesium, specific gravities, sedimentation rates, complement levels, differentials, eosinophil counts, Comb's tests, hapteglobins, PHs, acid-base balances, blood gases." Well. Compare *that* to Glasser's more conventional formulations of human concern—"He shook his head as he looked compassionately at the stricken child" and "But every now and then there's one who gets to you right at the beginning, a child with a special magic"—and you will see where Glasser's skills fall.

Still, this is a book specifically about human concern. It is a book with a thesis. Doctors, Glasser says, are so trained to believe in the miracle of medicine that they act as if they were gods interpreting disease to man; they no longer talk to patients and their relatives as if they were human beings with human anxieties and needs. To illustrate his point, Glasser presents to his intern an eleven-year-old girl dying of leukemia. The girl's father claims some knowledge of hospital procedures and insists that his daughter only be made comfortable until she dies. The intern rebels, of course: the child must be put on a protocol of drugs designed to obtain a remission that may, just possibly, last long enough for a cure to develop. To keep the child alive becomes a grisly business. The angry father stirs up the other parents of patients on the ward, convincing them that the doctors are either monstrous or incompetent. It is all very exciting. The intern pulls the plug on the child's life-sustaining machine when he has learned his lesson in humanity.

Except—except that the issues are never joined. The angry father is not simply a man who needs to be understood; he needs to be arrested. Pulling the plug on a terminal patient may be commendable, but it prompts more complex ethical reactions than a simple awareness of maturity and competence. Nor does Glasser really explore the questions attending the use of a protocol of drugs designed to serve better the needs of leukemia researchers than the child whose life depends upon it.

Two years ago in a book called *365 Days*, Glasser gave us a sequence of stories about American soldiers in combat in Vietnam. It worked better than this one does. Glasser knew no more about combat in Vietnam than he could deduce from service in a hospital in Japan. Yet his stories, equally as invented, equally as true as this one, worked in part because so little that seemed authentic had been written about soldiers in that war, in part because Glasser refrained from moralizing, and in part because combat stories are almost as old as storytelling itself. Here we have one story, and it is certainly readable. But it fails as fiction because its author is unequal to the moral situations he creates and because his characters have been plucked from the common reservoir of stereotypes maintained by novelists of tertiary talent. It fails as nonfiction because its author refuses to vouch for the accuracy of its design, the relatedness of the events he puts before us.

August 1973

AMERICAN NIGHTMARES

MANY READERS, I suspect, would pay the $15 that John G. Hubbell's *P.O.W.* costs to be excused from reading it. We know that American prisoners of war suffered greatly at the hands of their Vietnamese captors, and this knowledge has inevitably affected the way we think, or avoid thinking, about the war. Yet most Americans find it helpful not to think precisely about these prisoners, and certainly not about their ordeal. It's useful for us to perceive them fuzzily, not as individuals but as a unit that opportunely provided a demoralized nation with an example of courage, integrity, and resolution. The attempts by some prisoners to bring charges against others on their return were abruptly quashed because the country needed this unit to remain unified, to be what we had decided it was; something had to be right about that wretched war and what was right was our mutilated men. Besides, to think precisely on what happened to the prisoners is to realize that their misfortune was partly the fault of our society, which has never effectively defined the limits of what, in decency, it can require of its hostages in an enemy's jails.

In *P.O.W.* there's a grand confusion of the precise and fuzzy visions. Hubbell offers a detailed report on what Americans endured in North Vietnam's prisons, but declines to comment on his material, and provides no context or perspective whatever. Nevertheless, he or his publisher calls the book "a definitive history" when it really isn't history at all: it's dogged journalism. Hubbell and his associates conducted nearly two hundred interviews with those who returned and from the start seem to have intended their book to be a celebration of these men—a kind of Foxe's *Book of Martyrs* for our time.

In 1964, when Hanoi downed its first American plane, the Vietnamese didn't quite know what to do with their prisoners. Edward Alvarez was taken to Hoa Lo prison (later known as the "Hanoi Hilton"), where among rats as big as cats he ate rice that had been mixed with dirt and refused to answer questions. Other prisoners followed, including Robinson Risner, the top flying ace of the war, and in the fall of 1965 the Vietnamese launched their program of wholesale torture. Men were tortured for many hours, often many days at a time. As punishment for communicating by complicated codes involving tapping, coughing, and scratching, the men suffered broken and dislocated limbs; because they refused to bow to the guards, give information about themselves, or write incriminating "confessions," the Vietnamese "literally flayed the hides off their American prisoners" with rubber whips cut from automobile tires; because they refused to propagandize for the Communists or betray their fellow prisoners, they were bound so tightly that their shoulders nearly touched behind their backs, causing their ribs to crack and almost burst through their skin.

The Vietnamese were skilled and enthusiastic torturers and in time all the men broke and did what was required of them. Though most yielded no information about themselves that their captors hadn't read in the American press, and though the statements they signed resembled those made openly by American politicians, the prisoners thought themselves traitors. The Code of Conduct, which allows a prisoner only to identify himself, does not confront the problem of torture, and because it doesn't, the POWs suffered unnecessary physical and mental anguish. Late in 1969 the torture ceased, but the hard-line survivors among the Americans were dismayed by the arrival of a new breed of prisoner: men who deplored the war and were willing to cooperate with the enemy—some even volunteered to join the North Vietnamese forces.

Hubbell may be an uncritical collector of facts, but he is skillful at arranging his material. His prose ranges from the serviceable to the appalling—"a large expanse of him had been turned into a mass of oozing hamburger"—and his attentiveness to detail in more than a score of interchangeable episodes of torture verges on the perverse. Yet his book is undeniably informative and probably necessary, if only as a base from which future historians may build. I wish, though, that he had been able to breathe life into these men he means to celebrate. Incredibly brave men must be more difficult to write about than others, but Hubbell's prisoners are made real only in terms of their suffering. Nothing but literary incompetence is involved here, and yet when all these blows fall on men who seem to exist only to receive them, a certain corruption is at work. To pay proper tribute to the POWs we must try to understand them whole, as something more than Eagle Scouts toughing it out for their country.

December 1976

Since Homer's day, war stories have tended to run to some length; a good short one is hard to find. The shortest one I know, and one of the most resonant, appears at the beginning of Michael Herr's *Dispatches*. A half-crazed soldier speaks: "Patrol went up the mountain. One man came back. He died before he could tell us what happened." Here's another:

"You sit there at night with the infrared scope from a scout sniper's rifle and watch a Charlie come through four rolls of concertina wire. He started just about ten o'clock and he didn't get through the last strand of concertina wire until almost four o'clock in the morning. It took him six hours and we had every possible kind of trip wire you can think of inside there, along with mines, finger charges and Claymores. He came through and then we shot him.

"You go out there to take him off the wire the next morning, and it turns out to be the barber who's been shaving you with a straight razor for the last two months."

For all its brevity, that's a *literary* story: complex, eloquent, every word just so. I could teach it to a class, chalking arrows on a blackboard and concluding with a homily on "The Narrator's Tone of Voice." Now, class, before the bell rings, write an essay on why today's veteran talks in Early Hemingway. Nevertheless, the story is not intended to be literature. It comes from Mark Baker's *Nam*, which—like Al Santoli's *Everything We Had*—presents itself as an oral history of the American involvement in the Vietnam War, as told by those who fought it.

That two books so similar in intent should appear concurrently where none had been before is a coincidence familiar to publishers. And yet we need both, for though the two do not differ markedly in what they tell us about the war's horrors and confusions, they are, in emphasis and authority, strikingly unalike. Santoli fought in the war; Baker was a student at the time. Santoli's book is arranged loosely by chronology, from 1962 to the fall of Saigon. Baker's follows a soldier's cycle from induction through discharge and on to the veteran's difficulties reentering a hostile society. Both men take care to include testimony from one or two nurses and one or two blacks. Santoli interviewed thirty-three veterans; Baker—well, there's no way of knowing.

Santoli has drawn his witnesses from the more articulate combatants, those with an imagination or sense of responsibility that prompts them to want to leave a record. Like any good journalist, he identifies each by name, rank, and unit, his time and place of service. Baker, by contrast, identifies no one. He means to concentrate on the darker side of the war, and many of those he interviewed must have insisted upon anonymity as the price of their confessions to murder, rape, and atrocity. Still, the result lacks more than the authority documentation lends. People are *not* cameras; they interpret what they see and do and we cannot understand them or their actions if we cannot get some kind of fix on them. Baker's text is studded by rootless "I's" divorced from any condition except the shared experience of war. Have we heard from this person before? Is it a he or she, white or black, officer or enlisted man? Sometimes the text reveals these crucial distinctions, sometimes not. We never know anything, for instance, about the narrator of the story I quoted at the beginning of this piece; the imposed abstraction makes it seem less like journalism than literature.

That substantial reservation aside, *Nam* remains convincing—and the most horrifying book the war has yet produced. "I have to admit I enjoyed killing," one of Baker's witnesses says. And another: "I loved to just sit in the ditch and watch people die." A refrain that rings through both books is the pleasure war affords, particularly one fought by youngsters who took to shooting off heads as an extension of childhood fantasies. Baker's people confess to the fun of murdering old men and raping their daughters, of cutting off noses, ears, penises, and breasts. Bored soldiers test their skill by taking pot shots at a woman five hundred yards away. Angry soldiers, hearing that a detested sergeant is disabled, strapped to a cot, pour gasoline on him and throw on a match. One officer in the mountains orders his men to fire on generals arriving by helicopter; another murders an entire village on orders from above. In the book's most poignant story, a nurse who hopes to relieve her patients' anxieties allows them to show her pictures of sexual atrocities they have committed.

The absolute grimness of Baker's book is in no way relieved by Santoli's. A sergeant is shot in the back. A nurse reports that the medics as well as the patients on her ward were constantly shooting heroin. Wounded Americans beg to be killed. In the book's most effective testimony, a guerrilla warrior with the navy tells of a ritual called "getting wet," which involves cutting somebody's throat so that his blood splashes all over you. Here, as in *Nam*, the veterans agree that the real enemy was not the Viet Cong, who might well not trouble you if you left them alone, but your own officers, who would almost surely get you killed. Still, by virtue of letting his people talk more expansively than Baker does, Santoli manages a balance that Baker never intends. Santoli allows his people to be complex, which is to say normal; one is even something of a hero—a commander who actually looked after his men.

"I was insane the entire time I was in Vietnam," says Santoli's guerrilla. Oral history can't draw conclusions, but if these books do yield a moral, the insanity that this war bred is it. Why

so high an insanity quotient in this particular war? These very
young men came to the war for the usual reasons—patriotism,
machismo, because their country told them their participation
was required—and presently found the war to be purposeless.
There was not even a geographical direction. When everyone
may be the enemy, constant fear results. When, in a state of constant fear, one sees his buddies regularly blown away, a certain
brutalization sets in. All human life seems cheap, and the Vietnamese less than human. The evidence of these books is that the
highest American commanders condoned, if they didn't sanction,
the most appalling atrocities. What resulted can only be called a
war in a state of nervous breakdown. These books suggest the
consequences of that breakdown. They should leave any reader
with the conviction that we must learn how to control ourselves
the next time out.

May 1981

The problems posed by Watergate appear to have ended as
they began, with intelligent citizens paying them little mind.
There are now so many books about the scandal, and about the
attendant enormities of the Nixon administration, that the temptation is to read none. After all, the facts were eventually thrown
at us in gross lots, weren't they? And if we didn't have time then
to assimilate them, and can't now quite distinguish between Herbert Kalmbach and Herbert Porter, we did throw out the whole
horrible crew, didn't we? The System works (doesn't it?) and we
can think now about something else. Jonathan Schell's premise
seems to be that the details have been published and will be published again. His purpose in *The Time of Illusion* is to find a pattern among selected facts, to write as a historian, and if history
yields to polemic, to a warning that we haven't solved our problems at all, then histories have served honorably as polemics and
warnings before.

Schell argues that Nixon's administration developed "a new
form of rule, in which images were given precedence over substance in every phase of government." In short, by using the resources of the presidency, Nixon realized that he could control
what people thought of his performance and he therefore acted to
"compose scenes rather than to solve real problems." He could

appear to be working against crime and for the advancement of
blacks and the poor while in fact intending the opposite of what
he said in public. He could talk about bringing the country together while he deliberately exacerbated issues to effect a division
among Americans that would ensure his reelection.

According to Schell, when problems beset his presidency,
Nixon perceived all opposition, foreign and domestic, as part of a
unified conspiracy against presidential authority. It is Schell's
thesis that to counter this imaginary threat, Nixon set out to take
over the entire federal government, to assume a dictator's powers,
to "make war against Americans." Early in his incumbency he
attempted to weaken or destroy every institution that might oppose him: television, the press, private foundations, the Supreme
Court, Congress, his own cabinet. He and his cohorts bugged
their own staffs, waged a secret war against Cambodia, attacked
the rights of assembly and free speech, suborned critical government agencies into crimes, interfered with trials and grand-jury
investigations, extorted money from big business, and encouraged the kind of violence that occurred at Kent State. A master of illusion, Nixon rigged phony supporting letters and phony
opposition during his campaigns.*

And all of this illusion, Schell tells us, came about in an attempt to preserve a greater illusion still: that of America's "credi-
bility" with the rest of the world. According to Schell's
credibility theory, American leaders since Kennedy have resolved that we must maintain the *appearance* of great power and
demonstrate our appetite to use power abroad, if we are to avoid
nuclear disaster with the Soviet Union. Limited wars, like that in
Vietnam, are not about substantive issues like freedom or repel
ling communism; they are about our image as tough guys in the
world arena. Nobody cared much about Vietnam, Schell says,
but the credibilitists in government did care about avoiding
global totalitarianism and nuclear extinction. And so say all of us,
but it would be better if limited wars were not America's only alternative to brinkmanship as a means to show the world that it is

* Dave Brubeck, the jazz musician, told me that the bombing of Cambodia prompted him
to write the first political letter of his life. He told Nixon, in effect, to cut it out. The
White House replied, thanking Brubeck for his support of the administration's Southeast
Asia policy.

neither suicidally inclined nor impotent. The problem, Schell reminds us, remains unsolved. The proof is the temptation of President Ford's administration to show its strength by intervening in Angola's civil war.

Schell's provocative book is an argumentative essay set out as if it were historical recapitulation. Like most arguments, it is overlong, repetitious, ill organized, and intemperate, which is not to say that it is not entirely correct. Schell's graceful sentences nearly mitigate the rage with which he writes; his ironic juxtapositions nearly persuade me to accept his argument as fact. And yet his assumption of insidious design calls for more evidence. Schell neglects, I think, the muddle factor in government, the ad-hoc stupidity and random criminality of Nixon and his friends. Purposeless perversity is a human constant; that Nixon was the vortex of so much of it is alarming, but perhaps not proof of so grand a conspiracy as Schell construes. Never mind. Schell's book is a genuine chiller, if only because it reminds us of how far Nixon succeeded in dismantling our government and Constitution before Watergate, before he was reelected by a landslide, and how eagerly Americans cheered him on.

January 1976

Sitting in prison, Sir Walter Raleigh explained why he had written a history of the world rather than an account of recent events: "Whosoever, in writing a modern history, shall follow truth too near the heels, it may happily strike out his teeth. There is no mistress or guide that hath led her followers and servants into greater miseries." Massive transfusions of money, like those given to Bob Woodward and Carl Bernstein for their Watergate books, ease the pain some, but the reception of *The Final Days* may have left them counting their teeth. Angry people who know no more about the book than what they have seized from headlines or excerpts published in *Newsweek* have denounced it, and are defending their right not to know what's in it. I can understand their unease but think it misplaced. Questions about the authors' taste and possible vindictiveness subside when one has read the whole book, but questions about the reliability of this kind of journalism persist.

The Final Days belongs to that subspecies of journalism

called instant history. It was researched after Nixon's resignation and relies primarily on the memories of 394 people interviewed by the authors. The virtue of instant history is that evidence can be gathered while the participants' memories are fresh, relatively unreconstructed by hindsight. The liability is that the absence of the historian's perspective and accountability makes it impossible for the reader to assess the worth of what he's reading. Woodward and Bernstein can only say: trust us. I do, for their past courage and enterprise; still, their book makes me uneasy.

Gossip, for instance, is an integral part of their narrative. Woodward and Bernstein rely on hearsay evidence inadmissible in any court. They insist they have two sources for everything, but that is disingenuous: if a presidential aide tells two people he said such-and-such to the president, and those people independently pass his message on to the authors, then it becomes a historical fact that the aide did say it, though of course he may only have concocted a self-serving story. Much of what Fred Buzhardt told Nixon in this book makes Buzhardt look good, and since Nixon didn't cooperate with the authors there can be only one primary source for all this good news about Buzhardt. In those perilous days, a lot of people were worried about looking right while doing wrong, which should cast doubt on any scene where only one of them was with the president.

Then there's the New Journalism problem. "Buzhardt nervously tapped his hand on the armrest. His West Point class ring struck the metal." New Journalism dramatizes a scene rather than summarizes it, and such embellishment is usually justified by the writer's having been there. Woodward and Bernstein weren't: this kind of stuff may be documented, but it *sounds* like fiction. Even the suspicion of fiction throws all else in doubt. So does their choice of emphasis. In a crisis, doubters are more likely to provide reporters with cooperation and articulate responses than are the faithful, who retreat into clichés. Reporters tend to believe those who will talk to them, and then look for supporting evidence. Woodward and Bernstein rely heavily on evidence offered by those most nervous in Nixon's service; probably their conclusions are accurate, but the possibility of a serious imbalance cannot be disregarded.

Their worst problem is their refusal to cite sources for anything in the book. Usually we can guess the source of any scene—Buzhardt, Haig, Garment, and David Eisenhower were clearly helpful—but not always. Woodward and Bernstein apparently decided that since they couldn't attribute much of what they learned, they wouldn't attribute any of it. That way they have a smoother, unverifiable story, which varies in significant details from what J. Anthony Lukas has reported in his longer, broader book, *Nightmare*. Because future historians will have to rely on *The Final Days*, I hope Woodward and Bernstein have locked away a fully annotated manuscript.

These reservations considered, is their book worthwhile? Absolutely. I wish they had written it differently, but the book they have written will survive its critics. It is absorbing, nearly intoxicating in its fascination. We need to know almost everything in it: the complex portraits of the principals, the evidence of Nixon's isolation and disintegration, Kissinger's devotion to devious behavior, Haig's willingness to lie for his embattled employer, and the arguments among the lawyers about possible pardons for Haldeman and Ehrlichman. To its authors' credit, only the most flinty of readers could finish this book without feeling pity for this curious president who engineered his own destruction.

May 1976

OUT FAR AND IN DEEP

ONCE UPON A TIME, when I still smashed my overheads into the net, I sought enlightenment from a paunchy guru called the Pro. "What are you doing wrong?" Like all masters of his ilk, he repeated my question as his eyes narrowed against the strain of containing so much Oriental wisdom. "You've been reading tennis books again. It's always the same. You pay $7 for the tennis book, then you pay me $30 for lessons to undo the damage."

True, O Pro. But even though it is my karma forever to read tennis books and then hit overheads into the net, I approached Timothy Gallwey's *The Inner Game of Tennis* on my knees—the weary pilgrim attracted by vibrations of tranquillity. The epigraph suggests that tennis is but a metaphor of God's Great Game. The lack of illustrations, save one of a tennis ball metamorphosed by its seams into a diagram of Yin and Yang, and some jacket snaps of the author leaping about in long trousers, his face an impassive mask (no one since Bill Tilden has been composed enough to wear long trousers on a court). Inside, we are instructed to learn to love the tennis ball and scrutinize its seams as it hurtles over the net; also we are confirmed in our suspicions that the key to inner tennis is the key to everything else in life.

Gallwey's method is one of relaxed concentration: "The secret of winning any game lies in not trying too hard." In fact, what we must do is open ourselves to the perfect overhead smash that has always existed within us. We must stop analyzing what we do wrong, stop thinking about how to do it right, stop criticizing our shots, but rather approach our errors in an interested, somewhat detached tone." Nor shall we crow over our good shots: we shall simply become absorbed in the here and now of what we are doing because the good shots "come when the mind is as still as a glass lake." We shall not tell our body how to hit a shot (it already knows) but will instead visualize the perfect course of the ball zooming toward its precise target and let the body hit the shot that the mind wants. We shall rejoice in the game and in an "egoless desire to win."

There's a lot of truth in this, as well as a lot of the other stuff, and neither is particularly original because in *Zen and the Art of Archery*, Eugen Herrigel claimed the field before Gallwey was born. My final review of this book will be written on various clay surfaces in my neighborhood, but I must say I'm impressed by what Gallwey claims his discipline has done for him. By improving his concentration his reflexes have become so fast that he now receives the hardest serves while standing a mere foot behind the service line. As for me, the reviewer who is exhorted to abandon the judgmental process, I can detect two immediate uses for this book. One is to change my life and follow the Way, although I suspect that the kind of mastery Gallwey advocates, properly understood, is no simple achievement. The other is to give the book to my opponents, for it is certain to wreck their games. There may be Unity above, but in the Great Scramble here below surely anything goes.

June 1974

In 1970 an obscure law professor at Yale became a rich celebrity by publishing a toasted marshmallow of a book, *The Greening of America*. Warm, sweet, and gooey, it expressed a kind of undergraduate spiritual hunger, a hippie sensibility that its middle-aged author insisted would inexorably overtake all of American life. We couldn't know then what this dismal memoir* reveals: its author's wretched state of mind at the time of his success (he was forty-two and a desperate virgin), or his habit of assuming that when he feels unhappy the world must be at fault.

He believes his early law practice in Washington, D.C. violated his spirit: he wanted to feel "sensual" in the office, but wearing "a suit interfered with the free movement of my mind." Regression to a cradle mentality—"Touch me and rock me," he cries—helped; even better was to go to San Francisco in 1971 and hire a male prostitute. With Yale in his past (his departure was his students' fault: they had become increasingly prisoners of alienation), he finds freedom in the homosexual underground.

No one can hate a man who whines for a world of love and beauty—many good folk singers have done just that—but in charity I must not dwell long upon his book. A self-pitying affair, mired in clichés of thought and language, it is unredeemed by those graces necessary to the memoirs of all but the greatest of men: self-mockery, good humor, a sharp observation of others. Nor is his book altogether honest. "Many events and details have been fictionalized," he writes on the final page. "Some people who appear in the book are wholly fictional." Which leaves those who have the time and inclination to wonder which of this book's artificial people and unconvincing scenes are indeed fake.

November 1976

---

* *The Sorcerer of Bolinas Reef,* by Charles Reich.

I am often asked what is the best way to catch a flying saucer. The only method I know is that perfected by my neighbor
Harvey and his son, Terry. "It's easier than you think," Harvey
says. "We waited for a muggy evening. Heat lightning. Terry
took the Mini-Moog synthesizer out to the patio, plugged it into
the electric grill and played Pink Floyd space music: 'A Saucerful
of Secrets,' I think it was. Terry smoked Acapulco Gold and of
course I had my trusty bucket of martinis. Then we saw it: a
metal object hovering over our driveway. Four white lights below
and red and blue revolving lights above. No sound except a buzz-
ing between my ears. Two spacemen dressed alike came out of
what looked like doors and ordered us inside. They took us to a
brightly lit place where a funny-looking fella in a black cloak
warned us *not to try it again.* I think it makes them nervous, us
trying to trap them."

We must approach John A. Keel's *The Mothman Prophecies*
with a similar extraterrestrial charity. Keel, "an acknowledged
leader in the field of UFO investigations," wants to tell us about
the Garuda, a seven-foot man with feathers, bulging red eyes, and
a ten-foot wingspread, who haunted West Virginia in 1967. More
than one hundred people saw the Garuda, Keel insists, and many
of these were subsequently harassed by stubby men with olive
skins and pointed faces, who wore black suits and drove old Cad-
illacs that looked and smelled brand new.

During his investigation, Keel heard horrifying stories of
what he calls a "winged weirdo," saw some flying saucers, decided that "entities," as he calls them, or alternatively "strange
critters," were tapping his phone, imitating his voice in calls to
others, and generally trying to confuse him. "Somebody somewhere does not want us to understand," he says. "My own mind
was being tapped, just like my telephone."

Keel distrusts his fellow "UFO enthusiasts," but that's about
all he distrusts. He believes, for instance, in "cosmic clap," which
afflicts some men who have seen interplanetary visitors, and he
does not dismiss the testimony of acquaintances who returned
from the planet Lanulos with news that the people there run
naked. He believes he received precise details in advance of Martin Luther King's murder (but claims that he couldn't get King
on the phone to warn him). Perhaps, Keel suggests, saucers and

Mothmen are not from outer space at all, but are instead material-izations of energy from a dimension beyond our senses: it may be, he says, that they have always been here.

Well, it's as sensible an idea as any other that he offers. I wish that most of Keel's informants had not been teenagers, and that cameras aimed at these airborne aberrations did not suddenly malfunction, and that Keel did not tend to confuse cause and ef-fect: when people with damaged eyesight report weird observa-tions, he concludes that what they saw damaged their eyesight. Nevertheless, Keel seems to have had a rough time of it, what with phones beeping in his ear and black-suited men walking loose about the streets. I think he believes what he says; and I think it grand, what with the public tranquillity being troubled by authors mumbling that they can't get their damn poems, essays, or whatever it is they write published, that the Saturday Review Press is willing to demonstrate just how far it will go to accommodate an author with something to say. Clearly, with John A. Keel, we are dealing with something opposed to Occam's razor. Call it Occam's magnet.

March 1975

Once upon a time in the Olduvai Gorge, a lightning bolt split a baobab tree in two, causing the first or possibly second man to jump halfway out of his fur. Employing his newly evolved power of ratiocination, he arrived at a conclusion. Exercising his newly evolved power of speech, the first or possibly second man said, "That didn't happen," and shuffled on his way. Thus was invented one of our most engaging and persistent human quali-ties: the denial of reality. With two million years or so of practice, we have refined the art a bit: for unacceptable reality we have re-cently taken to substituting elaborate fantastical constructions. These three books show the process at work.* In each, the retreat from reality is more marked than in the one before—but each is more pleasant, more civilized than its predecessor.

Bruce Clayton's fantasy derives from the myths of frontier

---

* *Life After Doomsday,* by Bruce D. Clayton; *Casebook of a UFO Investigator,* by Ray-mond E. Fowler; *The Dictionary of Imaginary Places,* by Alberto Manguel and Gianni Guadalupi.

America: we have only to draw our wagons into a circle to survive a nuclear war. The war won't be as bad as you have heard. Assuming the Russians know what they are doing, 90 percent of America will be fallout free. You may think this a large assumption about the Russians, but Clayton is nonetheless interesting because virtually every point he makes will not have been considered by most of his readers. "What about sex in the fallout shelter?" he asks, and "How many members of your family are you willing to regard as acceptable losses?" (No, don't give us their names.)

His point is: you must do *something*. "The question of which assault rifle you should buy isn't nearly as important as the fact that you must get one"—to mow down ghetto refugees or your neighbors in search of your food supply. In fact, refugees won't be much of a threat because the roads will be blown up along with the cities, but as for your friend next door—well, the Heckler and Koch HK91 heavy-assault rifle firing a 7.62 NATO cartridge works very well. If you're on your roof hosing down the fallout, a Colt Commander .45 autopistol modified for combat is easier to carry. He shows us, too, how to convert our houses into efficient zones for firing, and suggests we store away five years' supply of wheat, milk, sugar, and salt. A wheat stew in every pot and an Armalite AR-180 in every loophole will see us through, as long as we've ordered our gas masks (Clayton tells us where).

I must say I found this all very impressive. Clayton assures me I will not be "shooting to kill" but "shooting to live." He reminds me that if I'm driving an escape car through a rioting mob and my wife is firing a Remington 870 Brushmaster from the back seat, I'd better have protection for my ears. It *had* occurred to me that if I spent next year shoveling my lawn up against the walls of my house I'd be better insulated against gamma rays, but still . . . what a deal of time, effort, thought, and money the Clayton program involves. Survival, for him, is a full-time occupation, fit mainly for the idle rich. If civilization increases in inverse ratio to the amount of time and effort required for survival, then Clayton's plan sets our gears spinning in reverse.

Like survivalism, the flying-saucer cult offers a systematic program for avoiding the reality of the nuclear threat. Medieval man assumed that strange objects would occasionally appear in the sky—the *Anglo-Saxon Chronicle* is full of them—yet only after Hiroshima did some of us conclude that they were the fruit of an inconceivable technology that would either destroy or redeem us. (Medieval man, of course, knew that he would be redeemed by an extraterrestrial force; he didn't need a saucer to do the job.) Nevertheless, a certain agnosticism is in order here. Just because a lot of screwballs claim to have seen, or even visited, a saucer doesn't mean such celestial crockery doesn't exist.

Raymond Fowler is no screwball; he is, like Clayton, a true believer and, as ufologists go, a reasonable man, if an unlucky one. His mother saw a UFO, so did his brother and his wife, but Fowler must make do with second and thirdhand accounts. To compensate, he subscribes to the true believer's logic. If UFO sightings increase with the threat of nuclear war, it is not because we are scared of our technology but because UFOs are interested in our development. If a man acts in a mentally disturbed way before seeing a saucer, his close encounter is not to be discounted: UFO technology controls our mental processes. If he reports other weird experiences, these, too, can be explained: proximity to a UFO somehow heightens psychic awareness. Fowler's book contains a lot of this kind of thinking and relies primarily on the kind of hearsay evidence that would be thrown out of any court. Nevertheless, the stories about little men in silver suits *are* entertaining and are told here in a manner more restrained than that of most pro-saucer tracts.

More entertaining still—and more strictly logical—are the fantasies collected in *The Dictionary of Imaginary Places*. Like Clayton and Fowler, the writers whose fictional geographies are summarized and illustrated here impose upon the inadequacies of the world we know elaborate constructions that are themselves commentaries on the way we live. Unlike them, most (but not all) of these writers admit to writing fiction. This *Dictionary* is a detailed gazetteer, including 250 original maps and illustrations of more than 1,200 cities, islands, countries, and continents invented by storytellers from Homer's day to ours.

Presented with mock solemnity and written with grace and wit, the book is a work of genuine scholarship that is also a pleasure to read. All the obvious places are included—More's Utopia,

Swift's Brobdingnag, Treasure Island, Oz, and Atlantis—and so
are many that less broadly educated lexicographers might have
missed: Brigadoon, for instance, Pepperland, and Freedonia,
scene of the Marx Brothers' movie *Duck Soup*. I regret certain
oversights—Al Capp's Lower Slobbovia and Cleopolis, where
Spenser's Faerie Queene presided—but there's compensation in
the wealth of obscure places that the authors have plucked from
sixteenth-century moral tracts and deservedly forgotten nineteenth-century novels.

February 1981

SCIENCE FICTION: THE STATE OF THE WHATEVER

*. . . listen:there's a hell
of a good universe next door;let's go.*

— e. e. cummings

SUDDENLY, THEY'RE ALL AROUND US. Too late now to think of
repelling them, or even of self-defense. They've conquered the
nursery and have sunk tentacles into the colleges. Disguised as
pimply kids and pallid biochemists, they look like *us*, and are
multiplying, communicating with one another in frequencies the
rest of us don't hear. They have a message for us, too: we're taking over. Pay attention. Be respectful.

They're the science-fiction people. Not Martians, but the
Martians' best friends: the people who write and read science fiction, and those who gape at science-fiction images on movie and
television screens. Nobody knows how many of them there are,
but their number grows and they are becoming noisy. Like in-

sects, the "SF" fans possess a swarming instinct; in groups, they migrate to exhibitions of pulp-magazine art at universities, to local, national, even international conventions. Their attitudes reflect a narrow, necessary unease about our future, yet their literary aspirations constitute a curious refutation of what other writers—they call them "mainstream" writers—have been about for decades.

This month, when the Modern Language Association meets in San Francisco, its members will participate in seminars devoted to two of SF's cult figures, Kurt Vonnegut, Jr. and Robert A. Heinlein, and two respected SF writers, Ursula K. Le Guin and Robert Silverberg. The teachers will then disperse to offer, in colleges from Barnard to Eastern New Mexico University, more than one thousand courses in science fiction, and countless more in high schools and in grade schools. And yet, for all this dispersion, most of what happens in science fiction passes unnoticed by the rest of the world. Barry N. Malzburg, for instance, has sold five million copies of his books, yet no one outside of the science-fiction community has heard of him. There seems to be some kind of contradiction here.

The problem goes right to the core of science fiction—no one agrees on a definition of what the thing is. Within the family, attempts at definitions are part of the game. Heinlein prefers "speculative fiction," which others have picked up, but it's too vague a term and encourages fans who insist that most great writers are science-fiction writers (the brotherhood has claimed, among others, Homer, Plato, More, Swift, Defoe, Borges, and Nabokov). Damon Knight, a theoretician in the field, has suggested that science-fiction writers, like Gnostics, alchemists, and depth psychologists before them, keep in touch with man's unconscious. It's a good claim, a nonliterary claim, but one not often heard. Nevertheless, some kind of heavy definition must precede discussion. Here's one: science fiction is a kind of fantasy that is rhetorically based on science or technology, either real or imaginary, or is based on a plausible extrapolation from present reality.

But it's more than that. Science fiction is a magnet that collects college professors, electrical engineers, teenagers, the semiliterate, and the preliterate in an enthusiastic community.

Science fiction also fills a vacuum in letters. Most people today cannot comfortably read our best practicing writers: Updike's novels, Lowell's poetry, and Barthelme's short stories seem to them impenetrable. Science fiction offers such troubled readers a plain story plainly told. Some of it offers heroes, monsters, epic battles in imaginary worlds. Some offers ideas of a sort: what happens if technology gets out of hand? If we encounter alien civilizations? If we ourselves were to develop differently? Some assuages the reader's conscience by taking seriously important questions of ecology, population, and sociology. And, in a time of drastically diminished markets for beginning fiction writers, science fiction offers a relatively uncritical place to start.

Like jazz, science fiction (at least as practiced by the professionals, not by mainstream writers who try it on occasionally) is an outgrowth of popular culture. "The kids are responsible for the whole thing," says Ray Bradbury, an old master of the genre. "They educated the teachers." He's right: most science-fiction readers are very young, between twelve and twenty-five. For a long time SF writers were what Harlan Ellison calls "young scientific hobbyists. Most of those guys were virgins until they were forty. They were not writers. They were more interested in scientific gimmicks than in mirroring life in any recognizable way." Many of today's promising SF writers began as fans—Ellison among them. "The fan usually gets started as a child," says Ben Bova, editor of the SF magazine *Analog*. "He is often an ugly duckling who cannot succeed at sports or other things—I was asthmatic and couldn't play ball. He compensates for this with intellectual stimulation and likes to imagine worlds and problems that others wouldn't consider. He usually grows up to be a scientist." The young fans attend the conventions, write imitative exercises for the fanzines. Few SF writers aim higher than what a teenage intelligence can grasp and the smart ones, like Kurt Vonnegut, carefully satirize targets—racism, pollution, teachers—that teenagers are conditioned to dislike.

Finally, science fiction is a siege mentality: *ghetto* is the fans' own word for it. Many resent being segregated from the general literary community. If a critic suggests that *Madame Bovary* is a sloppy excuse for a novel, no one stirs, but let him suggest that Frank Herbert's *Dune* and its endless successors induce instant narcolepsy—then a dance of the troglodytes ensues. The fans are organized. For a quarter of a century they have told themselves that SF has become respectable literature. Not hearing many echoes of this opinion from outside the ghetto, they present to outsiders a united, defensive front. Even Robert Scholes, an English professor and SF apologist, succumbs to the siege rhetoric: "There are some scores to be paid," he has written. "This is going to be fun." Nor do the fans readily forgive their heroes who make a run for the profits and reputations to be gained outside the ghetto. Vonnegut ran first; Ellison and Silverberg are poised to defect; and Anthony Burgess, whose novel *A Clockwork Orange* is often cited as an example of how good SF can be, claims it is not science fiction at all. "There has been no important science fiction since Aldous Huxley's *Brave New World*," Burgess says. The fans don't like to hear that kind of thing.

As it happens, science fiction's most important contribution to the way we have lived in this century has always had less to do with literature than with a habit of mind that views with skepticism the ballyhoo advanced on behalf of progress and technology. Modern science fiction is the shadow child of the utopian socialists who assured us, eighty years ago, that machines and the march to social equality were both the order of the future and the road to universal human happiness. As this cause was argued in countless tracts and manifestos, there arose a new kind of novel, scientific romances they were called then, some of which suggested that such optimism was a dangerous delusion. H. G. Wells managed to write exhortations to socialism with one hand while writing gloomy science fiction with the other. "An assault on human self-satisfaction," he said of *The Time Machine*, his haunting story of the final degeneracy of human society. He might have said the same of *The Island of Dr. Moreau*, which dramatized the blasphemy that technology becomes when so seemingly benign a matter as animal husbandry is taken to its logical extreme.

Taking possibilities, or trends, to their logical extremes is an important function of science fiction. "It's the only form of literature that has as its basic premise the fact that there will be change," says Isaac Asimov. "Science fiction leads from behind, really. It predicts only what seems logical, given certain scientific discoveries. It's a seed bed for scientists." For whatever good it has done us, SF writers have predicted such technological innovations as lasers, submarines, moon rockets, television, atomic explosions, tanks, pocket computers, air-breathing communities living under water, even night baseball. Today, says Asimov, science fiction can help us understand the need to exchange our extravagant ways if we are to avoid the destruction of mankind. "I mean we have to change our mind about *motherhood*. It's going to be awfully difficult. We may not survive because we may not be able to make the changes fast enough." Even now, some SF visions are being pondered seriously—not just the dream of killer satellites, but the idea recently advanced by NASA for a system designed to colonize space with a 500,000-ton, orbiting, wheel-shaped habitat more than one mile in diameter, with room for ten thousand people, as well as shops, schools, light industry, and agriculture. The project's designers see no technical impediment to this kind of thing—and don't ask whether this kind of thing is what we need or want. Whether a twenty-first-century kind of colonialism that takes its new territory with it is preferable to the thriftier nineteenth-century kind that seized it from previous occupants is a question that scientists and engineers don't ask. Science-fiction writers sometimes do.

> *Keep behind me. There's no sense getting killed by a plant.*
> —dialogue from the movie *The Day of the Triffids*

The science fiction available today may be divided roughly into four categories. Each has its own fans who are often scornful of the games being played in the other three stadiums. Two of the four, the heavy-money categories, are produced by television and Hollywood. The less affluent two are literary: one is the traditional hardware or space-opera story; the other, more restive, yearns for recognition as art.

Star Trek is more than a television series that died and was resurrected from the vault; it's a way of life. Today "Star Trek" thrives better on reruns than it did in its original incarnation—seventy-nine episodes produced between 1966 and 1968. Today children not born when the program was first shown nationally on NBC hold Star Trek parties. There are Star Trek stores in

California and New York that sell foam-rubber Vulcan ear tips and buttons warning, "I'm Scanning Your Body." In a forthcoming book, actor Leonard Nimoy admits that he has difficulty dissociating himself from the role of the imperturbable Mr. Spock that he played in the series. As many as eighteen thousand "Trekkies" have assembled at their own conventions. At Memphis State, East Texas State, and Lewis and Clark College in Oregon, seminars are offered in "The Philosophy of Star Trek." Paramount, which thought the series a bust, sold or destroyed its sets; now it must rebuild them for a multimillion-dollar Star Trek movie.

May they lose their shirts. Star Trek jellifies the mind. It began with some scientific playfulness, but as budgets and inspiration shriveled, the show became more "realistic." In theory, the starship *Enterprise* glides about the universe, its mission "to boldly go where no man has gone before." Perhaps it's easier to split an infinitive than infinity; in any event, the *Enterprise*'s more precise mission is to impose mid-twentieth-century standards of American democracy on alien civilizations. In one episode, the crew comes upon a planet run like a southern plantation: the white folk live in the clouds savoring art, while the dark folk work in the mines below, prevented by an invisible gas from attaining equal humanity. The boys from the *Enterprise* straighten *that* out, you may believe.

"Space: 1999," this season's surprise success on local channels, is nearly as stupid as "Star Trek," but much prettier. There's Martin Landau, whose stare will pierce concrete, and Barbara Bain, whose face seems frozen by Novocain. There are special effects, too, by Brian Johnson, which are indistinguishable from those he helped create for Stanley Kubrick's *2001: A Space Odyssey*—that is to say, we are obliged to spend a lot of time watching the undercarriages of space ships gliding above our heads. In SF television, innovation is to be avoided at all costs. The series is about our moon, which breaks loose from its orbit to go adventuring in space. Colonists marooned on the moon must soon cope with emergencies around the universe. Rudi Gernrich, who gave us topless bathing suits, designed the moonmen's costumes. Recently, Landau, in a white suit, faced down an evil alien in a black suit with impractically flaring cuffs. All that was missing was High Noon in Tombstone—but westerns are dusty and sweaty, and this is a clean and *pretty* show.

If literate science-fiction fans are contemptuous of SF television, they tend to be merely skeptical of SF movies. The fans sense that movie producers rarely strain their craniums in search of a challenging idea. Why should they, when giant ants or mobile, carnivorous cacti are all that's really needed? Take one space monster, freeze him in ice, then let him thaw while the humans fill in time with endless palaver. Mix with one woman, whose only role is to scream at appropriate intervals. Add one brave, stupid fellow who fights the monster and one smart fellow who figures out how to destroy it so thoroughly that nothing's left for the lab technicians to pick over. Presto: an SF movie classic.

The fans are aware, too, that the finger that Hollywood licks and holds into the wind is rarely pointed at art; it's pointed at money. The trend is the thing: you sense it, you exploit it, you let it go bust and turn to something else. "These things run in waves," says Roger Corman, who makes SF movies. "People are interested in all kinds of fantasy now: transcendental meditation, Carlos Castenada, as well as our space successes. It's like horror films. There's always a certain demand for them, and when they start to do well, they're overproduced." No one in Hollywood seems ready to make a case for science fiction as an art form, certainly not George Lucas, who calls his forthcoming movie *Star Wars* a story about a juvenile gang rumble against fascist oppressors of the galaxy. He doesn't even care if it's called science fiction. "It's a shoot-'em-up with ray guns," he says. "A romantic fantasy about as serious as a spaghetti western." Julia Phillips, who will produce *Close Encounters of the Third Kind,* calls her project "the *Jaws* of science-fiction movies." No wonder the fans are depressed.*

"As you remarked, Jacko, there's something wrong with the physics of this place."
—Colin Kapp, "The Pen and the Dark"

---

* The fans recovered when these two movies were released to wide acclaim, and denounced me for the derogatory terms they insisted *I* had used to describe them.

For all its hardware, visual science fiction is severely limited in its effects. "Everybody seems to be spending a lot of time on the look of things," says producer Si Litvinoff, "rather than on the ideas of the best writers on what things will be like. If you take a good notion and pursue it and stop worrying about the hardware, you're going to be successful." Certainly such joy as can be wrested from written science fiction lies in its ideas, in the abstract and sometimes exceedingly complex intellectual premises with which it is wholly concerned.

The golden age of science fiction began in 1939, the year that Asimov, Heinlein, A. E. Van Voght, and Theodore Sturgeon began sending stories to *Astounding Science Fiction*'s new editor, John W. Campbell. Campbell is an authentic SF hero. He gave his writers ideas for some of their best stories; he demanded real plots and plausible science; he was indifferent to complex characters and fine writing; and he insisted that human beings were never to be defeated by extraterrestrials. He paid his writers one cent a word (eventually four cents—about what SF magazines pay today).

For two decades science fiction bristled with robots and rocket ships, space and time warps, alien invaders (but not bug-eyed monsters, which were by then déclassé) and remote civilizations whose social structures were curiously similar to those on Earth in the thirties and forties. Most of the SF of this time was energetic, unliterary stuff; a faith in technology as the cure to problems caused by technology prevailed until Hiroshima and beyond. Most of it was written as long "short" stories, and a few of these, if swallowed as a teenager, will continue to nourish the adult mind: Asimov's "Nightfall," for instance, based on Campbell's idea that if the stars could be seen only once in a millennium, men would go mad with fear; Heinlein's "The Green Hills of Earth," a eulogy for a space poet; Ray Bradbury's "The Third Expedition," in which Martians destroy a manned probe from Earth by seducing the spacemen with an illusion of a 1920s Ohio town.

Then in the 1960s something happened to the genre. While some of the solid professionals ambled on as they always had, new writers like Ursula Le Guin and Samuel R. Delany showed themselves more interested in sociology and psychology than in physics and chemistry. "The New Wave," as they came to be known, wrote less about fanciful worlds and old-fashioned futures, and more about worlds and futures that develop logically from current social problems. Their books grew very long. Whereas the old guard tended to think in terms of a short story, which they were sometimes tempted to rewrite as a novel, with a lot of padding added, the new writers no sooner finished a novel than they began thinking of it as the opening of a trilogy—a good basic premise is hard to come by and it's easier to work variations on it than to think of another. These writers also began to experiment with what they called "style." In a fat anthology called *Dangerous Visions*, Harlan Ellison announced "a revolution." It was now okay, he told the SF community, to write about sex, religion, and politics in science fiction. We can act just like the grown-ups. In fact, we *are* the grown-ups.

Some who lived in the SF ghetto, and had grown to like it, shuddered. By experiments with style did the New Wave people mean the kind of prose that festered in Delany's tumescent novel *Dhalgren*? "The moon flung gold coins at her breasts.... He kissed her; she caught his wrists. The joined meat of their mouths came alive." Perhaps no one needed *that*, or Delany's twenty-page, bisexual, *Guinness Book of Records* orgies that sounded just like mainstream fiction orgies, only worse written. Even gritty science-fiction sex, like that in a recently published story "Lady Sunshine and the Magoon of Beatus," seemed less than desirable: "The gross dryad never let go the green boy's penis. She ripped at it with her nails. She gnawed at it with her skeleton teeth. She rubbed and snorted it in her decayed nose. Lady Sunshine could hardly bear to watch."

Crude as most of the experimentations with style and sex were to prove, they excited SF fans, who often confuse the attempt with the achievement. Many fans don't have a literary frame of reference, having preferred, as students, Ray Bradbury ("for his poetry") to Milton, Arthur C. Clarke ("for his relevance") to Shakespeare. Like his fans, Bradbury believes that science fiction is the only fiction relevant to the world we live in today. "Kids, when they get together, naturally want to talk about major problems," he says. "In the mainstream of our literature they don't find anyone talking about it. Saul Bellow and Norman Mailer aren't doing it." Bellow writes about what it

means to be an intelligent adult today and Mailer writes about curious concentrations of energy in our society, and from what they
write we may perhaps learn something about our collective future, but the fans don't believe it. "They read science fiction because its ethical and moral concerns are more clear," says Le
Guin.

Le Guin, in *The Left Hand of Darkness*, offers a thoughtful
alternative to the polarity of the sexes; Anthony Burgess, in *A
Clockwork Orange*, plays inventively with language—precisely
those areas that lesser writers find so resistant to innovation. That
these two experiments succeed is due in part to their authors'
understanding of what sexuality and language mean to us now.
The hermaphrodites who inhabit Le Guin's distant planet are interesting because they allow us to reflect on the extent to which
sexuality shapes culture. "Nadsat," the teenage language of the
future that Burgess developed, is interesting because it is not gib-
berish, but a clever, slangy blend of Russian and English that at
first distances the reader from its subject and then draws him
into it.

These two novels—one by an interloper, a man who uses the
gimmicks of science fiction in only a few of his books, the other
by a woman who is perhaps the best of the new breed of SF writers—may fairly be said to represent the state of the art today. Science fiction of this quality is very rare. An illuminating contrast
may be found in Heinlein's *Stranger in a Strange Land*, an ambitious and genuinely dreadful novel. Breaking awkwardly in the
middle, it is half a boy's idea of what a sex-and-adventure story
should be, and half a discourse on an impossibly stupid religion.
And yet it is probably the most popular novel ever to come out of
the science-fiction ghetto.

An argument can be made that the ghetto is precisely where
science fiction belongs, that it has enough to offer without suc-
cumbing to the pretensions of the New Wave. "What the New
Wave wants to do," says Asimov, "is through science fiction to
write whatever they want to write. Great literature, perhaps.
This is different from the people in my day. We knew we were
entering a ghetto." Le Guin applauds the social concerns of
today's better science fiction, but she warns against its getting too
close to mainstream literature. "Vital forms tend to be disrespect-
ful," she says. "If science fiction becomes respectable, it may die.

I wonder if it is really good to give full university courses on it."

Indeed, independence of mind, the disreputability that provides energy, may endure only if science fiction goes its own way. SF writers have yet to feel at home with the most important mainstream fictional techniques: irony, for instance, eludes them, as does wit and ambiguity, and a confident use of first-person narration. (In his film *2001*, Kubrick was able to impart a haunting ambiguity that his coauthor, Arthur Clarke, had not included in his original story and that Clarke felt obliged to clear up when he came to write a novel based on the movie.) Nor have SF writers come to terms with characterization. A writer who spends too much time on science fiction, Burgess says, "misses what is most important in literature: the human being and how human beings behave."

Disabling as these liabilities are to a genre that clamors for recognition as literature, they are immaterial to readers who remember what science fiction at its occasional best does well: to entertain, to provoke the imagination, to make different that with which we feel familiar. At its best, science fiction plucks from within us our deepest fears and hopes and shows them to us in the rough disguise of dreams: as monsters and as rockets.

December 1975

CONFIRMING OUR NEED TO KNOW LESS

ENCYCLOPEDIAS ARE LIKE loaves of bread: the sooner used the better, for they are growing stale even before they reach the shelf. In search of that perfect blandness most acceptable to the uncritical masses, the busy bakers bleach their flour, editors winnow authoritative articles, and the nutritious elements fall away. Never fear. We'll throw in a ha'penny's worth of vitamins to replace our more obvious losses and call our product "new, enriched." Who will know what else is missing—unless he once ate real bread, or read an old encyclopedia?

In evaluating the new, enriched *Britannica* (the fifteenth edition), we must remember that for all the information they contain, encyclopedias do not function as beacons for our time but only as reflections of it, and that the fashion of our present time is to know less and less about more and more. With that in mind, we may take note of two accomplishments in the first major overhauling that this venerable enterprise has endured in forty-five years: much, perhaps most of what it offers is as skillfully rendered as can be reasonably expected, and a genuine effort has been made to accommodate the consumer who doesn't want to know much about anything. Herein lies the genius of this edition: all over the world encyclopedias stand unused because, really, nobody wants to know much of what's in them. The new *Britannica* says, okay, we'll make your apathy respectable by systematizing it.

And it does. The fifteenth edition consists of three separate, interlocking parts, each with its own pretentious Greek title. The *Propaedia*, a single volume, divides all realms of knowledge into ten categories, with numerous subdivisions forming an outline by which a student may hop around in the other volumes, pursuing a subject of interest to him. The *Micropaedia* comprises ten volumes, which allegedly serve as an index to the rest of the set and as a collection of short entries (none more than 750 words), mostly on subjects *Britannica* feels are not worthy of further amplification. These are said to have been written in terms a junior high school student can comprehend. The *Macropaedia*, nineteen volumes, expands at length on major subjects: 313 pages, for instance, are devoted to two articles on visual arts. In all, there are 43 million words and 24,239 illustrations, making this the longest *Britannica* ever.

And there is a qualitative improvement, too. *Britannica*'s two-hundredth-anniversary edition, published in 1968, neglected to mention the Beatles, Marshall McLuhan, Ingmar Bergman, Jerzy Grotowski, Pete Seeger, Dave Brubeck, Helen Frankenthaler, and Malcolm X, all of whom had long left their mark on our culture and who are recognized in the new edition. A general attempt has been made to bring the encyclopedia up to date—at least in areas you are likely to notice, like films, which had long been neglected, and sports records, which are carried through 1973. The entry on Watergate goes up to the disappearance of critical tapes, that on Western art through earthworks (but not the neorealists); the deaths of Auden and Allende last year are noted.

There are other joys as well. Anthony Burgess's article on the novel is both comprehensive and stimulating. There are fine essays on Wittgenstein, parapsychology, and comic strips. The best people were picked to write articles on Ronsard, Thomas More, and eschatology. The bibliographies have been generally improved, though that on the U.S. Civil War is so short as to be nearly useless.

Still, the whole enterprise should make careful readers nervous. Not the selective stupidities—listing Utagawa Kuniyoshi under U, for instance, and Utagawa Hiroshige under H—but the pretentiousness, the inexcusable omissions, the sorry reductiveness of the whole.

An encyclopedia absolutely requires a first-rate index—*Britannica* used to have one—but here the experiment of combining the index with the short-entry volumes fails because the index, reduced in comprehensiveness, becomes inadequate. Many subjects thought worthy of discussion in the *Macropaedia* are not thought worthy of indexing, which means that this *Britannica* is of use only to students who know enough about what they're looking up to scout around in the principal texts; he who knows nothing learns nothing. I looked up "Peanuts" and Judge Sirica—and found nothing, yet these subjects appear unheralded in articles with other titles. I did find Erich Segal and Mario Puzo, however, which shows the kind of rush to obsolescence for which the *Britannica* is famous. Working from some table of priorities known only to them, the editors include Adolph Knopf, the structural petrologist (1882-1966), in the index, but not Alfred Knopf, incontestably this country's most important book publisher. (He recovers somewhat by being mentioned in the article "Publishing: History of.") Should the student be tempted to look up "Indians, American" in the index (as I would think he might be likely to do), he will find nothing. Asian Indians are represented by pages of entries, as well they should be, but our own variety are allowed only narrowly focused entries that all have to do with their oppression, e.g., Indian Removal Act, Indian Reorganization Act, Indian Territory. As for the blacks among us, the index contains a fascinating entry: "American Negro: *see* American Coloured local race." It's that English *u* in *Coloured* that undoes me. Haroun-al-Raschid, arguably the most important Arab leader of the Middle Ages, does not rate an entry in the index, nor does General Andrei Vlasov, who aided the Nazi war effort by leading Russian troops against the Soviets. Moloch is not mentioned, but *Moll Flanders* is, further evidence of the encyclopedia's high school orientation. You will look in vain for Wyatt Earp, General Israel Putnam, Secretary of State William P. Rogers, kleptomania, and Babi-Yar.

The lack of a competent index is bad enough, but the idea of ten volumes of the *Britannica* being written in language suitable for seventh- and eighth-graders makes me wonder whether these volumes are suitable for me. More important, why, in a set of books determined to eliminate repetition (as its editor insists), should the 4,207 entries in the *Macropaedia* be summarized in the *Micropaedia*—unless there is a need to please people trying to maintain as much ignorance as they can?

What is most disturbing, however, is the new *Britannica*'s conception of information we don't need. The entry on William Shockley gives his background in physics, but nothing of his famous ideas on race and IQ. The entry on Augustus John endows him with a wife he didn't have and maintains, in the best *virginibus puerisque* tradition, a studied silence on his interesting sex life. Military medals and decorations are no longer covered, nor is there a guide to the pronunciation of the Welsh alphabet—presumably because high school students are not interested; nevertheless, the alphabet could easily have been represented phonetically. Acting again (I assume) from an idea of what parents and teachers want their children not to know, the *Britannica* declines to print anything usable to guide a gourmet through the bewildering variety of wines.

Besides rejecting information outright, the new edition studiously diminishes what *Britannica* once thought worth knowing. Joachim Du Bellay, an incontestably important poet who was

thought worth a page in the eleventh edition, has been reduced
by five-sixths. John Ford, the great English dramatist whom the
eleventh thought worth two pages, gets no entry at all in the
Macropaedia. As for Attis, consort of the Great Mother of the
Gods, nothing in the new edition remains of the eleventh's patient citations of every variation of the myth, according to its
source. Of King Canute's apocryphal battle with the waves of the
Thames, amply described in the eleventh's well-written article,
the new edition has nothing to say: it's as if the modern *Britannica* had decided it can't cope with legends that point to some
fundamental human truth. In similar vein, the article on children's literature has been reduced by half from the preceding
edition and the illustrations discarded. And an elegant essay on
dragons from the eleventh has been hacked to shreds: etymologi-
cal and mythological information jettisoned and the language
vulgarized, presumably to suit student requirements.

Well, we live in a technological age, and each age gets the
encyclopedia it deserves. *Britannica*'s first edition emphasized
utility but did not shun controversy: Andrew Bell's graphic en-
gravings of childbirth, included to show an involuntary midwife
what to expect, caused a scandal. The fifteenth edition, edited by
Warren Preece (who has the gall to say that the eleventh, that
great monument to the humanist tradition, has nothing more to
offer us), is still determined to be useful—six and a half pages on
weed control, nine and a half on alcohol consumption—but in its
scramble for acceptance by the pubescent generation (or rather,
by those who buy books for it), it seems to have lost much of its
nerve. And so books for children, a French poet, dragons, the perpetual truths that they represent, the spiritual needs of man that
they reflect—these must yield to make room for information that
will change tomorrow. For all its virtues, this edition is a qualified
failure; it cares more for juggling its format than for preserving
knowledge.

July 1974

Postscript: The fifteenth edition of *Britannica* survived in its
original form for only eleven years. In 1985, *Britannica* revised it
to include a two-volume index, thereby making the enterprise
much more accessible—though the index needs work. Look up

Barabbas, as a student might want to do, and you won't find him, yet he appears in an otherwise inadequate article on Pontius Pilate. Look up Betty Friedan: again, nothing, though she and her influential book appear in an entry on the women's movement. Dragons are still a focus of *Britannica*'s neglect: the index forgets to mention its debased article on the subject. Useless to look up World Series winners; they can be found under "Sporting record," if that term happens to occur to you, but the index doesn't tell you that.

Nothing in the new version suggests that the editors have rethought their longstanding commitment to reducing the amount of information conveyed on once-important subjects. All but one hundred of the biographies in the long-entry volumes have been shortened and dumped into the short-entry volumes. How they choose who's ripe for reduction, no man can say—Robespierre and Thomas More have been demoted, Montaigne and Nietzsche not—but the damage is considerable.

The revised edition refers to the *Decameron* as a pornographic book!

BARBARA TUCHMAN'S CLOUDY MIRROR

As A WRITER of popular histories, Barbara Tuchman is as bold as she is adroit. With each of her last four books she has broadened her perspective. Most recently, in a biography of Joseph Stilwell, she tried to make her subject serve as an epitome of the American experience in China, and in *A Distant Mirror* she takes an entire century for her province. The mark she leaves on it may not be so deep as a well, but it is certainly as wide as a church door. It will serve the laudable purpose of introducing to her legion of admirers the fascination of a difficult and neglected era, and it will deserve its assured success—if only for its author's unblinking eye for drama and the clarity with which she deploys and describes the most complicated events.

The fourteenth century in Europe began badly, in cold, rain, and famine, and ended rather worse, mired in constant and purposeless conflicts that suggested to many the final breakdown of all social and religious order. Tuchman isolates four principal catastrophes that unraveled the fabric of the time. One was the wars: the war the English fought almost without remission for control of parts of France; the wars the French fought in Italy; civil wars in France and England; and, at the century's end, the appalling debacle of an ill-conceived crusade. Another was the Black Death of 1348–50, "the most lethal disaster of recorded history," which killed perhaps a third of Europe's population and left the rest wondering whether the end of the world was imminent. A third was the ravages wrought everywhere by displaced soldiers and brigands who formed companies to fight as freebooters and mercenaries. The fourth was the papal schism that, with the corrupt, even grotesque behavior of rival popes, threatened to destroy such stability as the church might impose.

Other horrors accompanied these. Madness infected popes and kings. Lawlessness and debauchery followed the plague. Any catastrophe provided an occasion for slaughtering thousands of Jews. Revolts of peasants and the bourgeoisie were ruthlessly suppressed. The chivalric idea degenerated completely as Europe's knights, the theoretical champions of justice, turned to aggression and predation. Debilitating taxation proved more damaging to society than the wars for which the taxes paid. And yet amid universal disorder some prudent men went honorably about their work. Tuchman offers us one: Enguerrand VII, lord of Coucy, one of the most important French nobles and commanders, a superlative knight who married the king of England's daughter and perforce became a talented diplomat as well.

The author intends Coucy, like Stilwell in her prior book, to serve as the focus for her broader history, but neither warrior can manage the assignment. Coucy is rarely onstage and, when he is, he moves (like all but a few medieval men) almost invisibly: we know where he went and how many he took with him and at what cost, but little more.

If this structural flaw is not particularly irritating, the book offers many flaws that are. The notes to the text are inexcusably skimpy, leaving delicious quotations unidentified and Tuchman's dubious claims about such complex matters as courtly love and the English course toward Protestantism quite unsupported. She relies, too, on secondary sources, many of which are out of date or long discredited. At one point Tuchman's text implies that she has read a long medieval romance, but the romance itself is not to be found in her sources; only a book about it is. She can be care-less with language, too: rhetoric, for instance, was not, as she says, the "source" of law, but a means of speech devised for orators to use; astrology was not the "determinant" of men's fate—the stars were thought to be.

Tuchman's fondness for magisterial generalizations tends to lead her astray. Here's one: "Woman was the Church's rival," she pronounces, though the Church knew well enough who its rivals were: the Crown, its own prelates, the interests that controlled land and commerce. Tuchman is probably thinking of the body of antifeminist literature promoted by the Church—a result of the Church's none-too-successful movement toward the concept of sacerdotal celibacy. We can only guess at the basis for her error; still, she should have known better than to go to the Do-minicans for a churchly perspective on women. Here's another: "Unperceived," she writes, "here was the start of the modern world." This fatuity follows a misreading of the theologian Wy-clif, who did not, as she suggests, believe man could work for his own salvation, and must not be confused, as she confuses him, with the English Protestants to come. (It's a common error to say that Protestants believe in "earning" one's salvation; that idea was, and is now, more Catholic than Protestant.) But even if Wyclif were what Tuchman says he is (and on Wyclif she works only from outdated sources), one could as easily attach the be-ginning of modernity to the invention of the stirrup, gunpowder, the telescope, the printing press.

Tuchman has read (or read about) Ariès's thesis on the "in-vention" of childhood and from it concludes that medieval chil-dren were neither treated tenderly nor valued in their formative years. Nothing could be further from the evidence we have from the time itself—the evidence of the way children are depicted in the mystery plays, for instance, or in Chaucer's "Man of Law's Tale." But then she appears to have misread both the drama of the time and Chaucer. She seems to think that the bawdry and violence of medieval plays conflict with their pious themes, whereas in fact the combination is all part of the point, part of a complex and ironic dramaturgy that represents a world in need of redemption. As for Chaucer, he did *not*, as Tuchman writes, "recant his own creation"—indeed, he said he was still pleased with his translation of Boethius, his legends of saints and other works. Following the tradition of writers in his time, Chaucer disparaged *some* of his work: "many a song and many a leccherous lay," which he dismissed as "worldly vanitees" that might lead others into sin.

To say as much is only to touch upon some of the problems *A Distant Mirror* presents, but then it presents significant virtues, too. Perhaps the best way to read it is to mistrust its author whenever she sallies into the life of the medieval mind and to rejoice in the rest, the parts devoted to politics and warfare—of which, as readers of *The Guns of August* should remember, she writes exceedingly well.

September 1978

THE WORLD OF FAERY

THE DISCUSSION at our dinner table peaked the other night when I said, "You'll only find fairy godmothers in stories. In the real world, fairies can't help out at Christian ceremonies." The thirteen-year-old girl who eats with us winced: "Fairies! *In the real world?*" Of course. Yeats once talked to a woman who denied belief in hell and ghosts, "but there are faeries and little leprechauns, and water-horses, and fallen angels." "No matter what one doubts, one never doubts the faeries," Yeats concluded, recalling a man who had told him, "They stand to reason."

Katherine Briggs clearly agrees. She has spent a long life studying fairy folklore and ten years writing *An Encyclopedia of Fairies,* an erudite and immensely entertaining volume that encompasses all supernatural creatures except ghosts, angels, and devils. As to whether fairies exist, Briggs professes agnosticism, though she emphasizes the "shock of authenticity" that some of the primitive tales convey: "their curious plausibility as if the mind leapt to receive them." It's this kind of reality that comes through so strongly in her book. What Briggs has done is to recover fairies from the nursery (and to a degree from formal literature and painting as well) and restore to them their diversity, complexity, and astonishingly subtle relationship with mortal men and women.

From the book's many entries (one should read *in* it rather than *through* it), a comprehensive fairy tradition emerges. Fairies have been with us since man first reckoned with his environment. Some say fairies are nature spirits; others, the spirits of the dead; still others believe them fallen angels not evil enough to go to hell. They are distinctly un-Christian and were, until Elizabethan times, generally human-size or even heroic-size creatures. Many— the Unseelie Court—detest human beings (the most malicious of these are the duergars, or black dwarves, of northern England), but others consort occasionally with mortals who treat them politely and incuriously, who do not thank them for favors or brag of their association. Fairies are counterparts of mankind, practicing trades, husbandry, and handicrafts, eager to dance and make music (one of them, a merrow, which is an Irish breed of merman, likes to compete at drinking with a fisherman). And many fairies need human beings—to deliver their babies or nurse them.

This encyclopedia has many enchanting qualities. Vividness of description, for one. A peddler speaks of a creature called the "Boneless": "A Summat as slides behind and alongside in the dark night. Many's have died of fright, through his following on." Weird bits of information, for another: the word *stroke,* in its medical sense, comes from "fairy-stroke"; the haunting "Londonderry Air" is a fairy tune, learned by mortal pipers, to which only mawkish human words have ever been fitted; willow trees have "a habit of uprooting themselves on a dark night and following a solitary traveler, muttering."

I like, too, the chronicles from the twelfth to the seventeenth centuries in which human involvement in fairy matters is reported as remarkable but not incredible. An English couple in Ireland, for instance, are troubled by a banshee and conclude that banshees flourish in Ireland because the natives are superstitious and lack a proper faith to protect them. Best of all are the fairy stories themselves, of which Briggs has collected hundreds from an impressive array of antiquarian sources. Some she has left in their original dialect, but most she has condensed with an authentic storyteller's skill.

If fairies do not exist, they are nonetheless necessary. Fairies fit our human imaginations: we need both those that will intervene in our lives and those that will have nothing to do with us. If they did nothing else, fairies would serve as a rebuke to our relentless denaturing of nature. But in fact they do much more. The stories told about fairies—the ancient, authentic stories—tell us a lot about human beings, about man's elemental wonder at and fear of the world: its mysteries, its losses, its changes. These stories, too, tell us how man learned to get along with his neighbor—a neighbor who often behaved most oddly. George Macdonald, a great teller of fairy tales, once suggested that they are designed to awaken consciousness—and that is exactly what the stories in this book do.

February 1977

Fairies retain their power yet. A serious critic—Leslie Fiedler, for instance, who wrote the introduction to Jonathan Cott's collection *Beyond the Looking Glass*—has only to enter the stories they inhabit, and thrash about in search of meaning, to be reduced to certifiable inanity. Titania strokes the critic's head and Bottom's a donkey again. "To hunt for symbols in a fairy tale is absolutely fatal," Auden once wrote; the figures "mean what they are." And Jung, who believed that the point of a symbol is to conceal, to protect the shell of truth, warned a pupil: "Understanding is a fearfully binding power, at times a veritable murder of the soul. . . . The core of the individual is a mystery of life, which is snuffed out when it is 'grasped.' "

That mystery of life, a representation through recognizable, though other than realistic, forms of the core of human experience, is what the best fairy stories are about. Drawing upon dream images, or figures from an imagined distant past, they illuminate our desires for a world without death, or a world where man is not alienated from other living things. They put into words (and many of the best of these stories are badly written, but lose none of their magic for that) our most inarticulate apprehension of quests, ordeals, bondage, and discovery. Most of them are, in their own terms, moral: Alice pits her slightly priggish decency against the sophistry of the caterpillar and the hypocrisy of the Walrus; the youngest sons in the Grimm stories succeed because they are dull, prudent, and listen to the advice of animals.

Cott's anthology of Victorian tales, some very long and most profusely illustrated, mixes with a surprising lack of discrimination the dreary and the excellent. Few authors are less appealing than the comfortable Victorian novelist, his paunch pressing against the buttons on his waistcoat, who is determined to be bright, amusing, and above all instructive to the young. "She thought it was sinful not to obey her husband," writes one of them; "all good wives should think the same." Another tells us that the good fairy will help us only if we "avoid petulance, impatience, grumbling and black looks. From those she always flies." I won't count on it, grumbling and petulance being my stock in trade, and I won't waste more space on the three longest stories in Cott's collection, which suffer from anemic inspiration, mechanical playfulness and, more important, a lack of numinous feeling, or of the Dionysian sensibility, that fearful attractiveness of the soul's destruction.

But Christina Rossetti's poem "Goblin Market" is here; with its hopping rhythm, erotic suggestiveness, and the broader attraction of forbidden fruit, it is surely her best. And there are two marvelous stories, romantic tragedies by writers unknown to me: Mrs. Clifford's "Wooden Tony," which develops through a well-sustained and developed metaphor the distorted world, removed from space and time, of an autistic child, and Mary de Morgan's "The Wanderings of Arasmon," which establishes the standard fairy-tale setup of a corrupt town under a spell that can be broken only by an innocent person and then modulates to a poignant variation on the theme of Orpheus and Eurydice.

The strongest stories here are two by George Macdonald, "The Golden Key" and "The Day Boy and the Night Girl." Macdonald insisted that "the greatest force lies in the region of the uncomprehended," and that a fairy tale is like a sonata, designed to awaken consciousness rather than to deposit meaning. He abstained from explanations: "So long as I think my dog can bark, I will not sit up to bark for him." His stories are not as brilliant as Lewis Carroll's, and are certainly less urbane, which may be why they produce a primal shiver that the Alice stories never do. Alice's simple leap down the rabbit hole becomes, in "The Golden Key," a leap of faith: the heroine, confronted by a hole in the floor of a cave, is told that if she wants to find her lover and the real world, "You must throw yourself in. There is no other way."

I mentioned earlier Leslie Fiedler's difficulties with what, for lack of a proper English word, we call fairy stories. The Alice books are for him "dirty" and their author a man who tried to persuade his friends to let him photograph their daughters in the nude. As much is lost by such reductiveness as is lost by Freudians who are damn sure they know what the Golden Key is, and the moss upon which the hero lies. Of course, a psychosexual element throbs within Carroll's stories, and Macdonald's, but does that make them "dirty"? Fiedler believes, too, that marriage and the propagation of children are the goals of most fairy stories, but of course they aren't: marriage, in most of these stories, is by itself of no more importance than the half kingdom that often goes with it, and offspring are seldom mentioned. It is the ordeal, the testing, that matters, the achievement by the hero of competence and wholeness.

Cott's longer introduction is of a structuralist persuasion, ambitious and distracted, but at least aware of the perils of symbol hunting. Skip the introduction; for all its faults, this is a useful anthology. Even at their worst, fairy stories can instill in children a sense of the wonder and multiplicity of the world, and that is enough.

February 1974

SPLENDORS AND MISERIES OF THE LITERARY LIFE

YOU KNOW, of course, that a new book by an author you've not heard of is like a hot-air balloon: it can't take off without heating up some gas. Blurbs are the gas of the book business. By blurbs I don't mean those adjectival phrases that publishers with artful scissors clip from balanced book reviews only to thrust naked into advertisements, but a sentence or two praising a newborn book from someone whose opinion presumably matters, someone soft of heart and mind, or in debt to the author, his agent, or his publisher. Beyond its ostensible purpose—to promote from the forty thousand books published each year one in particular for our attention—the blurb achieves other ends: it blunts the bite of crazed reviewers (or compensates for their indifference); it creates obligations; it affirms the superiority of the donor; it lets writers who haven't published recently see their names in print.

Thus Louis Untermeyer, almost forgotten, announces that one of this year's first novels is "wild and wonderful, breathlessly paced," and Frank Conroy, who wrote a good book once and a lot of blurbs since, says of its author: "A real find.... She's an artist." Only in fits of generosity can such language be shaken off. Cynthia Buchanan, who ought to write a second book, says, "This is knockout prose," making me wonder whether anyone who wrote good prose could endure the compliment. "A totally unique book," writes Marjorie Kellogg, which distinguishes it, I suppose, from the semiunique books that assail us from every side. Robert Ardrey calls Theodore White's most recent summary of current events "a story for the ages," which, if not a deliberate affront to common sense, suggests we need not hurry to read it.

"And do you think there are any who are influenced by this?" asks Sneer of Puff in Sheridan's play *The Critic*. Puff replies, "O, lud! yes, Sir; the number of those who undergo the fatigue of judging for themselves is very small indeed." The blurb business is nearly as old as the printed book: in the Renaissance, rhyming blurbs proclaiming a poet superior to Chaucer and Spenser were routinely bound into the books themselves. That good novelist and present Prince of Blurbs, Anthony Burgess, maintains the venerable tradition: "I have said before, though not publicly, that my fellow countryman Wilfred Sheed is probably the best living American novelist. I say it again, publicly." Sheed is a writer of several talents, but this is an indefensible statement disguised as a thoughtful, time-tested judgment. Graham Greene does this kind of thing rather better: "Brian Moore is my favorite living novelist." This carries even more clout and yet the careful consumer will detect that no more than a personal whim has been advanced.

The catalyst for these animadversions is *Slammer*, a first novel by Ben Greer, and a very decent, talented book it is, in spite of nine blurbs by other southern writers and two advance reviews that cling like suckers to its jacket, comparing Greer to Greene and Genet, Poe and Melville. The good ole boys have ponied up every adjective in the optimist's dictionary, and none of them has much to do with this sharp, flawed story of a prison riot and the people it consumes. I liked its authenticity (Greer became a prison guard to write it), but I didn't like its structural weaknesses. Nothing much to quote in that, so I offer the Prescott all-purpose blurb: "Quite a book indeed! I found it a very genuine novel (memoir, history, whatever) and more than a little unique, for no one has ever played with words in just this manner. You need only probe beneath its surface to find what lies below, and it is certainly long enough to keep you reading all night." Any publisher may apply this masterly endorsement to any book of his choice—as long as he doesn't call me first for permission.

July 1975

"The word *literary* does not apply. That's the first thing you have to understand." The Old Convention Hand and I were, just then, being gently trampled by a courteous throng in Washington's Shoreham Hotel. Around us the seventy-second annual convocation of the American Booksellers Association pulsed and perspired, while the Old Con insisted that I try to understand why it was important to be here with these people who fixed their eyes on my name tag and their feet on mine.

"This is *life*," he explains, "in capital letters. All through their lives book people are told they're missing out on life—and here it is. The contact with other book people, with live authors—maybe for the first time. Things of value are brought down to earth here, and that helps booksellers. The next thing you have to understand is that you can't sell books like Fords. Who buys a Viking book because he liked the Viking book he read last year? We sell a new product every time—that's hard. At the ABA, we pretend it's easy—like selling Fords or shoes. High heels are in this year, square toes are out."

For the book people, ABA is circus time. An estimated 6,000 booksellers, buyers, editors, authors, and hangers-on crowd the narrow aisles where 387 publishers, more than anyone has heard of, push their wares for fall. Lyle Stuart sits cheek-by-jowl with Harvard University Press, doubtless exchanging literary banter when the crowds grow thin. A new breed of salesman strides about: one in Levi's and a Mao cap sucks a lollipop, and others, young and thin, with flowered shirts and apostle beards, could sell a used book to anyone.

There are authors, too. In the old and tasteless days, ABA invited Tiny Tim and a girl with VistaVision breasts. Once a belly dancer gyrated every ten minutes or so, but this year ABA went literary: pro quarterback George Blanda is here to promote his book, and so is Jackie Robinson. Oscar the Grouch from Sesame Street autographs calendars in one aisle, and Dale Evans Rogers is signing one of her safe-in-the-arms-of-Jesus books in another. The second-longest line is for Mickey Spillane. His wife is with him, with her clothes on, though behind her are two hundred paperback copies of Spillane's book with his wife undressed on the cover. A tiny strip covers two of the three crucial parts of her anatomy; around the corner, the hardcover edition shows the whole works. Both Spillanes sign the books.

The longest line, however, is not for sex or even for new books: it is for Richard Bach, who is signing copies of *Jonathan*

Livingston Seagull. "What I need for my list," says the Old Con, "is a book about a baby elephant with mystical inclinations. You know: Father Wind and Mother Sea, and the elephant turns into a butterfly at the end. I could retire on that book."

Jostling us everywhere are the freeloaders: the dumpy people with shopping bags who are scooping up whatever is for free. Buttons, mostly: the largest shows the *New Yorker*'s monocled gentleman announcing "Books are my bag," and the funniest, written in Chinese to promote a Chinese cookbook, says "I can't believe I ate the whole thing." At the *New York Times* booth is a pink button proclaiming "Vaginal Politics," but you can see the book people shrink away. In an auditorium, a panel discusses problems of security—"Stealing is no longer a deviant way of life in America," the booksellers are told—and in the press room the authors are processed quickly. One talks about beauty for the black woman, another about ice cream. A masked airline pilot explains why we are about to die in the air; an Englishman who wrote a book about Clifford Irving's hoax fails to show, so a book critic in dark glasses impersonates him and fields questions from the press.

"Halfway through the second day," the Old Con tells me, "your knees begin to bend. It's not the gin, I think; it's the air." Walking through the exhibitions on the second day is, in fact, like walking on two martinis. Clusters of book people with glazed eyes pause wherever the air conditioners blow. Still, the drink helps; after the exhibitions close, the parties begin, and the trance generated by books continues by other means.

Repetition is the unspoken theme of the ABA: book after book, stall after stall, the same Balinese dancer print in all the Shoreham suites, the elevator doors opening each time to a blast of drunken hilarity. At a convention luncheon—"for those who have no better place to go," the Old Con tells me—after the vinyl chicken, Senator Ribicoff nominates Senator McGovern for president, and Jack Anderson, shouting in a hall where SST's could huddle together, makes our ribs vibrate as he challenges John Mitchell to sue him.

Oh, it is, as you can see, a time of literary togetherness, although a few people filter off to private parties. Anthony Quinn, another author, presides over lunch across town. "If it takes whips to bring women into line," he says, smiling bashfully, "then I say, bring on the whips." One publisher, the Old Con tells me, held a pot party—"I thought when I opened the door the whole hotel would be arrested"—and everywhere you can see the good book people staggering around, taking one another's measure. "I always heard you were better than me," one mumbles to a colleague, "but now that I see you, you aren't as bad as I thought." And, as the evenings grow older, the talk becomes political. Can McGovern beat Nixon? Are, in fact, the Communists taking over America?

More gin, more whisky. "I've never seen a falling-down drunk here," says the Old Con, "though I wish I had." Come on, I ask him, does anyone do any business here? Are any books bought? What, in fact, are you actually doing *now?* "I'm working up another sweat," the Old Con replies.

June 1972

Newsweek customarily celebrates Columbus Day by sending Peter S. Prescott to Vermont to review the Fall Foliage Collections. This year, however, Prescott was confined to the airless rooms of Manhattan's Roosevelt Hotel, observing an event called the American Writers Congress, which attracted more than three thousand writers and literary hangers-on.

Friday afternoon: Here in the hotel's Madison Room, every seat is taken, the door is jammed with people. Young women in designer jeans crouch by half-eaten sandwiches in the aisles, waving electronic gadgets. Television lights raise the room's temperature to a reading that matches my blood pressure. One light starts to fall, threatening fire, the rapid annihilation of all assembled, but is caught. I'm reminded of Hemingway telling Lillian Ross that when he came to New York he wanted to see an El Greco or two, but as for the places where writers hang out, "I want to give the joints a miss." So do I. Writing is not a collective activity; what makes the craft so rewarding is that we all write in our individual voices. Yet the loneliness that goes with the franchise prompts some writers to yearn for a kind of collectivity. Let's talk about our problems, get a little solidarity going. Bill Styron, surely, would like to read my poems, will put in a word for them at Random House. Writers acting together. The symbol of this congress is a clenched fist from which a pencil juts.

So here they are: writers talking. In the men's room, Swedish tourists giggle as they snap pictures of one another, but here in the Madison Room the theme is censorship. Former CIA operative Philip Agee addresses the congregation at length from his European refuge. A distraught young woman from a group called Redstocking assails Gloria Steinem for her past cooperation with the CIA. Her group's book, she says, was "rapidly put out of print by Random House," but she has copies to sell at a discount to anyone interested; for an additional $2 she will include the section that Random "censored," and for $2 more, a packet on the history of censorship. Rudolfo Anaya, a Chicano writer, denounces "the world of New York and the *New York Times*"; his book, he says, was "censored by the *Times*," by which he means the *Times* did not review it. Piri Thomas, whose books have been plucked from school library shelves, rattles off a litany of self-love: "I go with the flow, I'm beautiful, the flow is beautiful, let's get our beauty together." Applause follows this, as it does an elderly gentleman's account of his thirty years' persecution by J. Edgar Hoover.

The word *important* gets a lot of exercise this afternoon, often in conjunction with the phrase "received no coverage in the major media." Questions are invited from the floor, but speeches are offered instead. A man who calls himself "an assassination researcher" has a few remarks to make, so does a woman who says she writes pornography; her assumption that "you are all on my side" draws a few discreet hisses.

Presiding over the general paranoia is a shirt-sleeved Victor Navasky. Navasky is an author and the editor of the *Nation;* the congress is his idea. Writers, he says, face a crisis, and serious writers face extinction. Big government withholds the funds once available to writers and seeks to enact legislation crippling their access to information. Big business, caring only for profit, swallows up independent publishers. Publishers hold writers generally, and minority writers particularly, in contempt. Moral and immoral minorities are working to ban, burn, and censor books. Perhaps it is time for writers to develop a spirit of community, to gather for talk about whatever concerns them, to begin working on machinery to get something done. A writers' union, perhaps.

Such a congress would naturally take on a political coloration: from a bland center to the more alarming shades of left.

Friday evening: It's already clear that Navasky's brainchild is an enormous success: three thousand people will attend this event and five hundred more are now being forcibly barred at the door. Still, little alarm signals are already popping off. A pregnant woman sitting next to me is embarrassed that among all this intellect she demonstrates such mindless creativity. A witty writer worries that when his turn comes to speak, he should not, before *this* audience, attempt a joke: levity of any sort seems out of order here.

The program begins with the organizers asking people politely to go away, to stay away: "We may be breaking the fire rules." After a writer from the *Village Voice* refers to "our rights as workers"—not a noun that writers usually apply to themselves—a Puerto Rican critic brings us comradely greetings from a writers' congress in Cuba. His speech would have been okay except that socialism's great debility is that it cannot be brief; if the Marxists don't bomb us, they will surely bore us to death. ("If this keeps up," says an all-too-audible voice from the crowd, "I'll welcome the neutron bomb.") Nevertheless, the evening picks up when Toni Morrison delivers the keynote address. Most writers think they can speak in public—the congress is proof of that—but Morrison knows just how to say little with maximum effect: "The life of the American writer is under attack. We're *toys* to be played with. We are all workers. We are already at the barricades. We don't need any more writers as solitary heroes. We need a heroic writers' movement."

Saturday: Today and tomorrow we are obliged to choose among scores of symposiums with attractive titles like "Homophobia in the *New York Times*," "Latino Writing," even "Concentration and Conglomerates: The Political Economy of Culture." The program we all carry resembles a college course catalogue and contains such questions as "What, at bottom, are we doing when we write?" The short answer, "Sitting," seems clearly inappropriate because a lot of good writers are speaking from these panels and trying to be serious, even if they disappear as soon as their turn is done.

By now I'm wondering who these people are who pack each room beyond its evident capacity. Eavesdropping, I hear:

"I'm a secret novelist."

"I just wanted to get out of the Midwest."

"I used to read a whole lot more than I do now."

"And then I got into science fiction."

It seems reasonable to assume that the majority of what this congress calls "delegates" have yet to publish a book, or even many articles. A *Newsweek* colleague, conducting an unscientific poll, tells me that of the ten "writers" to whom he spoke none had written a book, one had written nothing, and all had nonliterary jobs. My guess is that they are here to feel like writers. Many young people want to be identified as writers before they become such; maybe, when they return to Butte or Tulsa, they will see a note in the hometown paper: LOCAL WRITER ATTENDS NATIONAL CONGRESS. They come here to hear Kurt Vonnegut and Gloria Steinem and James Baldwin say the same things they have said for years, but somehow it counts for something to hear these writers say the same old stuff again. Maybe, at the cocktail sessions, where the writers stand in line to pay $3.50 for a drink in a plastic glass, they can actually shake hands with Ed Doctorow or Don Barthelme. Aren't we all writers, just getting together?

Sunday: The togetherness theme dominates the day. At the Roosevelt, people are still denouncing Betty Friedan for selling out to the Moral Majority, but the real action has moved to Town Hall, ten minutes away, where the planning convention for a national writers' union is getting into gear. Navasky insists that the congress was not called to advance a union, but many delegates are interested in nothing else. Still, there will be a problem selling the idea to writers, who like to think of themselves as independent spirits and are willing to take less money if that's the price of freedom, or orneriness, or whatever it is that led them into the self-expression business. Not a few would write for free, if that's what it costs to get published. There are professional union organizers in this crowd who find such an attitude incredible: it surpasses naïveté to become cretinism, and these starry-eyed writers must simply have it shaken out of them. By contrast, many—perhaps most—writers feel that unions are best left to workers who need the protection of numbers, who don't love what they do, to teamsters and assembly-line mechanics who are willing to submit to union discipline and go on strike when told. Will John Updike take his fiction to Dodd, Mead if Knopf doesn't do right by one of his union buddies? Nobody knows for sure, but one could make an educated guess.* Besides, under present antitrust laws, writers (who are considered independent operators) probably cannot legally strike.

Little skepticism, however, surfaces at Town Hall, where a crowd of perhaps three hundred listens enthralled as a woman from the screen and television writers' union explains that for a script the length of a feature article her colleagues are paid at least $11,000. That sounds good to the writers, one of whom suggests we join this woman's union. One man challenges the union to place his rejected article on nuclear bombs: it seems clear to me that the people who most want a union are those who experience the most difficulty getting published.

After the stale rhetoric and the venting of ancient complaints, something does seem to have emerged. Last night, at a plenary session, resolutions were offered. Oppose U.S. interference in El Salvador. Support the striking air-traffic controllers. Support feminist writers, Latino writers, *all* minority writers. What may be important, however, is that the congress will attempt to perpetuate itself and the union will attempt to get going. Perhaps, if we are lucky, both will attempt to come to terms with venerable institutions like PEN and the Authors League, which have for decades been doing valuable work on behalf of writers in precisely those areas, excepting the political fantasies, that have been discussed this weekend.

The problems writers face are real. And the perceptions of pain, expressed so often during the past three days, are—even when most misguided—real as well.

October 1981

---

* I'm grateful to author Sidney Offit for the following scenario: Updike is at home, hammering at his typewriter, when the telephone rings. A husky voice asks, "Jack Updike? Is that you, Jack? Yeah, this is Lennie down at the shop. The writing going good? Nearly finished, are ya? That's swell, because some of your fancy friends at Knopf think they're too good to publish a book we sent them, so we're pulling everybody out. You go to Dodd, Mead. The book? It's real cute: things you can do with a dead hamster. [Long pause] Now, Jack, you really shouldn't take that attitude. We want you to be reasonable, Jack. Think solidarity. Jack, if it comes to that, we got guys here think nothing of coming up there and breaking your typewriter keys."

A NECESSARY SUPERFLUITY

ANGRY MOTHER: *You told me this suit was preshrunk and my son could wear it after it was washed! Just look at him!*

CALM SALESMAN: *He wouldn't look so bad, ma'am, if you shortened his arms and legs.*

PROCRUSTES, like the poor, we have always with us. We need him, I think, because he articulates direct, wrong solutions to complex problems. Of course, if you're an ogre, it's easier to whittle down a guest than buy a bigger bed at midnight. Of course, if book distributors can't move books, if bookstore clerks are ignorant and unhelpful, if librarians throw up their hands, Procrustes has a solution: publish fewer books. What a multitude of difficulties is set to rights with a single, cutting gesture! Procrustes was always efficient. And yet the book industry, like democracy, must not trouble itself unduly about efficiency. The book industry is (among other things) civilization's chief agent for developing and preserving such art as can be made from words, and for transmitting and preserving such ideas and information as may be worth considering the week after next. It cannot adequately fulfill either function if it withdraws, even partway, from the hurly-burly. Vitality does not spring from the cool recesses of balanced ledgers, but from activity and superfluity—or so the poets tell us—though few of *them* make profits for their publishers.

I revive these platitudes only because Mr. John P. Dessauer

has recently consumed six pages of the book industry's principal journal with the case for Procrustes.* His argument would be more dangerous had he been more precise about his terms, but it is nonetheless worth our attention if only because it has become recently fashionable among those who should know better. The occupational disease of all who must deal with more books than they can read themselves first manifests itself as apathy toward the surplus, then degenerates through cynicism to disgruntled mutterings: something must be done.

Mr. Dessauer exhibits terminal symptoms—yet he makes a show of pragmatism. Many of his points are unexceptionable: there is no pressing need to *increase* the quantity of titles published each year in America; reprintings of books are more profitable than initial printings (this point, known to publishers since Barabbas's day, is supported by several tables); persistent logistical problems frustrate the consumer in search of a book not currently displayed in his bookstore; and probably everyone would be better served if publishers tried harder not to print more copies of their titles than can be reasonably expected to sell.

But if Mr. Dessauer's argument is strong in these areas, it does not follow (as he seems to think it does) that we should cut back on the number of new books published each year. That the sales of the average title have not grown is no reason for retrenchment, only evidence that while our society produces an increasing number of literate citizens it does not produce more discriminating readers. That distribution facilities have become "dangerously overcrowded" is an argument for overhauling distribution facilities, not for choking off books from the printer. That "retailers can no longer find room for books that deserve the chance" is cause to rebuke retailers, who would rather stuff their shelves with get-well cards, Christmas wrapping paper, imitation pre-Columbian figurines and pretentious chess sets than with "books that deserve the chance." Retailers are not known to be immune from profit fever; when they lay in two hundred copies of Lawrence Welk's autobiography in preference to an ample supply of my collected works, or twenty varieties of backgammon

---

* Dessauer is the industry's leading statistician. His piece appeared in *Publishers Weekly*, as did my reply.

boards in preference to either of us, I assume they know what they are doing.

Passing over some of Mr. Dessauer's other curious arguments for cutting in half the quantity of new titles published—librarians would be pleased; special orders would be less of a problem; "the poor book buyer" might magically know which books are of interest to him—I come upon this assertion: "Less than half the books published can be reviewed." How does Mr. Dessauer arrive at that proportion? *Newsweek* will review between 250 and 300 of the year's 40,000 titles; the daily *New York Times* perhaps 350. I have no figures for the *Times Book Review*, but 1,000 to 1,500 titles reviewed annually might not be a bad guess. Does Mr. Dessauer really imagine that reducing new titles to 20,000 annually will significantly increase a good book's chances for review in major publications? Besides, virtually every book gets *some* reviews, often where they matter most: *Maximum Macramé* may be overlooked at *Newsweek*, but it will be featured in the *Macramé Monthly Review*.

Need we linger over Mr. Dessauer's doubt "that the majority of contemporary books on international affairs are as stimulating" as Aristotle's and Machiavelli's efforts? Or his supposition that most of us became addicted to reading through encounters with "genius and literary mastery"? Well, in the New Jerusalem (as shaped by Mr. Dessauer's scissors) we will have no need for Gunnar Myrdal or Bernard Fall, and infant fingers will fumble through the *Lives of the Poets*—not (as mine did) through *King Solomon's Mines*. Still, it is difficult to quarrel with Mr. Dessauer's cry that we should dispense with "fiction that is genuinely devoid of distinction." Most of the best-seller list would go, and that's a service to letters—but how are we going to persuade Viking, which publishes so much distinguished, uncommercial fiction, to reject *The Odessa File?* Mr. Dessauer has an idea that good books are all that need concern a publisher.

And that is where his real difficulty begins. "All publishers," he writes, "suffer every time a mediocre book is published that helps glut the market and keeps some good titles from reaching their potential." Doubleday suffers from *Airport?* Bantam suffers from *Valley of the Dolls?* Or does he mean, by mediocrity, books that sell, say, fewer than ten thousand copies? Sales of between five thousand and seven thousand copies of a nonfiction title, Mr.

Dessauer suggests, make that book "at best marginal . . . the title should probably not be published at all." We must learn to "cultivate true discrimination." Pause while authors shudder. Just such books have won important awards. Mr. Dessauer resumes. Here are the books we ought not to publish: "the marginal book an editor thought 'might just catch on,' the little talent an editor imagined might just be big enough. . . ." But let me interrupt him rudely in midsentence. Note the pejorative phrases. *Might just catch on*—with whom? The Literary Guild? Or three thousand readers who know what a good book is? *Might just be big enough*—for what? The "little talent" that produced *Chamber Music* and later *Ulysses?* Cut 'em off at the pass, John. To continue: Mr. Dessauer is doubtful about publishing "the chancy topic for which the editor believed the world might just be ready." *The Interpretation of Dreams. The Decline of the West. The Raw and the Cooked.* Aristotle may be better, but how can we *not* publish chancy books?

Enough of Mr. Dessauer. His dangerous argument is more important than is his inept presentation. Nearly half a million titles in print is not, as he implies, a cancer in the commonwealth, but rather a sign of national health. Let the distributors, librarians, clerks, and consumers sort out their difficulties as best they can. Probably we need a way to separate merchandise from art and information. There will be some overlapping, of course, but generally we can make distinctions: poetry here, investment advice over there. Book publishers need what other companies already have: a research and development wing, where people smoke pipes as you toss them little projects, and nobody expects much profit, or much anything, to surface for years.

Pending such enlightenment, an indisputable truth remains: when retrenchment comes, the good books are the first to go. Books by authors you and I have never heard of. Books that promote unpopular opinions. First novels that show glimmerings of developing talent. In short, the books that you and I want to read. It does no good to call for the elimination of mediocrity, or of specialty books that duplicate titles already published, for every publisher knows that these books cause him no financial difficulty. Indeed, without the profits they produce, the publication of "marginal" books would not be possible.

"Reducing the number of books you publish is dangerous,"

says a successful publisher. "You save yourself twenty loads of crap and one masterpiece. If we published only one-third of the books we do, we'd have passed over a novel we sold for $240,000 to the reprints." One need not look to a publisher's eleemosynary instincts to find his reason for publishing good books. "You can absorb mistakes of quality," says another. "A first novel can't lose that much. But not mistakes of greed. It's the advance which, out of vanity, costs you a million and a half that does you in."

"Getting and spending," as the fellow said, "we lay waste our powers. . . . We have given our hearts away, a sordid boon!"

December 1974

THE TIMES IN THEIR LIVES

Robert Burns got it wrong. The gift we hope for is not to see ourselves as others see us, but to arrange for others to see us as we see ourselves: our essential dignity, our triumphs, the luster we acquire when surrounded by our comrades or our possessions. Much photographic film has been expended in this pursuit. In *The Champion Pig*, Barbara P. Norfleet, a curator of photographs at Harvard, has assembled from studio archives around the nation a collection taken between 1929 and 1963 that reveals its subjects—prosperous white Americans—in attitudes of self-congratulation. The pictures are as far removed from art as they are from snap-shottery; they are professional photographs taken by craftsmen who knew they must please their clients. Norfleet herself has doubts about what we may deduce from such images, but the rest of us need not be timid. From so many icons of self-satisfaction, we may surely learn something about what has mattered to us as Americans.

What matters, or at least what is thought worth recording, are the enduring totems of untroubled times: Tupperware parties and family reunions, poolside barbecues and marching bands. Pride of ownership (of cars in particular) is a popular theme. A family poses in a new Plymouth won at a raffle. A shirtless man, sagging pectorals exposed, stands in his boat before a car, camper, and three admiring women. Rites of passage are even more important. A father with a cigar in his left hand examines as he might a Fabergé egg the baby he holds with his right. A rumpled, pudgy lad (like most children in studio pictures, an involuntary subject) is shown ill at ease just before his first haircut and in similar condition just after.

Doubtless we should be cautious in interpreting these photographs, but the temptation is irresistible. I particularly like two portraits that may reveal more than their subjects intended. In the first, an exercise in vanity, two images are joined to allow a young stud to advertise both his natty suit and his naked chest. In the other, four hunters stand about a car draped with four deer; the grotesquely ornamented vehicle proclaims the pride that they, with their slouching attitudes, affect to deny. And what can we make of the title photograph? Of the boy beaming behind his elegant, indifferent pig? Behind these two, only barely identifiable, the unprized pigs slumber in their stalls. And behind *them*, impassive, their faces shadowed by hats, stand the men whose ranks this boy will shortly join. There may be a statement here, but then we don't know who took the picture, or what—if anything—he meant us to infer.

June 1979

THE ESSAYIST AS AN ENDANGERED SPECIES

A FRIEND TOLD ME the other day that the last book about animals he had read was *Animal Farm*, his sneer implying that animal books are best reserved for readers at the Peter Rabbit level of literacy. For those who think they agree (on alternate Tuesdays *I* agree, having never recovered from once reading books for a publisher who sponsored an annual animal book award), let me say quickly that Edward Hoagland's essays in *Red Wolves and Black Bears* are never wholly about animals, though some contain a lot of wildlife lore, but are often about Hoagland's attempts "to rediscover the commonality of animal and man." By losing our awareness of animals, he writes, "we sacrifice some of the intricacy and grandeur of life." Bears and wolves, the subjects of the two longest essays in this collection, particularly delight him because in these large predators he finds resemblances to man—our anatomy and churlishness are not unlike the bear's, and our method of hunting is so similar to the wolf's that it recognizes us as superior predators, not prey.

Hoagland spends half of each year in the wilderness, the other half in the savage literary precincts of New York. He writes with intuitive perception about both, but better about the outdoors, on which he feeds expansively, exuberantly. "My own best premonition of life is of a rhythm like that of dolphins. Water, air, water, air. . . . Coasting in one medium, then down into another, and up briefly sailing again." And so, not in water but on land, Hoagland lives, diving from the city to Vermont to look for mountains, to Minnesota to stalk black bears, to Texas to see if the red wolf has a chance to survive. He seeks out the wildlife biologists and follows them through the woods. When he comes to write about what he has learned he writes complex essays in which a lot of good hard information is refracted through a distinctive, likable sensibility.

He has been compared to Thoreau through a kind of reviewer's reflex action; if we are to throw names at him, I'd reach first for Robert Burton or Montaigne. Whether his subject is houses in Louisiana or the ratio of a man's income to the number of dogs he owns, Hoagland is apt to hop around through history, geography, natural science, personal experiences, anecdotes told him by friends, the immediate focus of his attention shifting every two or three paragraphs as he adroitly develops tiny essays within the longer ones. "This roving humor," Burton wrote in *The Anatomy of Melancholy*, "I have ever had & like a ranging spaniel, that barks at every bird he sees, leaving his game, I have followed all." Burton's kind of roving personal essay, all style and intelligence and curious bits of information, attracts few writers today; it is so hard to do well that it, too, has become an endangered species.

Watching Hoagland work his way through a long piece is like watching a hunter stalk his game. More than most writers, he seems to use everything that has ever happened to him, everything he has ever heard. He chooses his subjects well: a seventy-year-old man, for instance, who dives forty feet into twelve inches of water; in the tackiness of this low-water act, and in its supreme daring, Hoagland isolates the urge in some men to push themselves to the limits of the possible. And he is by his own insistence an optimist—but his optimism is not of the smile button sort; it is tinged with irony and wit. "He married the same woman twice," he writes of a friend. "Although it didn't work out either time, she was well worth marrying twice, and to my way of thinking this showed that he was at once a man of fervent, rash, abiding love, and yet a man of flexibility, ready to admit an error and to act to correct it." It is hard not to be seduced by that view of what most writers would take to be a messy situation, but then few writers run on the fuel that Hoagland burns while working: joy.

May 1976

PRECOCIOUS MEMOIRS

BENVENUTO CELLINI tells us that no one under forty should write the story of his life. Had he read a dozen of the precocious autobiographies written recently by young people whose names will not be carved on obelisks, prison walls, or golden saltcellars, he might have made more of a fuss about his point. Cellini assumed that no one would trouble the reading public with personal details before he had done something splendid. His assumption has not endured. The quest not for glory but for a sensibility is the fashion now, as is a close look at experiences that are not exceptional but representative, or perhaps common to us all. The trick is to make a real book from the most ordinary material.

Still, those who write precocious memoirs are well advised to study irony and wit. If we who have done no great deeds are bent on self-exposure, should not our books assume a discipline and perspective, a lightness of touch, that our lives may have lacked? Sara Davidson doesn't think so. *Loose Change: Three Women of the Sixties* is graceless, tediously long; it ignores the one question that she should have put to her generation: how could these kids, while making such a pluperfect mess of their lives, insist that they alone could, indeed must, reform the world? But then this is not an analytical book, not a thinking person's book. *Loose Change* is both a participant's book and the book of a feeling observer. Candid, courageous, even poignant, it is redeemed finally by its thoroughness. Future historians will have more use for it than we will.

Davidson's plan is ambitious. She tells the story of three women, herself and two college friends, from the time they pledged a sorority at Berkeley in 1961 until, a dozen years and a sort of revolution later, they were pressing thirty and wondering what had happened to their lives. "We had thought life was free and would never run out," Davidson remarks. "We were certain we belonged to a generation that was special. We did not need or care about history because we had sprung from nowhere."

Three women: Sara, who became a journalist, reporting on rock groups and women's enclaves; Tasha, the most beautiful, who became an art dealer in New York; Susie, the leftist, who married the revolution. Among them, they saw everything: the free speech movement; the People's Park in Berkeley; Woodstock; Altamont; back-to-the-land communes; abortion; childbirth by Lamaze; drugs; meditation workshops; pop art; Sufi; gurus and encounter groups; Susie even went to Vietnam. Not one of these three had the sexual inhibitions of a goat, but their quest for an orgasm assumes an Arthurian intensity (Where is the damn thing? Does it exist? When and how long and by what means achieved?) that makes a kind of anxious counterpoint to the carelessness with which these women mate. "You really want to marry me?" Susie asks. "Why not?" Jeff replies. And so it goes; before she was thirty, Susie had slept with more than one hundred men.

Many books today suggest that the mass of women lead lives of noisy desperation. Desperation is certainly this book's theme: these women are drawn into bad marriages, bad liaisons, nausea, bleeding ulcers, frigidity, unwanted pregnancies, suicidal urges. Even Sara, skeptical journalist that she is, succumbs to the claptrap promoted by Richard Alpert, who played with LSD, went to India, and changed his name to Ram Dass. And yet *Loose Change* ends on a note of optimism, of survival. These women have somehow endured. Sara Davidson has made us care for them, and if she has problems with her diction, occasionally constructing wooden dialogue and falling into girlish modes of speech, she has recorded as well as anyone has to date her "generation's ease with sex and difficulty with love." What we need now is a book to tell us *why* such women lived the way they did.

May 1977

Euripedes had it nearly right: whom God wishes to destroy he first makes successful in show business. At eighteen, with her parents divorced and other fissures threatening to divide her family further, Brooke Hayward thought of herself for the first time as the audience at a Greek tragedy. "I already had presentiments of the ending." That, after all, was the classic form; it was not the surprise dénouement that one came to see, but the quality of the drama and performances. The drama Brooke watched was appalling, but the performances were strictly star quality. Her father, Leland Hayward, was an important theatrical agent and producer; her mother, Margaret Sullavan, was a talented and much-loved actress. Handsome, energetic, and rich, they led extravagantly disordered lives, recklessly consuming themselves and their three children. From the ruins their surviving daughter has built a book, *Haywire*. It's an affecting story, informed with love and understanding; but as surely as if Brooke were a castaway returned from a polar ice cap, it's a survivor's book, too. Its author is edgy and scarred.

Brooke begins her story with its climax: the deaths of her mother and younger sister, Bridget, in 1960, both probably suicides. At the time, Brooke was twenty-three, the divorced mother of two boys. Her father had been married five times, her mother four; her sister, Bridget, and younger brother, Bill, had all spent time in private mental institutions. Theirs was not what you could call a tidy family history, nor one to make Brooke confident about her own future.

In the early 1940s, Leland Hayward was not only the best theatrical agent, representing Fred Astaire, Gene Kelly, Judy Garland, Helen Hayes, Henry Fonda, and their like; he brought class to his craft of demanding outrageous salaries for his clients—the "Toscanini of the telephone," George Axelrod called him. Hayward flew airplanes and kept three hundred pairs of shoes in his closet. He was an urban man, at home in Hollywood and New York, unfit to be a husband or father. He turned to producing Broadway shows—*South Pacific, Mr. Roberts, Call Me Madam*—and worked himself to death. "What counted," his daughter writes, "was that he loved us—not whether he did so wisely or well."

Maggie Sullavan was a natural actress, though she always protested she hated acting and the star system. She did, however, star in movies (*The Shop Around the Corner, Cry Havoc*) and in plays (*The Voice of the Turtle, Sabrina Fair*), as she tried to shield her children from her professional life. Strong-willed and authoritarian, she had the romantic notion that the family could maintain a farm in rural Connecticut—though Leland was allergic to all aspects of the country. Maggie had, says a friend, "an essential arrogance, although she didn't know it, of wanting things the way she wanted them without regard for what Leland wanted." Shortly after their divorce, Maggie became particularly difficult with the children, later suffered a nervous breakdown and stayed, for a while, in a private asylum.

Being a Hayward child was both an ecstatic and a traumatizing experience. Shuttling between California and New York and educated by tutors, the children lacked the stability they needed. Leland often ignored them; Maggie was an overbearing presence. Brooke, the eldest, fought back and may thereby have saved herself, but the others watched and withdrew. Bridget's withdrawals in time became involuntary; as a teenager, she was institutionalized for two years. Frail and timid, she developed epilepsy. Bill, the youngest, angered his father, who had him thrown into the Menninger psychiatric clinic for two years. Sane when he entered, he quickly deteriorated.

Brooke, understandably, came to fear for herself. Her mother, depressed and desperate, had very likely killed herself; nine months later her sister died under equally ambiguous circumstances. Was this attraction to madness and suicide in her genes as well? Brooke decided not. Suicide was a luxury she couldn't afford. "Not with that background. Not with those odds. For me, it wasn't out of the question because of grave moral considerations but because I always resisted the predictable."

To write a memoir is to impose a deliberate and healing order on a life that may have hitherto seemed singularly lacking in structure. For Brooke Hayward, writing *Haywire* became a kind of therapy; the wonder is not that she wrote it but that she has written it so well. Organizing her material deftly by theme and character, advancing her narrative through a series of overlapping flashbacks, and bearing always in mind that this is a book about how the five of them affected one another, Brooke has wisely omitted all information about her life as a wife, divorcée, and mother. She has written instead a brave, honest, intelligent, and greatly moving book about how we must grow up to learn that in the real world monsters do not look alarming; that monsters, however grievously they injure us, can be understood and loved.

March 1977

Ever quick with his paradoxes, T. S. Eliot wrote in "Little Gidding" of "the unknown, remembered gate" that leads to self-discovery. Unknown because we have ignored it, remembered because it pricks at our consciousness, a hint that our collective past is significant to us as individuals. Finding the gate involves some damage to our preconceptions, and requires a kind of circuitous, backward movement, but once we pass through it we may "arrive where we started/And know the place for the first time."

Michael J. Arlen has gone through these motions twice now,

in two of his four books. In *Exiles* he wrote about his parents, who had been rich and famous before he was born and who, by the time he knew them, had slid into straitened, stylish inactivity. In *Passage to Ararat* Arlen looks for the Armenian heritage that his father, a popular English novelist who was born Dikran Kouyoumjian, had firmly put behind him. Arlen had grown up believing that "Armenians were somebody else," somebody second-rate, a people whose history existed largely as footnotes to the history of others: Turks, Persians, Arabs.

And yet Arlen was conscious that for all his Anglo-American education he was different, Armenian. With his wife and a load of history books he went to Soviet Armenia, "a complex journey, a journey on many levels." Detached, defensive, unaware of what he wanted, Arlen was made uneasy by the Armenians' sweaty conviviality, their reputation as wily rug merchants, their "tears. Stories of evil times. Dark interiors and the croon of old men." To be Armenian is to embrace "a chauvinism of misfortune."

Arlen traces the history of this protesting, mournful people, a mountain people who fought off the Assyrians, Scythians, and Medes and yet for whom all history is reduced to the atrocities wrought upon them by the Turks. The Armenians tell of priests crucified, of worshipers cremated in their church, "of disemboweling, of heads split by stones, of the rape of small children." In the 1890s the Turks killed three hundred thousand Armenians in two years, ten thousand in three days. The Armenians, said the Turks, had provoked such treatment.

Between 1915 and 1916, one million Armenians, half of all in Turkey, disappeared. Towns were relocated, men executed, women herded into concentration camps and sent on forced marches to be sold, raped, driven until they died. Arlen argues that this genocide was the first to employ modern communications and technology—the telegraph, for example—to promote official, plausible lies about what was happening. Hatred is contagious and Arlen broods about the self-hatred that afflicts his people. To live as an Armenian, he concludes, is to have become crazed by the past. But to accept that past is to achieve a kind of freedom.

Passage to Ararat, in which we share with the author his process of inquiry and discovery, is Michael Arlen's best book. In everything Arlen writes—television criticism, a study of a Chicago police assault on black militants, these memoirs—there is a unifying preoccupation: an attempt by the author to see himself and the rest of us precisely, and to examine both our seemingly inexhaustible need to rearrange reality and the evasions and technologies that we constantly develop to ease our self-deceptions. I cannot think of a more important undertaking for a writer just now; we should be pleased that one of Arlen's intelligence and sensitivity is committed to it.

August 1975

MEDICAL METAPHORS

A SURGEON WHO PUTS DOWN his scalpel to pick up a pencil is still intent on poking around in the human condition. Incisiveness is all. And yet even he who examines our guts with an informed regard is awed by their efficiency and organization. "I find there are many pieces in this one fabrick of man; this frame is raised upon a mass of Antipathies," Dr. Thomas Browne wrote three hundred years ago. Richard Selzer, a surgeon at Yale, must agree. He wrote *Mortal Lessons*, a collection of essays, "to search for some meaning in the ritual of surgery, which is at once murderous, painful, healing and full of love." For him the surgeon is a poet, a traveler in a dangerous country, a priest celebrating "a Mass served with Body and Blood," even a kind of sexual partner: "Bodies are stroked and penetrated here, but no love is made."

No enemy of metaphor is he. Indeed, as we read these pieces—these grisly anecdotes, these autobiographical excursions, these anthems to bone, skin, liver, and belly—we might conclude that the style, not the substance, is its author's point. Listen: "Now the scalpel sings along the flesh again. . . . One listens, and almost hears the whine—nasal, high, delivered through the gleaming metallic snout. The flesh splits with its own kind of moan." Or: "the Four Horsemen of Peptic Apocalypse come riding hard, galloping across the midriff, pillaging, raping tissue, laying waste." Surgery, it seems, must be prophylactic, but prose can be allowed to fester.

Ah, well. For all the baroque ornamentation of his book, Selzer is inclined to be modest, even reverent about his profession. To cut into the body is unnatural, he says; to do it at all requires "the quietude of resolve layered over fear." These brief essays are full of odd, perhaps disputable facts, curious tales, alarming revelations. Baldness, apparently, is indeed a sign of potency, and castration an effective preventative. Neanderthal man may not have stood quite erect because he was crippled by arthritis—from living in damp caves. Ben Franklin, troubled by a bladder stone, stood on his head to urinate and invented a catheter that he prized above his almanac.

Selzer's descriptions of cadavers preserved in medical-school tanks ("The hooks of the tongs are inserted one into each ear"), of the machine that vacuums a corpse's interior and them pumps it full of fluid, of a fetus resisting abortion, and of alcohol attacking the liver are enough to make a reasonable person forswear all further thought of willing away his body, of dying, of sex, even of drinking. Unreasonable people, however, may worry that Selzer cares too much for the ghastly, the sensational. His master, Thomas Browne, intended only to tease and provoke his reader, but Selzer, a child of our time, aims at coarser sensibilities. He aims to shock.

January 1977

HOW NOT TO WRITE A BIOGRAPHY

To PUT IT POLITELY, this won't do. To put it precisely, T. S. Matthews's *Great Tom* is so empty of real information, so ill organized, so badly documented, so vulgar in its language and proposals, so shabby in its homilies and deductions as to arouse rage in readers who have impatiently awaited a serviceable biography of T. S. Eliot. This is a pity. Eliot's stock has fallen in recent years; where once it was fashionable to say that he and Yeats divided between them the great poetry written in English since the death of Keats, it is now fashionable to shrug off the *Four Quartets* as if they were to his significant work no more than a prosaic coda, the more embarrassing for their Christian mysticism.

Studded as his poems are by personal symbols and references, an informed account of Eliot's life would assist the necessary reappraisal of his work. But the Eliot estate has not yet cooperated with a biographer, and Matthew's anecdotal effort provides few answers, perhaps because his questions ("Was he a phony scholar?" "Was he a Christian?" "Were his plays any good?") are so ill conceived as to inhibit any useful thinking on their subject.

Dutifully reporting such facts as are known—that Eliot, for instance, was born into a Unitarian family in Saint Louis in 1888—Matthews then deduces what is not known: that his mother and sister were "terrified of sex and disgusted by it, and ashamed of their female bodies" and that young Tom "could not stifle his deep horror of women." What might have been true becomes what is true: Matthews gives us all fair warning when he cites Richard Ellmann's dangerous precept that biographies are "hints followed by guesses" and that we must come to know the subject like "a character in fiction."

And so we follow Eliot to Harvard, where between 1910 and 1912 he wrote "The Love Song of J. Alfred Prufrock," and to Oxford, where he met Vivienne Haigh-Woods, whom he married in 1915. Vivienne was often ill, suffering from nervous diseases; she would not leave England and for her sake Eliot remained. Matthews speculates that within a few months of their marriage Vivienne was seduced by Bertrand Russell. Why? "One possible answer," he says, "is that she was a flirt, and flirts sometimes go too far." Sometimes they never get around to going far enough, but it hardly matters—Matthews has no other answer to offer.

Proceeding through his narrative in this manner, Matthews reports adequately on the skeleton of Eliot's life as we know it: his work as a banker and an editor, his lectures, dry periods, and adjustment to fame. As for Matthews's questions—"Was he a homosexual?" "Did Pound create Eliot?"—no new information is forthcoming. Letters have been denied him, others he may not print. We can almost see Eliot grinning. "Genuine poetry can communicate before it is understood," Eliot wrote, and he, the genuine poet, did not mean to be easily understood. Matthews stumbles into the most tempting trap for critics: he quotes Sweeney's claim that every man wants to murder a girl and says that Eliot is speaking for himself. Matthews's waffling about God, the Church, and Eliot's sense of guilt is wrongheaded and embarrassing, adding nothing to our understanding of what religion meant to Eliot or why he converted to Anglo-Catholicism.

Matthews knows where the problems lie and senses he cannot solve them: the only materials he has are unsubstantiated speculation and noisome homilies on man's condition: "In a sense, we are only a bad smell contained in a human skin." His vulgarity ("Eliot pondered all these things in his heart") is as persistent as his sentimentality ("He thought with particular fondness of his mother: how dearly he would like to see her again!"), and often, as if he were drowsing over his own text, he forgets to cite sources for his quotations.

He has few comments to offer on the poems, though he tries his hand at setting out the *Quartets* as prose—always a fatuous enterprise because the language of poetry is the language of energy and rhythm, however it is arranged. Matthews, I think, shows better judgment when, in the foreword to this book, he calls *Great Tom* "a biography of sorts." His diffidence is well deserved.

March 1974

THE RIGHT NOT TO WORK

READING THE BLEAK TESTIMONY assembled here,* I was reminded more forcibly than usual of a plain truth that complacency tends to obscure: not only does time change our
perceptions of man's most persistent afflictions, the problems
themselves change, too. Unemployment, in this instance: the
condition of not working because one can't, or won't.

Once there was a simple solution. Disturbed by the idlers he
saw about him, Piers Plowman, hero of a fourteenth-century alle-
gorical poem, called upon Hunger for vengeance "on these wasters who worry the world." Hunger swoops down and buffets the
wasters about; as long as he stays among them, the people are inclined to work. Times change. Now, thanks to unemployment insurance, union strike funds, and other modern amenities, the
out-of-work are not necessarily concerned about hunger, or even
thrift. One witness in these pages has just engaged a psychotherapist; another, collecting unemployment money, packs her friends
into her car and drives out to the Hamptons for a summer of
swimming, tanning, tennis, and "getting mellow and nice
again."

Well, my hat's off to them, I'm sure. Lurking within this
book is a paradox the author doesn't seem to notice: while he is
professing his belief that every American has a right to work, his
subjects are insisting on their right not to work—or not to work
at what doesn't please them. "I'm not gonna compromise and take
a job just for the sake of working," says one man. "I just don't

---

* *Not Working: An Oral History of the Unemployed,* by Harry Maurer.

want to," says a woman. "I just don't want to. I want to get up when I want to get up and do what I want to do."

What we see here is evidence of the extreme Pelagianism of our contemporary culture. If there were no Fall of man, if we live still in the American Eden, Adam's curse is irrelevant, perhaps presumptuous. "I don't want anybody controlling my income," a man says. "I want to make fifty grand and buy a sailboat." And why not? If we got rid of Eve's curse—bearing children in pain—why should men work? "I would never work for someone I didn't like," a jobless nursemaid reports. "Since I'm still getting unemployment, I don't have any reason to take a job until I find the right person." Anyone for tennis?

I don't mean to suggest that all of the unemployed who sat still for Harry Maurer's interviews are spoiled, or a threat to the common weal; far from it. Most present themselves as honorable victims of the marketplace, or of uglier currents in our society. Young blacks in Natchez have as much difficulty finding jobs today as young blacks in New York City. Men and women over forty find few doors open to them. A distinguished employment record, or even a college degree, may work against the job-seeker. What's more, we have recently created a new class of aspiring workers to discriminate against: the Vietnam veteran who, by virtue of his service in that country, is presumed to be an addict or otherwise mentally disabled.

Maurer traveled twelve thousand miles about the country to compile this record, talking to men and women of every social condition. His book contains much worth hearing, though some of his witnesses are more interesting than others. Maurer gives equal sympathy to all, takes everyone at his word, offers us edited but unanalyzed testimony of what being jobless means. He can hardly do otherwise—these are problems endemic in oral history—yet a nagging sense of insufficiency remains. Americans are great explainers, and was anyone ever fired from his job who did not have a plausible, self-serving version of what happened to tell?

April 1980

THE GREAT AMERICAN EAR

In Chicago, city of Third World taxi drivers, Studs Terkel slides across the passenger's seat to peer at the card with the cabbie's name. This one is Adewale O. Ogunfemi. "Hey," Terkel says, "you're from Nigeria!" The driver shoots him a look of alarm. "How you know that?" "From Lagos, am I right?" He's right. "Let me guess," Terkel says. "You're a student." Right again. "Circle campus at the university." By now the cabbie is having trouble keeping his eyes on the road. Here he is in the land of the CIA, but who is this rumpled man with the remarkable nose? "You're taking business administration, right?" "Man," the cabbie says, "how come you know so much about me?"

How come, indeed. Knowing who people are is Studs Terkel's profession. Talking to cabbies is simply reflex action. For twenty-five years he has conducted a daily, hour-long talk program on Chicago's classical-music station, WFMT. Choosing his subjects to suit only himself, Terkel may devote his hour to reading a story by Chekhov or Grace Paley, to playing old recordings of union songs, or to interviews with people who interest him: Dizzy Gillespie, members of the Fine Arts Quartet, the author of a biography of Walter Lippmann. Unlike most interviewers on radio and television, Terkel is heavily informed about his subject. He has not only read an author's book, he has taken massive, elaborately cross-referenced notes that enable him to move a discussion hurriedly along. "Either I have standards or I don't," he says. "It's the carpenter bringing his tool chest. I'm the carpenter. I can't say I forgot my saw."

These interviews with our society's articulate achievers

prompted a publisher, André Schiffrin of Pantheon, to suggest to Terkel something radically different: a self-portrait of Chicago composed from interviews with common people, "the man of inchoate thought," as Terkel later put it. Terkel took his tape recorder out into the city to talk with teenagers and octogenarians, cops and convicts, landlords and housewives, fascists and social workers, bums and aristocrats. The result, *Division Street: America,* was perhaps the first book to rely entirely upon oral history and remains a classic of contemporary journalism. Chicago, in Terkel's hands, became a metaphor for urban Americans everywhere in the mid-1960s, a matrix of our national fears and hopes. Other books followed, each developing from themes touched upon in its predecessor. In *Hard Times* Terkel recorded the memories of those who had survived the Depression. In *Working* he revealed in eloquent detail the physical and spiritual oppression of everyday labor.

Because it is not confined to a single city, or time, or a particular part of the human condition, Terkel's new book, *American Dreams: Lost and Found,* is his most diverse. Curiously, because we live in straitened, even painful times, it is also his most optimistic. The cast of characters is by now familiar (indeed, some are returning from appearances in earlier books): Indians, immigrants, and a folk singer; politicians, union organizers, and the grandson of a slave; policemen, aging executives, a grandnephew of Henry Adams. One hundred people speak in these pages—Terkel discarded the testimony of two hundred more—and most are old enough to be conscious of their situation changing: something has been lost, or found.

At twenty-nine, Miss USA of 1973 reflects sardonically on the crown she never really wanted: "They tell me I'm the only beauty queen in history that didn't cry when she won." A businessman observes that you can raise children better, more rationally, if you can keep yourself from loving them. A lumberjack in Oregon surveys the ruins of his territory: "The younger loggers were not here to see what was there before. If you've never known something, it's difficult to appreciate what has been lost." Yet for every bitter or disillusioned witness there are two or three who have experienced, or sense in themselves an untapped potential for, a better life. Terkel quotes a blue-collar housewife:

"What I'm beginning to understand is there's a human possibility. That's where all the excitement is. If you can be part of that, you're aware and alive. It's not a dream, it's possible."

People like this are the key to the book, the source of its optimism and best interviews. In one, really a poem to human survival, a woman tells how she has built her life around her autograph book, but when asked what would happen should she lose it, she shrugs: "*C'est la vie.*" In another, a Kentucky woman once ignorant as the dawn tells how she overcame her dislike of blacks and her fellow hillbillies to become an organizer of women in Chicago. In a third—the book's most remarkable piece—a former Klansman explains how he came to cooperate with a black activist woman he had long hated and opposed. "The whole world was openin' up," he says, "and I was learnin' new truths that I had never learned before."

These are Terkel's special people; he calls them his friends. Over drinks at Riccardo's, a restaurant in downtown Chicago favored by admen and journalists, he tells of a cabdriver who once asked him if he had ever seen the movie *Lord Jim*. While Terkel made noises about a book by the same name, the cabbie pressed on: "It's about someone like *me*. It's about a coward who finds his courage. That's why I joined the John Birch Society." "What he's looking for," Terkel says, "is some kind of self-esteem, but there's fear in his life. He tells me, 'I take my wife and kids to the beach every Sunday.' I say, 'To enjoy the beach?' He says, '*No:* to overcome my fear of the water.' You see, you can laugh at them, but that doesn't satisfy *me* at all. Everybody's more complex than we think and I want to find that out. I want to find out what the energy is, what makes people *tick*. The Bircher, the Klansman: the point is, they're *good* people."

As the evening matures at Riccardo's, the admen at the bar begin to whoop and sing. A glass drops, and then a chair. "I'm not too sure that absolute power corrupts absolutely," Terkel says. "I think to feel needed is terribly important." For a few moments he tries to explain his technique. He works by hunches. His subjects are people he meets by chance, or friends of friends. "I give people dough here and there, just a token, but even if I gave a thousand it wouldn't be recompense to that person who gave me something else. I won't deny I have this guilt. I always do. Here I am, Miss Lonelyhearts again. Am I not taking people's lives and here are best sellers made out of them? At the same time, they say to me: I never felt so good."

It is not difficult to get people to talk, even into a machine, because most people have never encountered anyone really willing to listen to them talk about themselves. By talking, people impose a kind of order on their lives. The order may be illusory; it may never have existed before, but to talk is to explain, to put a shape on things. "It's like you're Columbus discovering a new world. I can't tell you how exciting it is. I remember a woman saying, 'Let's play it back.' Because, you see, she had never heard her voice and says, 'You know somethin'? I never knew I felt that way.' And that moment is absolutely astonishing and exhilarating. And for me, too!"

This enthusiasm provokes from his subjects depths of revelation rarely offered to such notoriously unenthusiastic listeners as priests and psychoanalysts. "I'm as vulnerable as that person," Terkel says. "I think they recognize that. I goof up on the tape recorder. I say 'Goddam' and kick it, you know. Now the person, *they* see it's not working, it's not some man from TV saying are you for or against abortion. It's this guy who goofed up and they feel needed." Sometimes he forgets just how involved with him the people he talks to get. Once, after interviewing a fireman, after getting his entire life on tape, he said, "I gotta go, Tommy." "This guy says, 'You gotta *go?* Just like *that?* Here's my life I'm tellin' you about, you gotta *go?* I thought we'd have a little dinner, get some spaghetti, some beer.' I said, 'Course I'll stay, Tommy. Jesus Christ, I don't know what I'm doin'.'"

Terkel is sixty-eight, with silver hair and a well-used face; he wears a fatigued blazer over an open-necked shirt. "John Crosby, you know, the TV critic, said I looked like a younger Spencer Tracy. *Younger*, can you imagine." He has been a sportscaster, a disc jockey, and an actor. In the early fifties he had his own television show, "Studs' Place," a kind of benign, improvised prototype of "Archie Bunker's Place." On the streets, in bars, people stop him to talk. To get from Riccardo's to a Hunanese restaurant, where there are more drinks, and then to O'Rourke's bar out on North Avenue is an athletic event.

At O'Rourke's, where failed writers gather and there are

pictures of Shaw, Joyce, and O'Casey on the wall, Terkel finds an old friend, Paul Romaine, elderly and ailing now, but for fifty years a militant bookseller. Communist books, fascist books, books by Henry Miller and Frank Harris—Romaine sold them all, hating censorship as the FBI and Chicago's police tried to close him down. Terkel is genuinely moved to see the old man up and about and goes to buy more drinks. At the bar, people recognize him and persuade him to buy drinks for them as well. Terkel discovers he has no money for a taxi home. No matter: a man who looks and talks like Jimmy Cagney offers him a ride. He kisses Terkel's hand: "I love you, Studs. What you've done means a lot to me." He has a gun, he says, and will protect Terkel from "the bad guys out there everywhere."

Terkel, however, thinks the guys out there are generally pretty good. "I'm not a Pollyanna, but invariably there's someone, part of a community, and that person for some reason is able to have an insight. He is able to articulate the feelings that all his fellows have." In each of the interviews for his new book Terkel at some point paused to ask, "Did you ever hear that phrase 'the American Dream'? What does it *mean?*" Among the answers he received: "To be better off than you are." "Really money." "Maybe the American Dream is in the past." A bellhop says it is "to be famous." A migrant worker says it is "owning a piece of land." A Japanese-American says, "The American Dream? I think: for whites only." But a twenty-five-year-old man, who has recalled how he lied for TV commercials, says, "To me, it's people having control over their lives."

Terkel agrees with him. He loathes the ravages of technology: political polls, TV ratings, Muzak in elevators—the damnable devices that prevent us from thinking for ourselves. "We accept these daily humiliations. What's going to kill us, it's not gonna be a bomb, it will be banality. Think of our presidential candidates. Hannah Arendt spoke of the banality of evil, but the reverse is true: the evil of banality. What it does, it stunts the possibilities of the imagination." His own American Dream is to keep on doing what he is doing now until he reaches one hundred and falls apart like the one-hoss shay. But his dream for America is a plan to ensure food, clothing, shelter, education, and medical care for everyone, so that people may feel a sense of power over their own lives. "My goal is to survive the day. To survive it with a semblance of grace, curiosity, and a sense I've done something pretty good. I can't survive the day unless everyone else survives it too. I live in a community, and if the community isn't in good shape, neither am I."

October 1980

INDEX

A NOTE ON THE AUTHOR

PETER S. PRESCOTT is a senior writer and book critic at *Newsweek* magazine. He also teaches seminars in "Reviewing the Arts" and "Writing with Style" at Columbia University's Graduate School of Journalism. He recently received a Guggenheim Fellowship for a study of the juvenile justice system in New York City, first prize in the Robert F. Kennedy Book Awards for the book that resulted from that study, and the rarely presented George Polk Award for Criticism for essays reprinted in *Never in Doubt*.

A director of the Authors Guild and president of the Authors Guild Foundation, Mr. Prescott has lectured under the auspices of the U.S. State Department at universities in Syria, Egypt, and Ireland. He is the author of four previous books, all highly acclaimed: *The Child Savers: Juvenile Justice Observed; A Darkening Green: Notes from the Silent Generation; Soundings: Encounters with Contemporary Books;* and *A World of Our Own: Notes on Life and Learning in a Boys' Preparatory School.*